THE AGE OF
DISTRACTION

THE **AGE** OF **DISTRACTION**

READING, WRITING, AND POLITICS IN A HIGH-SPEED NETWORKED ECONOMY

ROBERT HASSAN

Transaction Publishers
New Brunswick (U.S.A.) and London (U.K.)

Library of Congress Catalog Number: 2011012445
ISBN: 978-1-4128-4306-5
Printed in the United States of America

Library of Congress Cataloging-in-Publication Data

Hassan, Robert, 1959-
   The age of distraction : reading, writing, and politics in a high-speed networked economy / Robert Hassan.
      p. cm.
   ISBN 978-1-4128-4306-5
   1. Time—Sociological aspects. 2. Distraction (Psychology)—Social aspects. 3. Information technology—Social aspects. I. Title.
   HM656.H377 2011
   303.48'3301—dc22
                  2011012445

"For Kate, Theo, Camille, and for rooms full of books"

Contents

Preface   ix

1   This Other Temporality   1

2   The Ghost in the Machine   21

3   Everything Nowadays is Ultra   47

4   We Are All Still Mesopotamian   83

5   The Chronic Distraction of Everyday Life   107

6   Canon   139

7   Considerations on the Prospects for Political Change   171

Bibliography   203

Index   215

Preface

So you will find here...only the figurations of the body's prehistory—of that body making its way toward the labor and pleasure of writing.
—Roland Barthes

Karl Marx's son-in-law, Paul Lafargue, wrote a remarkable and acerbic pamphlet in 1883 titled "The Right to be Lazy." For Lafargue, the right to time for oneself was the most important "right" that people should strive for. As he saw it, though, this fundamental human entitlement was being buried under the dead weight of industrial capitalism, a system that compelled people to sell much, if not most, of their time to the capitalist. An even worse assault on Lafargue's revolutionary sensibilities was that workers themselves had become complicit in the outrage. Instead of rising in rebellion, as his father-in-law had anticipated they would, they were willingly indulging in a kind of self-abasement by not demanding time to be "free," but demanding the "right to work," the right to become slaves to regular wages and to the rhythm of the machine.

By the late-Victorian era, it seems, we had already lost sight of the value of time—the value of time for ourselves at any rate. Time, in the more accurate predictions of Benjamin Franklin a century earlier, had become synonymous with money, and money was now the DNA of capitalism. The increasingly powerful and pervasive machine culture swallowed up the time that could be spent considering "The Greeks in their era of greatness." But in the culture of industry and capital the proletariat had dishonored themselves and allowed their consciousness and their understanding of the true value of time to be "perverted by the dogma of work." The solution, for Lafargue, was that machines must be brought under the control of people instead of people being the tools of an inhuman system. Only socialism could only bring this about, he imagined, and under such an enlightened and democratic rule, an "iron limit" of three hours a day would be the maximum amount of toil for all.

"The Right to be Lazy" was possibly the wrong argument at the wrong time, and was received (outside of the prison house where he wrote it) with a deafening silence. The term "lazy' had and still has all the negative connotations that grate against the "protestant work ethic" that supposedly underscores capitalism. Moreover, he seems to have anticipated its less than rousing reception amongst the masses, and concludes with a weak and lamenting cry into the teeth of much louder winds of change: "O Laziness, mother of the arts and noble virtues, be thou the balm of human anguish!."

We never hear much of Lafargue these days. Maybe the ghastliness of the industrial way of life was too much for him. The proletariat seemed not to be listening to his warnings of time robbery and machine dictatorship. In any case he and his wife concluded a suicide pact and killed themselves in 1911. This was the very year, coincidentally, that Frederic Taylor's *The Principles of Scientific Management* appeared, a book that revolutionized nature of the human interaction with machines and, some say, served fundamentally to harness people ever more tightly to the logic of machine-based production.

Today, the need to be free from the shackles of the machine sounds to many to be an odd and archaic notion. In the West at least we are often told that we have moved beyond the "dark satanic mills" that Marx's compatriot Friedrich Engels wrote about in the mid-nineteenth century. Today we are purportedly far more progressive and far more civilized. Certainly, people are still brutally exploited in the factories that make our shoes and shirts and electronic gadgetry in Latin America, in wide stretches of Asia and elsewhere across the world. But the prevailing notion is that it only has to be pointed out to Nike or Gap or whomever, that such unpleasantness is occurring in their sub-contracted production lines, and the problem will be fixed. Local exploiters will be told to raise wages and shorten work hours. Slowly, slowly, things are getting better. Such things take time. And in the fullness of time the Chinese production worker will also have her trainers and her iPhone; paid for with her own money. She will have joined the global leisured class, the class that does different kinds of work, with greater rewards, and are freer than ever from what drove M. Lafargue to suicidal despair.

The trouble is none of this is true. Workers in sub-contracted factories will work hard and long until they become too expensive and by which time they will lose their jobs to others who are willing to work harder and faster and for less. The West benefits from this exploitation, to be sure, but only in a strictly material sense—cheap clothes and cheap electronics. Hyper-exploited Latin Americans and Asians may have little time to consider the meaning of life, but neither do the service class or "information workers" in the richer zones of the globalized economy have that particular privilege, either. *All* of us inhabit a networked society that is, in the phrase used by time-theorist Hartmut Rosa, an "accelerated society" (2003). It is a society made possible by machines that run faster than machines have ever run before.

The machines in question are, of course, computers; machines that process information at a rate of speed that only increases, whilst dragging individuals, communities, businesses, governments, societies, and cultures into its hurtling and erratic trajectory that is heading to no-one knows where. And Moore's Law and new advances in "memristors," quantum computing and chemical computing are combining to ensure that there are no known limits to how fast computers are able to process more and more amounts of information. Yet, hardly anyone considers whether this is actually a good thing or not. The computers that suffuse every nook and cranny of society also accelerate it ways we barely understand. Indeed, in what is becoming the irony of our digital age—we do not have the time to think about the consequences of speed because our society is moving and changing so quickly. Not many of us any longer has the time to be lazy by choice, and therefore few have that precious time to consider whether a Lafarguian laziness might actually have benefits.

This book seeks to take some small steps toward a greater understanding of our temporal enslavement to the very machines that are supposed to free us. A big problem for us is that we are weak when it comes to information. Let me explain that statement. It is true that many of us throw caution to the wind when the next piece of super widgetry from Apple Inc. hits the stores, and we buy it whether we can afford it or not, or whether we have any practical use for it. But that is not what I mean. Our weakness in respect of information goes much deeper, and much further back into our species' history. Unlike other animals, we are unable to naturally filter out that which is not strictly necessary for our survival. As the philosophical anthropologist Arnold

Gehlen argues, we are prone to overstimulation by our surroundings because we lack the powerful instinct of most animal species that are able to ignore that which it does not strictly need to deal with. Uniquely, however, we are prone *to develop technology*. This facility for technology-building has enabled us to so something about information overload. It has allowed us to create material cultures, to construct habits and routines that allow us to focus our attention on certain things and the information they contain (or we impute to them). From the beginnings of our collective history, cultures, institutions, religions, civilizations have been assembled through technological development and these have served to focus our attention and allow us place emphasis on the forms of information (knowledge) and their application that best enable us (as we have judged it in our fractious and sometimes terrible estimation) to *construct* and *lead* lives instead of simply living them. In short, technology gives us the capacity to concentrate the mind or what we have deemed to be important, and prevents us from becoming lost in an ocean of information.

There is, however, a technology with which we have the deepest and most ancient of our relationships—which has now become a machine and yet we hardly know it: writing. Writing is a technology we barely recognize as such because it has so deeply entered into our consciousness and shaped who we are and the worlds that we have constructed. Tony Judt tells us that "words are all we have" (2010, 155). But we all too easily neglect and abuse this treasure because we take them for granted—and because we are awash with them. Today we swim in fast-flowing torrents of information and it is this digital overload that is causing us to regress to our infantile and weak state in terms of how we relate to information. We lived for thousands of years in the culture of print. And as mass literacy created the mass society with the rise of industrialism, print became a way of life. But we lost our respect for its power, and as it insinuated itself into our consciousness it ceased to be a tool for us, it seemed instead, as Walter Ong pointed out, simply to be a part of what we are as humans (1992, 293). The tool has now changed, but we do not realize what this means, we do not recognize the implications this change has—for just about everything.

Theorist of technology, Bruno Latour, tells us that technologies are enfolded with the heterogeneous temporalities that reflect the context of their creation (2002, 249). And so our "oneness" with writing meant that in its original form it was encoded with human and environmental temporalities. The practice of writing and reading is fundamentally biological and organic and its rhythms constituted the baseline rhythms of early civilization right up until recent times. The processes involved in the practice of reading and writing "matched" the speed and physical capacities of humans and the lives they led. And Judt was surely correct in his summation of the value of words. Writing and reading made everything possible that we have today. Industrialization, Enlightenment thought, democracy, modernity-as-project—all were the "effect" of writing and reading and thus these large-scale social and cultural processes were themselves encoded with the human and environmental rhythms of time—with one pretty significant, not to say, *revolutionary* addition: the clock. This is another technology that we too often taken for granted, because it too has suffused its logic into the core of our being, individually and collectively. People born into modernity were born into the rhythm of the clock. One had to learn how to tell the time, but once inured to its infallible linearity, the individual was primed to synchronize with the wider tempo of society. Clock time as habit and as institution means that for the first time in human history, the world becomes plannable, schedulable, and organizable.

When the clock became an entrenched and institutionalized regulator, developing industry along factory lines thus became thinkable and doable. Capitalism could likewise flourish; and both in combination would give Adam Smith pause to consider the provenance of the wealth of nations in the late eighteenth century. Smith himself was an influential member of the world's first information network. This was the circulation of ideas though what came to be known as the "republic of letters"; an information work of the highest order whose ideas on the nature of democracy, science, and philosophy constituted the basis of the Enlightenment. We can say, then, in a chain of causation that forms the principle arguments to come in this book, that a biologically and environmentally entimed technology of writing made possible the rise of organized and proto-rationalized societies. Rationalization in its turn was made possible with the adoption of the technology of the clock that sublimated organic and ancient rhythms (though not completely negating them) to the rhythms of machine and industry. Individuals and societies and civilizations could flourish within this fundamentally print-based ordering of human relations. Institutions could arise to shape cultures and polities and form the larger historical developmental trajectory of modernity. The pace of life would speed up slowly (and sometimes rapidly), but always inexorably, to challenge the physical and cognitive capacities of humans. For most of our history we could cope with this pressure, just.

Times, however, have (literally) changed. The world has a new information network through which to conduct its business. And not just the business of business—but the business of almost everything we do. Indeed it is increasingly the case that everything we do is a form of business. Networks of electronic communication are supplanting much of the human interaction that formerly was conducted face-to-face. Not only that, whole new (and previously unimaginable) realms of relationship and experience are opening up—witness, for example, the rapid rise and vast scope of social networking. Virtual worlds of culture and politics and entertainment blur to form a common logic based upon the power of a new and invisible (to most of us) kind of writing: code.

Our transformed relationships are not simply confined to those that we have with each other. Underlying these changes are new experiences with temporality and with writing. The time that Lafargue wanted freed up to allow us to be human beings instead of automaton, has instead become commodified and compressed into what Ron Purser termed a "constant present" (2002, 13). In our accelerated society the demands of the digital network press in on our experiences of time, filling our time and shrinking its phenomenological textures down to the flat temporal horizon of the *now*. Past and future become more difficult to retrieve and project—because we have less and less time to indulge ourselves in our own time.

Not so long ago the primary media for information networks was still print. In newspapers, in magazines, in books, in libraries, words remained fixed in time and space. We consumers of words also wrote them in a form primarily set upon paper, either longhand or typewritten or mass produced through industrial presses, that would remain material and solid until archived—where its meaning fell silent until once more read—or it was discarded in some way for it to disappear. The mass media of television and radio for all their global and electronic forms were nonetheless "informed" at their roots by words on paper, and "conditioned" by the relative space–time fixity of the ultimate baseline media of the printed word.

Information and communication technologies (ICTs) have accelerated time and accelerated how society lives it. Crucially, ICTs have destabilized the ancient fixity of words and their meanings. Destabilized words have now created ontologically destabilized worlds. Writing has become liquid, and digital representations of meaning have begun to pulse and flow at an ever-quickening pace that militates against the pause and the traction and concentration and the reflection that meaning-construction demands. Our weakness in respect of information is increasingly becoming pathological. Expressed in what I see as a 'chronic distraction' we are at risk (individually and collectively) of becoming disconnected from the rhythms of time and the technologies of time that have made the worlds that we still take for granted. When living in a constant present, and where knowing 'less about more' becomes the default position, the institutions that created out modern world begin also to slip their ontological moorings. Our chronic distraction is in many ways a *distraction from uncertainty*, an uncertainty that the unplanned trajectory of our late-modernity generates in its speed fetish. As Zygmunt Bauman notes in his *Liquid Modernity*, quoting Gerhardt Schulze, "this is a new type of uncertainty: 'not knowing the ends instead of the traditional uncertainty of not knowing the means'" (2004, 61).

A lack of understanding of both "ends" and "means" is our lot today in the network society. Chronic distraction—caused by the entrenched logic of acceleration through ubiquitous computing and neoliberal ideology—is how we respond to this lack. And much slips through the crack in our collective attention span. The following pages will discuss what I see to be the most important effects of our collective uncertainty.

There are a couple of things we can be sure of, though: time and the technology of writing have been transformed at their heart. And like the network society more broadly, they have become digital and highly unstable. We are losing our grip upon the world at its ontological core, and the network system as presently constituted prevents us from regaining any sort of democratic control over it—at the local level as well at the global. What to do? Answers do not come easily, but we need to make a start and if words are all we have, then we need to use them to better understand our relationship with them.

President John F. Kennedy once said that Americans "must use time as a tool, not as a couch." This could be construed as a sideswipe at Lafargue and his paean to the freedom found in idleness. Rather more likely it was meant as a straight invocation against the "wasting" of time. But to use time as a tool we need first to be able to control it, in our individual lives as well as at the collective level. We do not. Driven by the market and by the "dogma of computing," a new *network time* is a tool that is spinning out of our control. This leaves us only with the couch, M. Lafargue's couch. Why not take a seat?

1

This Other Temporality

Do I Have Your Undivided Attention?

This is a book about a contemporary cultural cognitive condition called distraction. Attentive readers will have possibly noted the rather inelegant and overdone attempt at alliteration in that sentence, where five "Cs" collide, albeit quite gently, one after the other, causing a kind of speed-bump effect that serves, ideally, to slow the reader down a little bit. Longish sentences, like the one you have just read, can have a similar effect. There are a couple of points to be made in this observation. One is that advertising professionals (as well as book editors and publishers) tell us that to sell something to somebody, be it a brand of toothpaste, or car, or book, or idea, there must be a tactic employed, whereby the "hook" catches the attention of the reader and pulls him or her toward where you want them to go. The other point is that what is happening—and what is happening if you are still reading—is that a certain amount of cognitive traction is taking place, the effect of "interest" keeping you here on this page for a while longer. On the Internet, website designers routinely aim for something similar. They call it "sticky content" and it is the kind of stuff—and could conceivably be anything—that keeps eyeballs from wandering too quickly from Website to Website. The search-engine colossus Google has made a business out of tracking "stickiness" and selling advertising on the back of it. There will be much more on the Internet (and Google) later. What I want to do in this first chapter is to think from a different perspective about what is happening in the traction–distraction dialectic. The value of stickiness (or anti-distraction) to advertisers and booksellers is obvious. But what (commercial concerns aside) is actually happening when we are being distracted, or when efforts are made either by people in the world "out there" to get and sustain our attention, or when we ourselves make the conscious effort to remain with the process of reading and writing a little longer, and resist the impulse for the mind and the attention to wander? Why, indeed, does the concentration tend to lapse? Are we innately shallow creatures who are easily distracted and endlessly diverted? Or can we see this restlessness in another way, as some do, where instead of terming it distraction we can put a positive spin on it and call it "multitasking", something that is supposedly a useful, efficient, and industrious skill for today's world? Does it actually matter very much?

Writing this book would indicate that I think that it does, and deeply. As children at school we all learned that distraction is a bad thing. For the eyes to stray out the classroom window to the clouds or the playing field, or for the mind to roam to untold realms of fantasy and idleness was always seen to be to the detriment of the purpose of schooling—which was to learn, to absorb information and knowledge, and to become more or less rounded and functional individuals and citizens. Doubtless, some of us continued longer in our visual and mental wanderings. But we could be trained to moderate this and learn the discipline of sustained concentration. Others could learn to be creative within a distracted state. And yet others, indeed, learned to be more flexible and develop the ability to move in and out of all three modes. However, that age-old problem for kids and for adults too has come up against the unprecedented challenges of the "network society," where lightning-speed information processing and its application have transformed the contexts in which we relate to information and knowledge. The classroom has changed; the workplace and the home space have changed. The effect is that never has it been so difficult *not* to be distracted, and never has our resistance to it been so low and feeble.

Why this is so will not become clear, nor solutions thinkable, until the problem of our now-chronic distraction is properly identified. Accordingly, I want to locate the ground zero of the malaise of chronic distraction in the realm of *time*. At one level this is obvious. If we try to concentrate on something, such as reading another page of Wittgenstein on a park bench when your mobile phone is buzzing, or when an e-mail delivery icon pops up when we are trying to write an essay at home or a report at work, then we are dealing with a specific relationship with time, a contextualized one where different things are competing for your time (your attention). At this surface level of analysis, the problem may be brushed aside as simply a fact of our busy networked lives, examples of what Dale Southerton (2003) calls the "time squeeze," and is something that we all just need to cope with as best we can. However, unless we understand the nature of social time and our relationship with temporality, then not only will these problems become worse—which then becomes a political problem—but we will also *understand them correspondingly less*, because the network society, as I will show in Chapter 3, is one that is set on a path of open-ended *acceleration*, that is to say, if you think life today is getting faster, then you ain't seen nothing yet. Today the imperative of needing to understand time as a changing social phenomenon is acute, because the new relationship with time—like the network society itself—permeates so much of our lives.

The first job then is to make clear and definite links between the experience of what may *prima facie* seem to be quite different phenomena. These are: *time, technology*, and the processes of *reading and writing*. I want to show how these have functioned together in a particular way to build the world as we have known it for nearly three hundred years. This has been the world of modernity. In very recent times, however, these interacting processes have been transformed at their core and are now building a very different world, a late-modern one where the sureties (such as they were) of the previous world are fast disappearing and being displaced by what I see to be a chronic and pervasive mode of *cognitive distraction* that is the expression of a world increasingly devoid of the Enlightenment impulses that gave it meaning and purpose in the first place.

The foregoing sentence reads like the beginning of a serious, if not familiar, tale. But this is not another whingeing critique of a dissipating late-modernity—nor is it just one more pleading case in support of an ossifying modernity. It is another way of looking at these ways of being and seeing through a very different lens. It is a perspective that is permeated above all by a *theory of time*, which, in its turn, throws a different light upon technological development, beginning with the invention of writing and the development of the skill of reading. Taken together, these will provide a unique view of the trajectory of modernity into a late-modernity, and illustrate how the arc of "progress" has been transformed into its opposite: that is to say, into a negative circle (or cycle) of presentism where past and future are compressing steadily into a constant now. It is here that new modes of time, new modes of technology, and new modes of reading and writing help create a faster and shallower world and more instrumental world where we know less about more—and forget what we know every more quickly.

Adorno and Horkheimer in their *Dialectic of the Enlightenment*, argued that reason and rationality had become "negative" and evolved into a "mere construction of means" where there was no way back to a logic of emancipatory reason (1986, 42). There is no doubt, as this book will show, that they were right and that a world obsessed with "means" has reached such heights of intensity that even Adorno and Horkheimer could scarcely have dreamed of. But that is not the end of the story. I am telling quite a different tale regarding the evolution of the Enlightenment-created world, one that suggests that if there is indeed a way back, then it will be through the finding of new intellectual, cultural, and *temporal* paths to follow. To do this it will be necessary, however, for the reader to persist with a challenging (challenging for me at least to think and write about) few opening pages, to then perhaps be rewarded by what I see to be a fresh perspective on our current reality. This new reality, a "temporalized" reality, is one that, *contra* Adorno and Horkheimer and their generations of adherents, is in fact full of promise and potential and ways of seeing that are not possible through the many current, and largely baleful, modes of analysis.

So to begin with some framing questions with which to consider the nature of and the relationship between the processes of temporality, technology, reading and writing: What is the "time" of a thought? Is it possible to measure thinking? Can we consider knowledge or information (a crucial distinction to be taken up later), or reading and writing, as having their own temporal "rhythms"? Can time move too fast for us? Questions such as these might seem akin to trying to grasp fresh air with your hands. So unfamiliar are we to thinking in such terms that such ideas sound (and feel) impossible. By contrast, so familiar are we to thinking and experiencing as "individuals," that we assume, intuitively at least, that what goes on in my head, what I carry around as "thoughts" and "knowledge" may indeed have a generalized association—after all we share a common world, do not we? However, to borrow a phrase from the existentialist and psychiatrist R.D. Laing, "I cannot experience your experience. You cannot experience my experience" (1967, 16). To a significant degree, it seems, time, thinking, and many forms of knowledge are the fruits of subjective experience. These are ways of understanding, processes, and modes of being that we cannot *really* and *fully* share. We connect our experiences only at the most superficial level, where what you experience and what I experience may be objectively the same, but our interpretations will always diverge in respect of the "reality" we confront. Like two friends experiencing a football match. They will likely see the game in very different ways, with a myriad of factors shaping each interpretation, be it boredom, or excitement, or knowledge of the game in general or perhaps a comparative lack of it. Never can we "match" exactly our subjective experience of the world.

At one register of consciousness this observation on the apparent nature of experience is banal and expresses something we all "know" to be the way of the world. Experience—so this reasoning goes—is singular and is a manifestation (or possibly cause?) of our innate individuality. And so to say that thoughts and knowledge can have rhythms, pace, and a particular *speed* seems faintly absurd. Consequently, in our western, modernist culture, the subjective nature of experience and the elusive nature of time make for a rather difficult dovetailing. Indeed, it is even more problematic to think of "measuring" such interaction temporally. Time's intangible qualities and its capacious elasticity between past, present, and future are sunk deep into our literary culture and we can glimpse here the extent of the challenge we face to properly grasp the nature of time. The French novelist Marcel Proust made a career out of such an approach to time. Somewhat ironically, he guaranteed himself in the process the "timelessness" of being admitted into the Western modernist canon. In his *Remembrance of Things Past*, Proust continually describes time as being an element of both social and individualized contexts. But he inscribes these with a special evanescent and dreamlike quality, ones that he is nonetheless careful to differentiate from the actual practice of sleep. In his discoursing on the subjective unconsciousness nature of sleep at the liminal portal of waking, Proust writes that: "… on those mornings (and this is what makes me say that sleep is perhaps unconsciously of the law of time) my effort to awaken consisted chiefly in an effort to make the obscure, undefined mass of the sleep in which I'd just been living enter in to the scale of time" (2006, 326).

Julia Kristeva has analyzed Proust's approach to time and noted that his "style outlines *this other temporality*, which transcends measurement, space, and duration…" (1996, 233) (my italics). The philosopher's perspective of time's subjective essence continues with Elizabeth Grosz who, following the phenomenology of Husserl and Bergson, writes that "Time is neither fully present, a thing in itself, nor is it a pure abstraction, a metaphysical assumption that can be ignored in everyday practice. We can think it only in passing moments, through

5

ruptures, nicks, cuts, in instances of dislocation, though it contains no moments or ruptures and has no being or presence, functioning only as continuous becoming" (2004, 5).

The multifaceted, subjective, ostensibly elusive and *malleable* nature of time is pretty clear in these texts. But this essence also forms the unconscious—and largely unreflected upon—backdrop to our collective social and public lives too. We only have to consider how, in many instances in many social and political cultures, what time "is" is always up for grabs, and therefore not readily "measurable" as real-world temporal rhythms. For example, there is a common view of history which states or implies that it unfolds over the "passage of time," down through a great chain of events involving particular people and places, armies, inventions, revolutions, and so on. In this view, "traditions" can form as a result of this temporal congealing through ritual and practice, and their relative fixity as facts and events in written records seemingly allow us to be in touch with our collective pasts. History, then, might seem to have its own temporal rhythms, punctuated by patterns and sequences that may act as the basis for a chronologically measurable, historical time. However, as Eric Hobsbawm observes in the opening to his collection, *The Invention of Tradition*, many of those reassuring social and cultural rituals "which appear or claim to be old are often quite recent in origin and sometimes invented" (1983, 1). Similarly, Benedict Anderson, in his *Imagined Communities* argued powerfully that the concept of the nation, something that is the very epitome of "tradition" and historical time, is a figment of our collective imaginary, something we agree to be true, because the scope and "substance" of a nation is impossible to appreciate as a individual, if only because he or she can only ever experience a tiny part of the larger totality: so we "imagine" it, so as to give "confirmation of the solidity of a single community...moving onward through calendrical time" (1991, 27).

The social dynamics of invention and imagination working upon our sense of time is a continuing feature of the contemporary world. In the former Soviet Union, for example, the forward march of progress through "calendrical time" was a *telos* set in concrete by the Communist Party and its particular ideology. Through its hegemonizing grip upon the educational, industrial, and media institutions, the past was able to be invented and imagined and projected toward the future in such a way as to place communism, Soviet history, and the Party itself, in the best possible light. Post-1989, however, the psychic structures of history and tradition began to collapse and the institutions they formed began to crumble to reveal a sort of time void. New inventions, new traditions, and new perspectives [through, for example, the articulation of new historiographies (e.g., Brent 2009)] rushed into the space to give past, present, and future new shapes and textures and potential modes of experience. Accordingly, Russia's past is presently being rearranged and reordered in accordance with the changed exigencies of new Russian power formations. Today there is a largely subterranean (in that it receives little media attention), but hugely significant battle being waged in Russia over what might be called, to use Proust's title, "the remembrance of things past." It is a battle between progressive civil society groups such as Memorial and the quasi-totalitarian state that is now in the saddle. Memorial wants to reclaim or simply to discover, through free and open study of the State Archives and other sources, alternative pasts that had been expunged from popular memory through Stalinist repression (Figes 2007). However, the new regime in Russia, threatened by this challenge to their own twenty-first-century brand of soft-Stalinism, continues to invent and inscribe narratives of the past that suit their present and future projects.

An example of these ongoing time wars surfaced in the seventieth anniversary of the outbreak of World War II in September 1939. In an article published on his official website, Russian Prime Minister Vladimir Putin described the Nazi-Soviet Pact of August 1939, which cleared the way for the Second World War, as "immoral." Such a statement was on the face of it highly significant, as it seemed to suggest a new candor on the part of the Russian leadership, one that might be open to a fuller accounting of the past. However, this was as far as the criticism went. Putin's article went on to throw a heavy obfuscatory blanket over the past by arguing that the "immorality" of the Pact was justified by the context of the times. The fact that the British had *also* treated with Hitler at Munich the year before, was held up as evidence by Putin that there were no innocents in the diplomacy of the late-1930s; and anyway, the root of the problem lay in the Allied *diktat* expressed through the Versailles Treaty of 1919 that placed an insurmountable burden of reparations upon Germany—something in which Russia played no part. And so a closer reading of Putin's essay reveals that the Nazi-Soviet Pact was something supposedly *forced* upon the Russians, through circumstances created by the West (Putin 2009). All this is debatable up to a point. However, the essay makes no mention (and this would have been significant) of the "secret protocols" attached to the Pact which allowed for the brutal dismemberment of Poland in the war that was to come, nor of the systematic plunder of Poland by both the Nazis and the Soviets, nor the murder of fifteen thousand of the Polish officer class by the Soviet secret police in the forest of Katyn in 1940 (Snyder 2010).

As these instances show, temporality is rooted in the social, is subjectively and collectively experienced, is impressionably formed and reformed according to context and circumstance and ideological position, and is—as a consequence of these foregoing qualities—wholly and essentially *dynamic.*

It should be stated here and now that this broad view of time is for me deeply compelling. Time, because it is social, is also as diverse as the social. Time can be mysterious, but it is also as plain as the nose on your face. We can "possess" it in the form of individualized experience and memory, but modalities of power can also remake it for us in ways that are not necessarily to our advantage as thinking beings that wish to understand the reality of the world. Through being rooted in the social, time in this perspective is constituted by what social theory has termed "embedded" times. These are the "complex times of nature and social organization" that are at the very core of life (Adam 1998, 49). As we shall see, these embedded times are, in fact, the many and variegated rhythms that inscribe and modulate the tempo(s) of life in all its diversity. These embedded temporalities act as an internal and environmental force that comprise the baselines of existence, and are expressed, for example, in the cycles of dawn and sunset, in the repeating of seasons, in the emergent process of reproduction and death, in variable sequencing of waking and sleeping, in the patterns of cardiac beating of the heart, and in the rhythms of breathing.

Times that are embedded in the body and in nature are thus irreducible and act to shape our consciousness and so are of course elemental parts of what it is to be human. However, we barely give them a second thought. We move through these times unthinkingly because they (and therefore a possibly more intimate and insightful relationship with them) have been over layered with, to employ the phrase from Kristeva I just cited, "another temporality," one which in fact does *not* "transcend measurement." Indeed, this one has its *very basis in measurement* because it is produced by *technology and by the specific path that technological development has taken.* The core thesis of this book is to show that the embedded times of the body and nature, and the subjective times of Proust and phenomenologically derived experience have, since the development of the *key technology of writing*, been increasingly displaced and dominated by the rhythms of a technologically produced temporality. To be sure, the development of writing and the transformed human consciousness that emerged from this dialectic made us what we are today, and much of this has been progressive and positive. It is a relationship that has allowed us to imagine (and to create) worlds through the development of science and philosophy, and allowed us to take steps beyond our infant species' ignorance and its primal fear of nature. But the dynamics of the interaction—the dynamism of technological development, and the dynamism of our relationship with time—has brought us now to a moment of crisis, one that has its origins in the practices of reading and writing.

The period from when the first cuneiform marks were scratched onto slate tablets in Mesopotamia around four thousand years ago, to the present day where billions of words that are produced digitally every day has been, relatively speaking, a bat of the eyelid in the geologic or evolutionary timescale of nature. Nevertheless, so much has changed so quickly within this short timescale, because speed and acceleration became locked into the relationship with technology with the rise of capitalist industrialism. We read and write more than ever, but we are (individually and collectively) less able to exert less control over the processes governing what we read and write—and to what uses we put the forms of knowledge that emerge from it. Moreover, the physical temporalities of our hand and eye movements, the movements that allow for the production and consumption of reading and writing, have not speeded up appreciably since humans first learned the skill of literacy—but economic and technological imperatives that now drive the production and consumption of information and knowledge has accelerated to an unprecedented degree with the rise of the network society. Today, technological speed and acceleration have been let loose upon the social world, and in our pathetic efforts to synchronize with the new pace of life and of change, we simply find ourselves reacting to it, being distracted by it, and being diminished as a consequence of it.

And so it is necessary, indeed it is now essential, to explore the largely neglected interrelationship between the ways in which humans experience and produce forms of time—with that of the development of writing, possibly the most important technology ever to have emerged from the brain of our species. I want to explore this interaction, because the balance between temporality and our production

9

of knowledge (or what today may be more accurately described as a *dominance of information*) through writing has become seriously out of kilter. The inquiry is doubly important because this desynchronization is something that we ordinarily do not recognize as a problem, so in thrall to technological development are our societies and the economic structures that now shape and dominate them. Today, technological development is guided more than anything else by "efficiency," and "efficiency" in its turn, is largely expressed and measured within the very narrow criteria of simply *doing things faster*—and doing this increasingly by means of computer automation (Hassan 2009).

Which brings us back to the question of time. Most of us would acknowledge, if pressed, that too much speed or haste in, say, the driving of a car, or in the coordination of air-traffic control duties, or the filing of a job application, could have potentially negative outcomes. Speed is not always the best course of action, in other words. We intuit this fairly easily across a whole range of common-sense scenarios in everyday life where we know that it is best to proceed sometimes with care and caution. However, when it comes to *computing* we simply gape in awe and admiration at what the clever fellows at IBM or Intel or Apple or MIT Media Lab can come up with, week after week. This generalized *sang froid* becomes rather more worrying when it is remembered (or when it is realized) the tremendously powerful position that the logic of computing holds in our societies. For example, in long ago 1984, just as those (now) impossibly heavy and slow "personal computers" were being delivered to our office desks, courtesy of IBM and Bill Gates and Apple Corporation, J. David Bolter, writing in his *Turing's Man: Western Culture in the Computer Age*, was both emphatic and prescient about the importance of what was then happening. The computer, he maintained, was quickly shaping up to be the new "defining technology" and the key to understanding the tremendous changes taking place in our age. This was because computers were special in terms of their technological effects. Bolter argued that they do not wholly replace other "defining" technologies such has the combustion engine—but they do create a *new technological context* within which other technologies must adapt, be adapted, or else suffer inexorable marginalization. As Bolter puts it:

> Computers perform no work in themselves: they direct work [...]
> The computer leaves intact many older technologies, particularly
> the technologies of power, and yet puts them in a new perspective.

With the appearance of a truly subtle machine like the computer, the old power machines (steam, gas, or rocket engines) lose something of their prestige. Power machines are no longer agents on their own...now they must submit to the hegemony of the computer that coordinates their effects. (8)

Just over a decade later, Manuel Castells drew our attention to the scale and significance of computer-driven change in Volume One of his *The Rise of the Information Society* where he observed that the information networks that were emerging out of the desktop revolution "constitute the new social morphology of our societies [and] the diffusion of networking logic substantially modifies the operation and outcomes in processes of production, experience, power, and culture" (1996, 469). Computing, then, "defines" our world, and "substantially modifies" the reality we knew prior to its rise to dominance. Yet this new logic, or morphology, speeds up exponentially through computing in ways unprecedented, to leave us gasping in its wake as we inevitably fail to keep up with its inhuman and unstinting pace. But even in our breathlessness we still view this to be "progress" and as the mark of "efficiency."

Before continuing, and before you put this book down early and for good, I should stress that this is not yet another anti-computer technology tract—one that implies or argues explicitly, that things were better prior to when Steve Jobs of Apple Corporation, or his spiritual sons, Sergey Brin and Larry Page of Google, came along. The computer revolution has brought much that is truly useful to humanity: for example, the sequencing of the human genome has prised open the mysteries of our genetic constitution, and all manner of wonderful discoveries await; we see it too in the fairly unalloyed positive transformation of such disparate realms of inquiry such as medicine, or archaeology, or pharmacology, or astronomy, meteorology, and so on. Increasingly new fields of vision regarding what we might hope to understand and accomplish would not have been possible without powerful and fast computing.

However, I want to concentrate on the *social and temporal* effects of Castells' "new morphology" claim. In particular, I seek to make the temporal aspect much more salient than has been the case previously in social theory critiques of computing and society. By making the temporal an explicit factor in how we understand our reading, writing, and thinking lives in the twenty-first century, the book shines a critical light on the effects of out-of-control computer speed in the neoliberal economic contexts. This is speed that works upon the social world—upon individuals and upon societies—in ways that we have barely begun to consider. To get the critique properly underway, it is necessary for the sake of clarity to unpack the main elements of my argument before putting them back together in a theoretical synthesis. The present chapter will thus articulate the context for the rest of the book by focusing on three subsidiary components that will be analyzed separately ahead of their reintegration back into the larger framework. These subsidiary components are: social time; technologies and time; and writing, thinking, and knowledge in time. We will look at these in their turn, but first it is necessary to say something about clock time and its relationship with social time.

Time Expressible as Number

On a surface level, at the level of the everyday, the idea of temporality, and indeed the practice of time itself tends to be (whenever we do actually think about it) pitched at the plane of the abstract; something, akin to "the economy," a "thing" or "process" that deeply affects us, but is nonetheless not something that is constituted by flesh and blood and by the natural world in the ways described above. In the West, since at least the eighteenth century, powerful historical forces have functioned to extract time from its embedded and experiential realm—with all the contextuality and heterogeneity that such provenance would naturally convey—and to locate it within the larger and rather more singular dimension of physics and mathematics. What this meant was that time could be thought of as a rational and ordering force that worked its logic (and its magic) upon the irrationality and disorder of man in society.

Abstract, machinic, invariable, and linear time—a disciplining time that would rationally arrange the social world, and rhythm it to synchronize with a universal and cosmological order—was at the very heart of what was to become *modernity*. And its introduction was revolutionary. A key figure in the establishment of this doctrinal principle, something that would achieve the status of natural law, so powerfully would it reorder human time consciousness, was Isaac Newton. The influence of Newton's theories on time cannot be understated. He was at the forefront of the seventeenth-century transformation in rational thinking and in the development of science that indicated the possibilities for alternative explanations for the nature of the universe. Newton perhaps epitomized the focus as well as the scope of the intellectual concerns of the Renaissance, the period that made possible the efflorescence of the European Enlightenment that would come in the next century. It is his work on physics, in particular, what came to be known as Classical Mechanics that are of most concern to us here. Classical Mechanics or Newtonian Mechanics described, through the use of mathematics, the motion of objects in space. Time is obviously implicated here. However, as Barbara Adam (2004, 29) explains, Newton:

> ...was not concerned with time in its own right, but with the operational value of time as measured in motion. He conceived of time as a quantity: invariant, infinitely into space-like units, measurable in length and *expressible as number*. Newtonian time is time taken, the duration between events, which is unaffected by the transformation it describes (my emphasis).

As the intellectual father of modern mechanics and of the theory of the motion of objects in space, what Newton contrived was nothing less than a *mechanics of time*, one that argued explicitly for a mechanistic underpinning of the universe. As the philosopher Arran Gare has argued, this constituted a hinge-point in the development of what he terms the "mechanistic way of life" that had been slowly building in Europe from the time of Plato (Gare 1996). Indeed, Newton propagated the idea that the cosmos, the world and its proper working processes, were analogous to a machine, a particularly *clockwork* universe that moves in celestial harmony—a gigantic space–time action which people and nature existed *within*, and perforce could be best understood *through*. Out of the works of Newton and others such as Hobbes and Descartes, the machine metaphor began to infiltrate the consciousness of men and women living at the threshold of modernity. As Gare describes its longer historical context: "while the idea of what constitutes a machine has evolved from a clock in the seventeenth and eighteenth centuries, to a steam engine running down in the nineteenth century to an information processing mechanism in the twentieth century, the machine has remained *the dominant metaphor* to understand nature..."(1996, 134). Time was now viewed as independent of the social world, and therefore as a machine force that the social world had to align with if it sought harmony in place of chaos. In his famous definition at the beginning of his 1687 *Principia*, Newton declared that "Absolute true and mathematical time, of itself, and from its own nature, flows equably without relation to anything external." He regarded moments of absolute time as moments that follow a continuous linear sequence and, moreover, the rate at which these moments succeeded one another is independent of the universe and its processes (Whitrow 1988, 128–29).

So powerfully has the idea of clock time stayed with us, and of course it deeply permeates everyday life still, that it continues to form a psychic barrier to other ways of experiencing time and thinking about time—such as through the brief phenomenological outline that was sketched above. I want now to build on this experiential perspective, using both my own work and the relevant thinking in social theory that informs it. What I hope to do is to show what the mechanistic thinking of clock time has *displaced* from our temporal consciousness, and then theorize about what this displacement suggests about our speed-filled present-day world. "Displaced" is a key term. We live by the clock, still, but we "know" and "feel" other times. However, our connection to (and with) these have become attenuated through a machine-based modernity and capitalist logic—and so to understand these times more clearly we need to put the time of the clock into its proper context as a social construction.

The Humanness of Time

There is no time without man.
—Martin Heidegger (1972, 16)

Time reckoning—or the cognitive ability to think about time, to reflect on the experience of time, and to consider the meaning of time—is, as far as our current thinking goes, a uniquely human trait (Zimmer 2007). Some animals may recognize and produce temporal patterns and routines and rhythms. Certain domesticated animals such as cats or dogs may learn to be familiar with the daily schedules of feeding times, times to go for a walk, when someone is due to arrive home, and so on. In contrast, humans, through the development of self-consciousness (and more on this later) have learned to inquire about how duration, rhythm, and tempo are constituted. We have reasoned that time is multivariate, is socially embedded, and in time's imbrications, diversities and transformations, form part of the substance of evolving social interaction. To be able to reflect upon the experience of time, though, does not automatically open the doors to perception and understanding. My experience, as Laing stated, can never be yours, and vice versa. So how then is it possible to about the experience of time in a way that is mutually shared to an extent that is meaningful? The problem is an ancient one. Indeed, we humans have been grasping to find a common understanding since at least the time of Saint Augustine who lived and wrote in the first century, and posed the following conundrum in his *Confessions*: "What, then, is time? If no one ask of me, I know; if I wish to explain to him who asks, I know not."

Sociology and social theory has taken us some way toward dealing adequately with this problem. This has only been tentative, however, and within the sobering context of a mechanically (or now electronically) dominated instrumental culture that still thwarts a deeper temporal understanding of social life. Let us look at some of these contributions.

Emerging from the pioneering works of Emile Durkheim (1964) and Robert Merton (1937), the writings of Norbert Elias has been a major contribution to the sociology of time and his emphasis on its social (as opposed to its mechanical) nature acts as a lodestone in this realm of inquiry. For Elias it is the process of change and our ability to cognitively and reflexively experience it, which constitutes the starting point for an understanding of social time. This insight leads him to a working definition of time. The experience of time, he observes in his *Time: An Essay*, "...is based on people's capacity for connecting with each other two or more different sequences of continuous changes, one of which serves as a timing standard for the other (or others)" (1992, 72). Elsewhere in the book, Elias expresses this concept within a slightly more expanded field of vision: "...the word 'time' is a symbol of a relationship that a human group of beings biologically endowed with the capacity for memory and synthesis, establishes between two or more continua of changes, one of which is used by it as a frame of reference or standard or measurement for the other or others" (1992, 46).

I have on the wall of my office a sheet of A4 paper upon which, in bold 44pt Sans-Serif typeface, there is a beautifully condensed summation of Elias' idea of the nature of social time. It was written by Simonetta Tabboni in her majestic essay "The Idea of Social Time in Norbert Elias' and it reads: The social construction of time...goes back to a *specific human ability to work on the experience of change, to react, to organize and confer meaning on the experience*" (2001, 7) (emphasis in original). In this reading, time can only be understood—properly and in its essence—as social time, time created by humans in their social world and recognized as such because they are human. Uniquely as a species we impute meaning into things and through meanings that are elicited from change we also generate the basis for the recognition of the process of time as change. Admittedly this is still somewhat difficult stuff to understand. This cognitive problem is nonetheless ironic because social time, thus understood, forms the backdrop to our social lives, and we unconsciously navigate these temporal shoals of change every day. The difficulty, as already noted stems from the fact that mechanical time displaces, disturbs, and clouds this awareness through the weight of its historical presence and through its continuing economic imperatives (Nowotny 1994). It is, nonetheless, worth cracking the nut of social time in order to consider its contents so as to develop a better understanding of social time in practice.

In her essay on Elias, Tabboni notes that in the general literature on the origins of time awareness "two types of awareness are indicated as central: that of continuity/discontinuity and that of recurrence" (2001, 7). When considering the awareness of continuity/discontinuity, Tabboni writes that these are "polar categories" but that they are defined through their opposition and are "...only capable of consideration in their reciprocity." She goes on to elaborate that we experience these: "...when we realize that a change has taken place in some part of our reality: in our body, in our thoughts, in the physical and social world around us" (2001, 7). Change is movement, and this is characterized, as Tabboni explains, by "events...in relation to which one can see a before and after, something commonly referred to in expressions like 'from then on', or 'from that day on'" (2001, 7). The idea of recurrence is equally fecund. This is "the regular cyclical return of the same phenomena: pulse beats, sleeping and waking, day and night, Christmas and Easter follow each other and provoke behaviour that seems unchanging. The seasons of the year alternate with social seasons and give place to recurrences, not of events which can be seen as having a before and after" (8). Event-generated change and patterns of cyclical recurrence thus comprise the grids of temporal reference that constitute our temporal being. The fundamental elements that make time human, then, are the embedded temporalities both in our living bodies and in the natural world that surrounds us.

This perspective is still rather individualized and does not fully convey an impression of the actual *social* dimensions of social time, of people moving through a social world, constantly in interaction with others within shared environments. However, Henri Lefebvre, a thinker known mostly for his writings on the social production of spatial forms, makes a bold and insightful theoretical move in this direction. Lefebvre saw time as inextricably linked with space in the social production process. In his *The Social Production of Space*, he illustrates this through lucid description of the temporal "rhythms" of the body that are "deployed" into what he calls "'real' abstract space" (or socially constructed) space:

> Rhythms in all their multiplicity interpenetrate one another. In the body and around it…rhythms are forever crossing and recrossing, superimposing themselves upon each other, always bound to space…if we attempt to specify them we find that some rhythms are easy to identify: breathing, the heartbeat, thirst, hunger, and the need for sleep are cases in point. Others, however, such as those of sexuality, fertility, social life, or thought are relatively obscure. Some operate on the surface, so to speak, whereas others spring from hidden depths…. (1992, 205)

Lefebvre's original French language edition of the book was published in 1974 and it helped to generate a literature that, from the time of Durkheim and Merton, had still not become a proper school or movement, but was nonetheless beginning to orient toward a broadly sociological and critical theory approach to time (i.e., Cottle 1976; Hendricks and Hendricks 1976; Koselleck 1979; Sherover 1975). More recently, Bruno Latour made social time an aspect of his Actor Network Theory (ANT) that is based on the interactive agency between networks of humans and technologies. Latour saw temporality (or the creation of social time) as part of the functioning of the ANT dynamic. In an echo of the quote from Heidegger above, Latour asserts that "The connections among beings alone make time," and that only humans "have the capacity to produce both time and space." Indeed, Latour goes on to say, and this will become apparent in my later discussions, "it was the *systematic connection of entities in a coherent whole* that constituted the flow of modern time" (1993, 77) (my emphasis).

All this moves us some way forward in our understanding of the social nature of time, and the foregoing few paragraphs constitute what would be the very basis any understanding of a sociology of time. Nevertheless, it does not yet form a functionally robust framework that links the subjective experiences of time and their multiplicities (embedded in bodies and in nature) with the ongoing creation and emergence of time in everyday-life situations. It still does not fully promote the temporal dimension to a salience that places all other dimensions of the social in a new and revealing light. To move to this level of synthesis we need to consider the work of Barbara Adam. Adam achieves this fusion through the introduction of a new concept, which she terms "timescapes." It has been the life's work of Adam to make salient the function of temporality from the perspective of sociology, and her 1998 book *The Timescapes of Modernity* contains the introduction of the concept and the initial systematizing of the supporting theory.

The "scape" in Adam's idea of "timescape" is significant. The definition of "scape" is "a scene" or "a view," and these suggest a strongly spatial element which is evident in the everyday use of the term in compound words, such as in "seascape" or "landscape." One of Adam's signal contributions is to rebalance this spatial bias, and necessarily so, because as the physics of Einstein tells us, and as the philosophy of Lefebvre re-emphasizes, space and time can no longer be viewed as separate processes. As she puts it:

> Where other scapes such as landscapes, cityscapes and seascapes mark the spatial features of past and present activities and interactions of organisms and matter, timescapes emphasises their rythmicities, their timing and tempos, their changes and contingences. A timescape perspective stresses the temporal features of living. (1998, 11)

The timescape, then, stresses the priority of the spatial–temporal whole in place of the historical dualism that has permeated our modernist thinking on time and space, and raises to prominence the dynamic of time in the always-emergent human condition. A cityscape, for example, in its living, growing and changing form, is more than the spatio-geometry of its buildings, the grid or maze of its streets, alleys and boulevards, or the serrated horizon of its skyline. The cityscape also thrums with the traffic that flows through its arteries; the machine rhythms of capitalism temporally mark the city's days with opening and closing times of businesses; and people swarm to the city to experience (and also to create) its "buzz" of activity and its uncountable multitude of temporal diversities—from the fast-paced excitement of a night club, to the quiet and reflection of study in a public library. Adam highlights the "symphony of rhythms and temporalities" that go to the production of social time (1998, 13). The metaphor of the symphony is apt. It illustrates the diversity of timescapes that can come together to create the temporal whole. In the social context, the kaleidoscope of timescapes "gives a dynamic structure to our lives that permeates every level and every facet of our existence" (1998, 13). Within this temporal framework "all aspects interpenetrate and have a bearing on each other. All coexist and are lived simultaneously" and this "underpins our development as humans and as living organism. It marks us as creatures of this earth, as beings that are constituted by a double temporality: rhythmically structured within and embedded in the rhythmic organization of the cosmos" (1998, 13).

When the idea of "social time" is spelled out like this, courtesy of penetrating and illustrative thinking, such as that of Elias, Tabboni and Adam, then the deeply temporal nature of our lives become more apparent and clear. We can see that we contribute to, and derive temporal experience from, the multitude of timescapes that comprise the taken-for-granted backdrop of time that we are so used to, and the theorized level of the abstract becomes apparent through the efforts of such social theorists. But therein lies the problem of an adequate understanding of social time in our modernist context: it needs a conscious theoretical effort to render it more insightful. This is because the "social" in social time is not a pure, unadulterated entity. The "social" reflects our messy humanity, and its baleful proneness toward hierarchy, exploitation, the concentrations of power, increasing layers in the complexity of life, and so on.

Our relationship to technology and technological development becomes an important factor here. The technologies we use and the tasks that we assign them similarly reflect our complex social structures. Adrian Mackenzie makes the very useful point that far from being empty, neutral and autonomous abstractions, things that simply are; technologies (and technical practices) are in fact *signifiers* or expressions of specific (or generalized) social relations (2002, 205–6). An aircraft carrier battle group, for example, may be said to signify a masculinist power projection in the context of modern interstate rivalries (Mackenzie 2002, 205). The battle group example may also be read in the context of modern state *inequalities of power*, whereupon only the mightiest of nations have the technical and economic resources to build and use them. By way of contrast, an example of what might seem a radically differing signification can be seen in, say, a doctor's stethoscope. On one level, this relatively uncomplicated technology, invented in the early nineteenth century, may be viewed as a positive and unquestionably humanist technology. Such a reading would see it as a signifier of the fruits of Enlightenment inquiry, where a form of logic freed from superstition and religion could develop technologies and techniques that are designed to improve the health and well being of our species. On another level, however, the humble stethoscope may be read as a signifier of the *medicalization* of the body. In the work of Michel Foucault, for example, medicalization can be seen as the negative expression of a form of social power through specialist technical knowledge (Foucault 1980). And so a Foucauldian deconstruction of the social context of the stethoscope therefore may offer more complex readings. For example, in the one-to-one medical encounter the stethoscope can be seen as a tool that helps give the physician complete control over a passive body; or more broadly it may be seen to fit as one technique among many medical practices and discourses that can render the individual or class as subject to a diminished authority or control over one's own body and its care (Illich 1975).

As social constructions, technologies can alienate or empower. Indeed, the same technology can do both at the same time: we see this in Marx's critique in *Capital* of the factory system as the font of working class alienation. It is a perspective that is as valid today (where the logic of the factory system is essentially the same as it was in the 1860s) as when Marx first dissected its inner workings. But other readings are possible. It is easy to appreciate, for example, that whilst holding down an alienating and soul-destroying job, the worker also gets a wage that may allow him or her to save for a better education that could someday be a passport out of the factory. The point is that humans have a powerful and complex and often defining relationship with technology. But this role, this interaction, is malleable, contextually contingent, and historically unfolding—both in the context of the individual and wider society, and in the context of the development of individual technologies and systems of technologies.

The further point of this line of inquiry is that it leads us to a consideration of the idea of technologies containing their own temporality. Like the idea of time as social and as being embedded in social processes, the idea of technologies containing a specific temporal logic is one that a Newtonian mechanical modernity does not allow for. But what does it mean to say that technologies, indeed simple technologies such as a pen or a sheet of paper are encoded with their own forms of time—and in the case of machines, with their own temporal logic? Further, what does such an encoding and logic portend for our understanding of the practice and effects of reading—and most especially—of writing?

2

The Ghost in the Machine

In advance of moving the discussion toward the nature and effects of technology—and to the temporality of the technology of writing in specific—I want first to undergird that argument with a general analysis of the temporalization of technologies.

We begin then with a basic question: what does technology do? In one sense the question is easily dealt with: technologies allow individuals to *act* upon the world. That is to say, he or she is enabled to make an intervention that can make a difference both to the world and to the experience of the technology user. For example, the development of the spear in ancient hunter-gatherer societies meant that possessors of that technology could hunt more efficiently and make war more effectively. Their surroundings were immediately transformed into both a context of potential, whereby the range of prospective game is massively expanded, and to one of risk wherein others who possessed spears constitute a possible danger in a situation where food may be scarce or hunting grounds depleted. The dialectic between the individual (or the group) and the world through technology, we can see, is immediate and powerful. In our own hyper-technologized society, the dialectic may not always be so apparent and forceful, but it occurs everyday and in a growing diversity of ways that make for (taken as a whole) a highly dynamic world where social change (social time) is in constant flux. And so for example, sitting behind the wheel of a car transforms the man or woman into a *driver* who is the bearer of a multitude of possibilities and potentials in terms of the ability to act upon the world. Among other things the driver becomes a *mobile consumer* who enters the massive complexity of the global economy as soon as the ignition key is turned and petrol begins to be used. The driver also becomes a site for the technological world to act back upon, as directions and instructions need constantly to be read and observed, obstacles negotiated and behavior modified accordingly.

All this is fairly mundane stuff. But it is nevertheless a vital starting-point toward an understanding of the central problematic of technology—that of *agency and domination*. When and how do technologies enable and when do they constrain—and what does time have to do with it?

Marshall McLuhan is famous for his work on media and for the critical conceptual breakthroughs he made in this field during the 1960s. In terms of media his work is usually associated with its electronic forms such as television and the telephone. Moreover, he is justly celebrated for his knack for illuminative aphorism—thus allowing generations of students to get to know something of his thought through one-liners such as "the medium is the message" and the "global village." A key insight of McLuhan's that I want to develop here is concerned not simply with media technologies (although these will become important later on) but with technology per se. And so to answer in another way the question "what do technologies do?" McLuhan tells us in his *Understanding Media* that they literally become "extensions" of the natural capacities our body. The idea is uncomplicated, but when it is dissected and analyzed—and the temporal aspect is brought into view—then the effects and consequences of "extensionality" go to the heart of what it means to be human and social in the technologized world. At the very beginning of his book, McLuhan observes that: "During the mechanical ages we had extended our bodies into space. Today, after more than a century of electric technology, we have extended our central nervous system in a global embrace, abolishing both space and time as far as our planet is concerned" (1967, 3). Contemporaneous technologies such as telephone, radio, and television comprised the technical processes that enabled the rise of McLuhan's "global village," where an interconnected "nervous system" of media simultaneously shrinks and accelerates the social world. David Harvey, as we shall later see, would later use the more critically suggestive term "time-space compression" to frame the same process (1989, 240).

Moreover, technology use is dialectical, wherein to use another of McLuhan's aphorisms "we become what we behold. We shape our tools and then our tools shape us" (ref). Here, McLuhan suggests that extensionality occurred prior to the invention of the machine, or electricity, and indeed is a property even of the most basic of tools: the knife thus may be seen an extension of the hand, the telescope an extension of the eye, the bicycle an extension of the legs, and, most centrally for our following discussions, writing becomes an extension of language and of memory.

Through the development and application of technology, then, the world (our physical and social contexts) is transformed and is continually transformable. So deeply is this imprinted upon our species that is impossible to think of human existence without the extensionality offered through tools and their techniques of application. Agency and domination interact in the development of the human potential, casting also the long historical shadow of what Feenberg calls the "agency problem" where Frankfurt School critiques of "total administration" and "technological rationality" are seen to create a "technocracy" wherein the potentials of agency and freedom are subsumed under the weight of a "negative dialectic" that is expressed in a growing autonomous and automated technical logic (Feenberg 2004, 101).

If we peel back the idea of extensionality to its essence, we come to what I see to be the very nub of the argument in this book. Through technological extension, space and time may be said to shrink or to compress, but what does this mean in respect of our relationship with technology in the context of space and time? To put this a slightly different way: *what happens to our constructed dimensions of time and space at the point at which we extend ourselves into these through the use of technology?* The act of extension itself transforms the space–time construction by giving it a new context. The fact that a one-hour walk thus becomes a five-minute drive by means of a car is only the surface manifestation of the transformation, the taken-for-granted experience of space and time—but what *really* happens? In his *Physics* book IV, Aristotle emphasized the inseparability of space and time when he argued that our understanding and reckoning of time depends upon measurement. As he phrases it: "time defines the change, being its number, and the change the time" (this may be read more simply as time being the number or measure of movement) (1993, 220b). In this he prefigures Newtonian clock time. However, Aristotle suggests something more profound than that. If we agree that time and space are socially created, then to extend and simultaneously create these in a social context (in a "scape" of space and time), then not only does the socially created time extend *from us* to create the context of a new "scape"—but also, being humanly created, the time becomes a *property of* the technology itself. In other words, when we create technologies in order to extend ourselves, we also and unavoidably, "entime" them.

It is necessary to step carefully here, so let me break this down a little, and firstly think some more about the idea of extending our bodily selves into space and time before considering the temporality of a technology. This book will later concern itself with information technologies as comprising the machinic architecture of chronic distraction, so let me illustrate what is meant by the idea of extension by drawing upon the example of the mobile phone. When we pick up a mobile phone and press out a number, at the moment at which the connection is made we immediately *apprehend* the extended spatiality of the world through time—our action causes the physical distance between speakers to dissolve and inhere into the virtual space of the connection. If the call is made between, say, Canada and Australia, then the space of half the physical planet becomes apprehended (becomes subject to) the virtual space context, the timescape that is created by those at either end of the link. If time is the number of movement, as Aristotle argued, then through the mobile phone we take the *measure of the distance* and reduce it to the fantastical in terms of natural human capacities. Through this apprehension of space and time our extended selves radically transcend the embedded temporalities of the body and of nature. In this information and communication technology ICT -enabled timescape, the diurnal time of the bodies and the seasonal rhythms of the environments in which they exist are displaced by the powerfully augmenting force of a networked technology. This might suggest a positive and all-compassing agency or power on the part of the mobile phone user, the final realization of a world where we can conquer planetary space–time and the natural temporal capacities of our bodies with the effortless push of a button. In one sense that is obviously true. The "global village" has shrunk to a size we can hold in our hand and we can traverse it in a matter of seconds. But this "power" comes with a very substantial cost, including a panoply of negative aspects that emerge and are created through an imbalance in the agency-domination dialectic, and these constitute today the primary features of our hyper-distracted networked lives. Those discussions will come later. Prior to that we need to more clearly understand how technologies are themselves entimed.

Before considering that question it may be constructive to give an example of how technologies can be encoded with specific social relations. The illustration is useful because it will show how technologies can embody distinctly human subjectivities, and therefore suggests that they can also be "temporalised."

In his essay, "Do Artifacts Have Politics?" Langdon Winner maintained that "technical things" do indeed "have political qualities" (1980, 121). In broad terms Winner makes the point that in technologically developed societies, the forms of technology in use are not random, or neutral or one-dimensional expressions of the interplay of social forces that anyway gets lost or dissipated in the deepening and widening of technological systems. For Winner, "certain technologies *in themselves* have political properties" (123) (emphasis in original). In this approach Winner builds on the phenomenology of Edmund Husserl and the idea that the reality or nature of an object is to be found in the thing itself. Power as the elemental force of politics thus becomes the identifying property of certain technologies and of arrangements of technologies that are manifest in society as "forms of order" (123). Winner discusses the case of the architect Robert Moses who was a key builder of parks, roads, and bridges and so on in New York from the 1920s until the 1970s. Politics and power, as Winner compellingly argues, reside in and are constitutive of the numerous technological artifacts that Moses conceived and built. Describing, for example, Moses' New York bridges, Winner observes that "many of the overpasses are extraordinarily low, having as little as nine feet of clearance at the curb" (123). Winner makes the point that we rarely give such technologies (or their dimensions) a second look, unless they make some kind of powerful aesthetic statement to us. In his career, Moses constructed two hundred or so of this type of low bridges. But they concealed within their plan a particular intentionality: to be precise they were "designed to achieve a particular social effect." The "social effect" was to discourage (or make impossible) the routing of buses that were too high into certain sections of the city, to the "upper class" and "comfortable" areas. Winner argues—drawing from a biography of the polarizing figure of Moses—that this specific engineering decision to exclude buses was in fact the technological encoding of Moses' racism. It was well known that the poorer classes in New York, mainly the black working classes, traveled by bus because they were unable to afford personal automobile transportation. The bridges were thus encoded with a politics whose primary purpose was to exclude the black working class from being able to use the roads by the main means of transportation available to them, and therefore effectively barring them from the more affluent white sections of the city.

In his 1990 book *Cities of Quartz*, which was a critical study of the Los Angeles-built environment, Mike Davis makes similar observations concerning the technological arrangements of that city. For example, in areas of Downtown Los Angeles that were being earmarked for gentrification, the problem of endemic vagrancy was hindering the scheme to attract the wealthier middle-classes and the business investment they would bring in their wake. Moving the homeless on was proving only to be a short-term measure, as they inevitably returned to sleep on park benches and in bus shelters. The "final solution" (as Davis phrases it) for the City authorities was to construct a "new barrel-shaped bus bench that offers a minimal surface for uncomfortable sitting, while make sleeping utterly impossible" (1990, 233). Such "bum-proof" benches are now widespread across United States and also in many other parts of the world, such as the UK and in Australia where shopping centers quickly grasped the economic advantages of not offering sheltered accommodation for those unable or unwilling to shop. What looks on its surface, then, to be largely an aesthetic choice in the construction and deployment of civic furniture, after closer scrutiny often turns out to be the intentional siting of political technologies for specifically political purposes. A similar case may be made for a whole range of technologies, such as CCTVs, that also constitute a very distinct "form of order" under the guise of "public safety," as do certain forms of ID cards or tracking software, where political intent is inherent to their conception, design, and function. It is clear that politics can clearly be encoded into artifacts, and this may be recognized if we interrogate the political economy context of the artifact itself. But how is time encoded in a technology?

If we recall the illustration of the mobile phone, we see that it has a definite temporal function in that it compresses the time necessary to speak to someone half a world away. But how does time reside *encoded* within its assembled parts? In an important essay titled "Do Technologies Have Time?" Karl Hörning et al. make a useful inroad into this question, and establish an argument that I will develop further for the purpose of my own claims. The essay makes a similar grounding case to my own in that it argues that "time is part of our physical involvement with the natural and technological world; our daily involvement with the world is temporal to its core…[and humans] are locked into the material and technological world that they create" (1999, 294). Here the authors convey strongly the idea of extensionality, where the creation and application of a technology also serves to temporalize it. Technologies, as they put it, are "time-loaded" with the "regimes of time" that form the temporal context or timescape of their temporal becoming (303). And so, for example, within the dominant time regime of industrial modernity, the time of the clock begins to encode technologies from the moment of their abstract conception in the head of the designer through to the point of their material reality acting upon the world as artifacts. More broadly, the timescape generated by the clock began to permeate the social world as an ordering regime that gave organization logic to the Industrial Revolution and was indispensable in its rise and eventual domination (Thrift 1996). Moreover, through the dynamics of "practice" in the world, through repetition and through durational unfolding, the time loading of the technology *reinscribes* its machinic and clock-based temporality back into the rhythms of the user (Thompson 1967). I am arguing here that clock time specifically is encoded into industrial technologies, and in this I go through a more deterministic trajectory than Hörning et al. are prepared to. They see a vague and diffuse social time as being encoded into the technology, one that is able through "practice" to offer more open potentiality in how that "temporality of practice" unfolds through use (296). However, I see a rather more instrumentalized process, where the "temporality of practice" tends to dominate and foreclose, and opposed offering a context of enhanced agency. Let me offer the reasoning behind this more deterministic viewpoint.

Along a similar phenomenological line concerning what might be called "the time of things," Bruno Latour tells us that the "time" of an axe is immeasurable and not reducible to one time. It "takes" or "apprehends" its time from its direct use and its context of creation. In his essay "Morality and Technology," Latour describes the interactions of time, humans, and technology with some fluency. He writes:

> What is folded in technical action? Time, space and the type of actants. The hammer that I find on my workbench is not contemporary with my action today; it keeps folded heterogeneous temporalities, one of which has the antiquity of the planet, because of the minerals from which it has been moulded, while another has the age of the oak which provided the handle, while still another has the age of the ten years since it came out of the German factory which produced it for the market. When I grab my handle, I insert my gesture in a 'garland of time'. (2002, 249)

Latour argues that temporal dimensions are "folded" into technologies like ingredients into a cake. This is cognizant with much of what I have maintained thus far. But I also add another element: the *history*

27

of the tools' "becoming." Under capitalism the time of a machine is *measurable and generalized* and is based upon the tempo of the clock. Think of a classic industrial machine such as a lathe used for turning metal. As Latour's hammer contains the age of the minerals from which the head has been formed, and the wood which forms the shaft, so too the components of the lathe contain the effects and traces, the history of the convergence of social, political, ideological, scientific, and technological contexts that brought it into being. The lathe is a precision instrument whose rationale is constructed through the same mathematical rationale (of measurability) that conceives of all things as number—the same logic that divides the flow and emergence of time into seconds and minutes. The lathe contains the effects and traces of a designer imbued with the heritage of Enlightenment thinking, with a rational cast of mind and a planned and relatively restricted instrumental perspective where what the machine will do in the future is knowable and predictable. It has a planned "lifetime" measured in years. It contains also the logic of the industrialism of which it is a part, of commodity production, of competition, of efficiency, and of speed of operation. The lathe, in other words, is not conceivable without the intersecting tangle of the differing contexts of modernity that made it thinkable, requirable, and actual. The present-day lathe is the latest in a *generational development* of lathes and related machines that has *evolved* down this instrumental and narrowly delineated line that is time-loaded with the timescape of the clock and the social, economic, cultural, and political rhythms that corresponded with the clockwork baseline that Newton saw as "absolute" time. The "folded" and "heterogeneous temporalities" that Latour speaks of have, since the rise of the industrial way of life, ceded to and been displaced by a strictly homogeneous form of time that is based upon numbers, is "absolute" and subjectless and has "established the trajectory of European technological development that has continued to the present" (Gare 1996, 103).

I have tried to argue in time is fundamentally social. The very essence of time is grounded in the embedded rhythms in the physical and natural world and we are able, at the most unmediated and subjective level, to perceive time and become conscious of it through social change. However, at least since the time of Aristotle—and with world transforming power since the time of Newton and industrialization—a mathematically based and technologically developed form of time began to dominate. The domination by clock time has been encoded into the technologies humans developed and the societies they created, to invent a *modern* world.

I want now to look at the most fundamental of all technologies, that of writing. In the remainder of this chapter I will show that writing itself is time-loaded, and writing has entimed the modern world in a specific way; giving it specific rhythms. I will further show that writing and reading which are the thought-bases of modernity have been transformed by computerization, and that the "network time" of computers has placed the contemporary world on a new temporal plane—with profound consequences for almost every element of our late-modern world.

The Technologizing of the Word

It is with the acquisition and development of language that humans began to distinguish themselves from other primate species and to act upon the world and space–time in ways that were fundamental to the evolution of consciousness and the rise of civilizations. Increasingly complex forms of communication gave rise to increasingly complex and technical forms of organization. The first of these was the invention of writing. The earliest forms of writing emerged in the ancient Near East region that is now Iraq around 8000BCE. This "proto-writing" was more a form of accounting by means of marks on clay tablets, or tally-sticks, knotted ropes, or painted sea shells, and so on, that expressed property marks, or functioned as mnemonic devices that would indicate who owned or owed how much of a particular thing, be it livestock, or bags of grain, etc. It is significant that the earliest form of this most important of technologies emerged as a form of accounting. It indicates a deep-seated tendency in humans to orient toward number and, later, toward the development of number systems as a way to profoundly act upon their environments. Like the example of the mobile phone used earlier, even simple marks (commonly understood as being encoded with specific meaning) were a way of effectively apprehending time and space to the social dimension. Thus, the scratching of a series of marks on a tablet could indicate, for example, that an individual has in the past borrowed five goats (these may have been eaten or sold on, but still "exist" in virtual space and time as represented by the marks), and will return them or their agreed equivalent, at some point in the future.

Rather later, around 3000BCE, a profound technological innovation took place with the invention of phonetic writing. Remarkably, this invention occurred independently in Babylonia, in China, in Mesoamerica, and in India, with each emergence expressing differing systems of logographics (Daniels and Bright 1996). With this common effulgence of communication, the form, function, and trajectory of human relations would change forever—and change at an increasingly rapid rate. And so we see, for example, that the cuneiform writing that emerged in Babylonia evolved in to a technological system (or *technique* in that it had to be learned) that soon supplanted the oral systems of communication that had hitherto dominated human relations in that region of the world. Ideas, concepts, agreements, sureties, pacts, histories, and so on, could be fixed on the media of the time and given the status of something real—the status of fact. The fixing of words onto readable and preservable media greatly expanded the organizational potential of nascent societies, creating a "memory" of all kinds of things that spurred trade, commerce, art, philosophy, and the building of whole civilizations. The fact that something was written gave a powerful reality to the subject written about. It is interesting to note that the word "anecdote," a term we use today to relate something personal or autobiographical, something that does not quite have the power of "truth" or "reality" (only an adjunct to it), comes from the Greek word *anékdota*, which means something that is unpublished. If it is not published or written, then, its authority of being "real" and "factual" is diminished.

The practice of writing began to change what is it to be human in the world. It enabled a radically new form of interaction based upon information creation and dissemination, but it also began to change the ways in which we *think* as humans; indeed, the changes have been claimed to be neurophysiological in that the very organization of brain function was altered. Walter Ong, for example, in his essay "Writing is a technology that restructures thought" (1992), argued that with the development of writing and literacy, the technology of the written mark "takes possession of [human] consciousness" (1992, 293). Writing, it seems, is endowed with almost supernatural powers in that, as Ong observes, "it tends to arrogate to itself supreme power by taking itself as normative for human expression and thought" (293). The inherent power of writing and of literacy stems from the fact that it has grown in to a process that is both a necessity and something that seems so natural. It is this duality, according to Ong, that tends to "block understanding of what writing itself really is" (293). The technologizing of the spoken word was thus the technologizing not only of human consciousness, but the technologizing and transformation of "the early human lifeworld" (297).

The consciousness-altering power of the written word is especially significant. That it transformed what it meant to be human was underlined by the psychologist Julian Jeynes who made a remarkable claim (a claim later supported by Ong) in his 1977 book, *The Origin of Consciousness and the Breakdown of the Bicameral Mind*. In it Jaynes argued that prior to the development of writing, humans had not developed self-consciousness, as we know it today. He maintains that in the period between the estimated emergence of our species around 130,000 years BCE, to the development of alphabetic script in Babylonia about 4,000 years ago, the ancient human mind functioned in its natural state in something close to what we today term schizophrenia. The mind (as the expression bicameral suggests) was—for the majority of our species' existence on earth—split into two spheres. Communication, information, and understanding were possible primarily through speech. But in this aural world, as Jaynes suggests, "human nature was split in two, an executive part called a god, and a follower part called a man" (1977, 84). Man listened to the voices in his head, the "auditory hallucinations" that were the product of the brain's natural state, and acted upon them. "Neither part was conscious," Jaynes argues, and precisely because we are today fully self-conscious, we find this other mind-state as "incomprehensible" (84). However, Jaynes argues that with the development of writing, the "judgments of gods...began to be recorded," and in regions such as Babylonia, writing was also put to civil use. Jaynes continues that:

> This is the beginning of the idea of law. Such written judgements could be in several places and be continuous through time, thus allowing for the cohesiveness of larger society writing was a method of civil direction [and] method of social control which by hindsight we will know it will soon supplant the bicameral mind. (198)

Writing *exteriorized* and *spatialized* and *temporalized* the words in the heads of people who gradually began to see themselves as separate from these. The bicameral mind of voices and its "auditory authority" (201) began to dwindle and as a consequence, neurophysiological changes began to occur through the human "effort to find out what to do when voices are no longer heard in hallucination" (246). This technologically induced transformation is the origins of our consciousness.

Sufferers of schizophrenia today, Jaynes suggests, are individuals who retain vestiges of that ancient bicameral brain state.

Technics as Time

Through the action of the dialectic the technology of writing not only allows us to transform the world, but our actions upon the world also work back upon us, and—in its most significant early development—created the basis for the evolution of consciousness, and the capacity to think in terms of the analog "I." It is necessary to critically interrogate this dialectic further—with temporality as a key factor—because this will tell us something significant about both the logic underlying the specific reality of our world, and the *human threshold* we have vis-à-vis our temporal relationship with technological development.

The technological dialectic (or interaction) initiated by writing has had both positive and negative aspects. On the positive side, as already noted, the world bequeathed to us though civilization, a world of art, of reason, of Enlightenment science, and so on, has been made possible through our discovery of the amazing potency that stems from agreeing the meaning of marks upon paper. On the debit column, to be sure, the horrors made possible by the logic of rationality have been incalculable, and may even outweigh the good that has emerged from it (Adorno and Horkheimer 1986). It is increasingly apparent that systemic technological power and its logic expressed through such processes as nuclear fission, genetic manipulation, and continued fossil-fuel addiction are indeed propelling humanity along upon a "journey into the unknown" (Jonas 1985, 21). The most important point here is that although we created this world, for good or ill, the possession of consciousness means that we are *still able to reflect upon it* in order to understand it more, and so to imagine and posit solutions for the creation of a better arrangement of things. So let us analyze the actual processes of acting upon the world through writing, and consider how time and technology are mutually constituted through this process. Let us see, further, how this new perspective casts light on important aspects of the present-day world, aspects that are blocked by what Ong (1997, 293) saw as the imperiousness of technological development that writing has made possible—and how this imperiousness has blocked a greater understanding of the nature and potential of social time.

In terms redolent of McLuhan's "extensions" thesis, the philosopher Bernard Stiegler in his *Technics and Time*, observes that the practice of writing, or technology use in general, functions as a "prosthetic." The etymology and sense of the word "prosthetic" is important. As Stiegler writes:

> 'Prosthesis' does not supplement something, does not replace what would have been there before it and would have been lost: it is added. By pros-thesis, we understand (1) set in front, or spatialization; (2) set in advance, already there (past) and anticipation (foresight), that is temporalization. (1998, 152)

Through Stiegler it is possible to view writing as the *prostheticization of thought*. Writing extends thought. It sets it out in front and into the created social timescape wherein written thought becomes a site of measurement; and as writing is a technology, writing becomes a measure of time—the "technics *as* time" that is the core thesis of Stiegler's book (1998, 83). Writing, in other words, does not simply record resemblances to reality in its descriptions, but *records time itself* and is *recordable as time* through our experience of change (Tabboni 2001, 7). We have seen that the entimed machines of industrialism, such as lathes or motorcars or cash registers, are encoded by the world of capital that moved to the rhythm of the clock. But how is writing entimed? Or more precisely *with what* was it entimed during the seminal phase as far as our world today is concerned—the phase of classical antiquity where Greek and Latin writing began to lay down the intellectual, moral, philosophical, and political basis of what we recognize as normative social and civic life?

At this time the spread of writing as the prostheticization of thought began to affect the world "out there" through the dissemination of ideas, edicts, laws and a growing diversity of technical, social, cultural, civil, religious, and political knowledge that in combination served to give the social world its forms of organization and increasing rationality. Writing also reflected the timescape context that dominated at its time of creation and dissemination—and in this early phase this was the embedded times of biological life that is constituted by humans and nature in interaction. And so the writing of classical antiquity, and earlier, reflected that world, and that society, and the ideas that it produced. This was a pre-machine and pre-clock time world and so that its writing was entimed—and thus reflected the entimement—by human biology and the natural environment. The temporality of bodies, of presences and proximity, of the spatially constraining and temporally limited (in terms of quickness) physical movement of the hand and the eye meant that ideas expressed and the world reflected though its expression were encoded with a kind of *ingrained physicality.*

This critical juncture was described by, almost matter-of-factly, and buried underneath a surfeit of facts and other points of interest, by Patricia Fara in her book *Science: A Four-Thousand Year History.* Fara notes that the basis of clock time numbering, the sixty seconds, sixty minutes, one hour that we are so familiar with today was invented by the Babylonians in Mesopotamia around four millennia ago. When you think about it, "sixty" seems a queer number to post-rational decimal societies. However, what Fara reveals is that the Babylonians were constrained by the technologies and the raw materials that surrounded them—and by the physicality of human hand–eye movements. As Fara describes it:

> The raw material the Mesopotamians used—the clay, the reeds—affected the numbering systems that they developed: they counted in blocks of sixty, which seems strange for people brought up with tens and hundreds. However, if you try to write with a stylus (diagonally cut drinking straw works well), you soon realize that sixty was a more sensible choice than it might seem. The Babylonians used two basic symbols, vertical for single numbers and diagonal for tens. They grouped the first nine digits in threes, one row beneath the other, because the human eye can immediately distinguish between one, two, and three adjacent vertical marks—but not four. Reading the horizontal wedge-marks is more tricky, and scribes developed a system enabling them to recognize a set of up to five instantaneously. So after 59 (five horizontals, and three groups of three vertical), they moved everything over one place to the left and started again.... (Fara 2010, 11)

Fara thereafter quickly moves on to other matters, because her subjects are different from mine. However, what she relates here is in many ways the fundamental point of this book, and that it is the *physical and environmental origins of both time and writing*—and the fact that this basic principle still underpins our world today. Clock and script were developed as immediate expressions of immediate bodily capacities and immediate material surroundings. This profound fact has not been lost in the mists of historical time, but its vital importance has simply been overlooked. If physicality and materiality are the basis of clock time and the written word, then what does it mean for a world where the clock and the printed word have been made digital, and the digital version is becoming dominant? How far can our natural capacities be pushed by technology? And what does it mean if (as I will argue) our physical–temporal limits have already been passed?

At the early stage of the development of writing, the prostheticization of thought through writing still meant that thought and its entimement were still contiguous and close to (and circumscribed by) the embedded times of body and nature, and so what was expressed and concretely made reality was more-or-less in temporal synchronization with the times of the body and the natural environment.

What this meant in the context of the dialectic was that written thought could spread and grow, and the world that this helped to create acted back upon the embedded times of the biological world in ways that did not (and could not yet) contain the incipient or actual accelerative dynamic in technological processes that would be sufficient to undermine or displace the times of humanity and nature. Taking the measure of the world through writing in all its forms was thus in a very real sense to explore it with a power and authorial authority that has probably not been surpassed in terms of the truly open potential that these tentative first few steps represented in our realizing of the world through the agency of the technologized word. The prostheticization of thought through writing extended enormously the capacities of humans to take the measure of their world through the dissemination of almost *pure thought* at a time, to repeat, when the technological echo of writing's acting upon the world was not yet fundamentally undermining of the rhythms of thought by the imperatives of modernity and its machine logic.

It is intriguing to consider the idea that the time of classical antiquity, the time whose thought still deeply underscores our own world, was the time when the ideas of the philosophers, the discourses and writings of Plato, Socrates, Aristotle, and others reflected the freest expressions of thought—protheticized and technologized and temporalized thought—that humans have achieved. It is quite possible that their still powerful resonances today reflect that idea. *Immensely consequential* thought was able to occur because of the concatenation of forces arranged at that time in history. The societies of Greece and Rome were rationally organized, and functioned on a hierarchical basis whereupon, at base, slave labor and a militarized culture functioned to create the context in which philosophers could consider the nature of the world and its processes from a kind of ground zero, a *tabula rasa* where elite contemplation would be a continually innovative and path-breaking swathe cutting through our profound ignorance. Plato, indeed, in his *The Republic*, maintained that society must ideally be ruled by "philosopher kings" who alone would have the power to rule wisely (Pappas 1995, 114). He was not thinking in precisely these terms, but what Plato was arguing was that "philosopher kings" should rule because, freed from the drudgeries and preoccupations of slave and military and commercial life, only they *had the time* to think and to reflect and to debate.

Plato has a topmost place among philosophers, and his influence reverberates still. It was he, for example, who laid the basis for the mathematical forms and logic that would influence key figures in our narrative such as Isaac Newton—who in his turn, influenced a whole intellectual tradition that delivered the science and theory of computing to the world. More broadly, it was Platonism that made such a world thinkable and thus possible through the articulation of the philosophical basis of mechanism, the assumption that organisms, humans, nature, and the universe, together comprise a harmonious order that worked as a machine. This thought-process of mechanism and harmony is what made the very conception of a machine possible. And so in ancient Greece, through writings that would prosthetically enter the time–space of philosophical history, Plato planted the germ of what Arran Gare terms "mechanistic materialism" that would come into budding flower in the intellectual luminosity of the seventeenth and eighteenth centuries (1996, 114–15).

The most important point I want to emphasize is that at this profound phase of Western intellectual and philosophical thought, the time of the forming and entrenching of the *canonical* thought that underpins our western world today, was a time when writing, the texts they created, and the ideas they expressed, were *not yet machine-driven*. From the time of classical antiquity, and from there to be resurrected in the Renaissance through to the early Modern Period, ideas circulated by means of time-consuming handwritten texts that were disseminated by the muscle power of beasts of burden or by foot, and/or by technologies based upon the wheel or ship that had been in existence for many hundreds of years. Ideas and their written expression were entimed by the hand–eye temporalities of physical writing and reading and by technological contexts (those governing space and time) that remained little unchanged over the span of centuries. This was not a phase of stasis, however, either cultural or technological or temporal. For example, the growing spread of mercantilism that was the precursor to capitalism, had a differing approach to time and to information than that of the European ecclesiastical authorities who had until the sixteenth century almost a monopoly over the written word, and whose logic was of course opposed to that of classical Greece or Rome. Jacques Le Goff (1980, 30) explains the cleave from religious time and the crucible of social transformation that it exposed:

> The merchant's activity is based on assumptions of which time is the very foundation—storage in anticipation of famine, purchase for resale when the time is ripe, as determined by knowledge of economic conjunctures and the constants of the market in commodities and money—knowledge that implies the existence of an information network and the employment of couriers. Against the merchant's time the church sets up its own time, which is supposed to belong to God alone and which cannot be an object of lucre.

This nexus goes to the heart of the motivation for technological development. The raising of time and money to central importance in human affairs in late Medieval European societies gave the quest for technological fixes an unprecedented impetus and dynamism. Rapid technological development began to move to the centerstage of history, and a rising wave of mostly unheralded revolutions in technological innovation was underway across a whole range of areas by the time of the Renaissance. As Frances and Joseph Gies (1995, 2) argue, the Middle Ages can be seen as a period of:

> ...gradual, imperceptible revolutions—in agriculture, in water and in wind power, in building construction, in textile manufacture, in communication, in metallurgy, in weaponry—taking place through incremental improvements, large or small, in tools, techniques and the organization of work.

These "gradual, imperceptible revolutions" were oriented, inexorably, toward the spreading and deepening through writing and literacy and through practice (the technical application) of a Platonic mechanistic materialism. Gare articulates the movement of this powerful technology–ideology dialectic:

> The development of mechanistic materialism was the crystallization of a large number of such forms of thinking. Forms of relations within society provided the analogies for the development of this view of nature, which was then analogised to comprehend society.

This comprehension reincorporated these forms of thinking into new social practices. (1996, 115)

With the rise of mechanistic materialism and the creation of the world as the reflection of its idea, technology (and the human relationship with it) would from now on be set upon another, and more complex, level. Here the entimement of technology and technological development would be seeded by machine logic. The logic and limits established by the physical confines of the embedded times of the body and of the natural world would be increasingly adrift from a gradually more autonomous logic of machine technology and machine time [a process McLuhan termed "autoamputation" where control over the "extension" that is technology becomes lost or is attenuated (1964, chap. 4)]. Before that, however, the process and practice of reading and writing was itself to undergo its own revolution—a turning of the dialectical screw, if you like—to become the "machine that made us," and become entimed with a very different rhythm to that of the body and nature (BBC 2008).

Triumph of the Machine

Around 1439, and following many years of tinkering and experimentation, Johannes Gutenberg, citizen of Mainz, goldsmith and printer revealed his own "defining" technology in the form of the moveable-type printing press. As with the invention and normalizing of the clock and its machine time, it is difficult to overestimate the significance of this invention. Writing became forever detached from the rhythms and time–space limits of the hand–eye practice that had been the stock-in-trade of the medieval *scriptorium* for a thousand years and more. Ideas, laws, stories, technical descriptions, gossip, political tracts, and so on, could now be printed in potentially unlimited numbers at far lower cost and at what were then unimaginable speeds. As mercantilism was moving toward a more organized and rational capitalism in the Renaissance period, the higher rate of productivity became an important factor in this information revolution. The imperative of productivity provided a powerful and indispensable prerequisite for capitalism to function in the way that it does today. As Jeremy Norman calculates in his *From Gutenberg to the Internet*, the increase in productivity attained by the printing press when measured against the average speed of a scribe was "roughly 160 times, or 16,000 percent" (2005, 29). The informational world had never before moved with such rapidity, and this launched, as McLuhan observes in his *Gutenberg Galaxy* "the take-off of the machine" (1962, 155). And so with the development of a machine that would contribute directly to the development of every other machine that would follow it, we see the beginnings of the realization of the Platonic idea of mechanistic materialism.

Writing, functioning as a prosthesis that inscribed ideas and thought, as well as a biologically rhythmed temporality into the world, was transformed by the printing press. A key transformation is that the extensionality that writing derived from media technologies that were described by McLuhan would suffer its foundational "autoamputation" through the mechanization process. McLuhan's idea of autoamputation in the development of media technologies introduces the notion of the obsolescence or diminishment of one process—in this initial instance the physical process of the painstaking writing of everything in longhand—in favor of the intensification of another, which here is the printed word (Federman 2005). By continually extending ourselves into the world through the transformation of mediation we began to experience a dual positive–negative effect that we can see to be very significant in terms of the temporal consequences for the human–technology relationship. On one hand, the inroads that we make into the world through technological extension allow humans all manner of benefits in respect of their ability to affect, organize, and control their environments. On the other hand, the farther we extend ourselves, and the more we make obsolete prior forms of media whilst intensifying others, then the process of autoamputation becomes like a burning of bridges on our collective journey into unknown world that we have virtually no preparation for. The burning of bridges takes us away from, and renders it difficult to return to, our temporal essences and their innate physical limitations. And as the "feel" and proximal physical aura of our extension into the world attenuates through expanding layers of technological mediation, then so too does the technological process become more abstracted from our human–temporal essence.

The process and practice of writing now increasingly begins to take place within the realms of machinic systems that takes on an additional logic of commerciality, of marketing and of selling. The book trade, which grew rapidly in the wake of technological progress, became the vector for what writing produced and how it was consumed. Of course, not everyone either in the time of the Renaissance or today, was or is a writer. For most of us, the wider social world is met with and comprehended through literacy and through reading. The technological realm of productive systems, and systems of marketing and distribution are either invisible or irrelevant to us, and we see only fixed words on paper, or screen, and through it our worldviews, our forms of knowledge, and what we perceive as the reality of the world are largely constructed through that reading process. Underpinning the apparent progress that emerged with the invention of Gutenberg's miracle, however, was an industrialization of thought that had superseded the physicality of the prostheticization of thought inherent in the act of hand-and-eye writing. And so increasingly cut adrift at the frontiers of new innovations, and increasingly dependent upon the latest advance in media technology (book, daily newspaper, telegraph, telephone, and so on), we adapt to new forms of compressed space–time, and adapt our lives in order to synchronize with its machine-time rhythms, thereby displacing or sublimating or forgetting or having no opportunity to discover, what time actually is and where it actually resides: in us.

The Gies' "…gradual, imperceptible revolutions" (1995, 2) that had been underway since the late Middle Ages began to gather a connected and coherent momentum generated by the now-rapid transmission of ideas made possible by Gutenberg's invention. Indeed, information networks were beginning to form as more and more people in more and more places began to impose themselves on the world through technology in unprecedented ways. The Enlightenment and the Age of Progress and Reason began to beckon. The power of thought had been enormously strengthened through new media technologies, and this power had a historic–temporal–secular dimension that was unprecedented. Words written on paper and distributed in large numbers across increasingly wider spheres could now describe and propagate the reality of the world in new ways and in a new technological context that drew upon illuminative pasts in Greece and Rome; words proposed and created a living present of constant transformation; and words sketched and projected sublime futures. As Voltaire, a leading French author and philosopher of the Enlightenment thought put it, "No problem can withstand the sustained assault of the mind." But this was a protheticized mind, one that was increasingly reliant on machinery and abstract systems that produced abstract thoughts concerning the world "out there" and how it was to be understood, controlled, and shaped. The proto-modern world and its leading thinkers (philosophers, politicians, scientists) thrived in this machine-drive space–time context, imagining, like Voltaire, that there was no limit to what humans could do—but oblivious (and how could they not be?) of the seeds of acceleration that had already been planted into the machine-logic of their exciting new world.

The Platonic mechanistic worldview was both cause and consequence of the emergence of the machine, and industrialization and the Enlightenment were its material and ideational expressions. These processes also served to crystallize modern political thought, and although modern political thought was steeped in Greece and Rome, it transcended this organic thought and was catalyzed by what industrialization and Enlightenment made possible. Mechanical writing producing mechanically oriented worldviews that produced a mechanistic material world, really came into its own in the so-called Age of Enlightenment. The self-consciousness that both Jeynes and Ong saw as a consequence of our relationship with the technology of writing became, for possibly the first time, a *social* self-consciousness in that major Enlightenment figures such as Immanuel Kant could reflect upon the Age that they themselves were creating. This was evident in Kant's essay from 1784, which asked "An Answer to the Question: What is Enlightenment?" It is a question he answers in the essay's opening sentence, in which he affirms: "Enlightenment is man's emergence from his self-incurred immaturity" (1784/1996, 58). Indeed, Kant saw writing and the processes of publishing as the essence of "the public use of one's reason" and the necessary means through which to propagate and give material concreteness to the ideas that Enlightenment reason gave expression to (Laursen 1996, 254).

The effect of writing and "the material forms in which it was transmitted" enervated this period in history and has been raised to a necessary salience by Régis Debray (2007, 5). In his essay "Socialism: A Life-Cycle," Debray outlines his thesis when he argues that it is: "Impossible to grasp the nature of conscious collective life in any epoch without an understanding of the material forms and processes through which its ideas were transmitted—the communication networks that enable thought to have social existence" (2007, 5). The "communicative networks" that acted as extensions and propagators of rational thought were, of course, the books, pamphlets, treatise, newspapers, journals, and magazines that gave intellectual life to this first print-based information revolution. This information revolution is part of what he terms a "periodization of the history of ideas" (5).

Debray sees two main phases within what he terms a vast historical "arc of time" (6). These are the "graphosphere" and the "videosphere." The former, based upon writing, emerged with Gutenberg's invention and constituted the "medialogical basis" upon which modernity, enlightenment, and the politics of liberal democracy and socialism grew and spread within growing information networks. The latter, a rather ugly neologism emerges in our own time, the time of the Internet, of globalization and of neoliberalism. Debray brackets these periods as: "a printed Europe [and] a wide screen America" (28). The videosphere, the age dominated by the fast-flowing image, will of course be a central focus in the following chapters, where the pathology of outwardly directed chronic distraction displaces the relative fixity and inwardly directed effect of the reading of the textual word in print. Before that, it is necessary to understand what the graphosphere meant in terms of the extension of the technologizing of the word—and the technologizing of the world itself.

Debray's term (grapho-sphere) is well chosen as it exactly describes what the Gutenberg invention did for the power and force of the technologized word and the mechanical process of mass printing. The dissemination of ideas (out there) into the physical world attenuated their connection with the original author, and words as books, pamphlets, newspapers, and so on began to take on a life of their own, a potentially limitless reconstituting of itself through each readers' understanding of the particular text and the subsequent writings they would produce as a consequence. The grapho-sphere was literally the burgeoning of an unprecedented print-based *networked world of words* (ideas) on increasingly diverse subjects—often wholly new subjects—that coined more and more new words, and creating the momentum for a spreading literacy in its wake. We can see an analogy of this (albeit at a much faster temporality) in the current practice of blogging. Here words (and images) flow from the computers of millions and are taken up and reconstituted and globally disseminated through the computers of other millions. The resulting "interaction" is the chaotic, essentially unmanageable and essentially digital *cacophony* that Zittrain (2007) terms the "generative" net, that drives economy and society through the exponential production of information—that is leading to no-one knows where.

In the early phase of the graphosphere, indeed for almost the whole phase of domination by the mechanically printed word, there was a much slower rhythm and tempo to the working of the written word upon the world. The elites who wrote and read and formed the graphosphere itself knew where they were going—or at least imagined they did. Their sense of certainty and their confidence in the potentials of modernity—to deliver them from being fortune to history (Hutchings 2008, 28–54)—created what has been termed the "Republic of Letters." This was an imagined space (a virtual network) where prominent philosophers in Britain, France, Germany, and the emergent USA could, in the Socratic fashion (and at one technological remove) debate the main Enlightenment preoccupations of science, philosophy, and democracy. As Robert Darnton put it, the eighteenth century was the "great era of epistolary exchange" where the Greek dialectic of truth-seeking and discovery was animated through the swapping of letters:

> Writers formulated ideas, and readers judged them. Thanks to the power of the printed word, the judgements spread in widening circles, and the strongest arguments won. (Darnton 2009, 11)

Such "epistolary exchange" was the basis for the abstracting of individual ideas to a level of transcendent universality that imagined a new world free from the absolutism and ignorance of pre-Enlightenment times. If philosophers knew where they were going, then so too did the early capitalists who were midwives to a new economic system (one that was often full of horror and misery). However, those with any sensitivity to the revolutionary effect they were having upon the world could draw comfort in the vision of a new and improving world written up for them by thinkers such as Adam Smith. Smith's 1776 *Wealth of Nations* rather conveniently depicted a world where competition and innovation and relentless production would eventually bring out the best in people and in economies, leading to more dynamic and individualistic world, where the individual, acting rationally in his or her self-interest, would nonetheless eventually contribute to the greater good. In politics, Smith's contemporary, David Hume, envisaged a new politics based upon a "social contract" (with "contract" conjuring up the law-bound written document) where, reaching back also to Greece and Rome, argued that "...all government is...founded on a contract, and that the most ancient rude combinations of mankind were formed chiefly by that principle" (1980, 211–12). From such philosophical conclusions, emerging from Darnton's "strongest arguments," the world was seen to be changing for the better, notwithstanding the enormous upheaval wrought by industry. The key point is that it was justified and rationalized and planned and propagated (and often harshly critiqued) through simple words written on paper that had created the abstract "Republic of Letters."

From the eighteenth century onward, the mechanization and rationalization of the world made possible through the revolution in printing, gave material and ontological reality to modernity. The *actual* writing of the world through cartography and geography had already, since the sixteenth-century Age of Exploration, instigated another consciousness-changing effect. The world was already becoming globalized through networks of trade that was pushing capital and its mechanistic materialism "over the entire surface of the globe [where] It must nestle everywhere, settle everywhere, establish connexions everywhere" (Marx and Engels 1975, 34). The world, for the first time, could be conceived as a singular and orderable and controllable and appropriatable place. What this meant was that the consciousness we had of ourselves as existing within a strictly confined social and geographical context, began to open out to a consciousness of the wider world. The increasing numbers of the literate could read about it, and the growingly mobile class of merchants and traders could experience it firsthand. Accordingly, there developed a new awareness of a widening of the ancient bounded locality toward the beginnings of a national community; and then, and rather earlier than we customarily think, this first systematic globalizing process enabled the literate and the mobile to be able to conceptualize what Roland Robertson termed "the compression of the world and the intensification of consciousness of the world as a whole" (1992, 8).

In summary: the technology of writing, as we saw through the arguments of Jeynes and Ong, made us a species with defining characteristics. It restructured our consciousness, and made us self-conscious. For Jeynes, writing unified the bi-cameral mind by externalizing authority through its inscription on portable and distributable media. The voice of authority in our head, the voice that commanded us, thus receded to become (as Ong suggested) our own voice, through the conversation we have in our heads as a result of the "interiorization of the technology" that the act of reading and writing encourages (1982, 83). By "interiorising" the technology of writing, by becoming dependent upon it as the fundamental means of communication, it also became "second nature" (Ong 1982, 83). Indeed so fundamental and so second nature has writing become, that through many generations of embedding it no longer seemed a technology, and so its effects have been masked or little understood. This, as we saw, has had immense implications for our relationship with time and temporality. Through the act of writing we began to extend ourselves into time and space, and the "technologized word," to borrow Ong's phase, became our "exteriorized thought," as Stiegler has suggested. The act of writing, and the world that was written onto was entimed, initially, by the "embedded times" of the body and the natural environment, whose "natural" and fundamental times were underpinned by the human capacities—and constraints—of hand and eye. The ideas contained within increasingly sophisticated and technical writing, of course, led to increasingly sophisticated technologies, and these in their turn promoted the organization and rationalization of economies and societies. This world acted back upon its creators. It extended us out into the new world itself—but it also, though the effect of McLuhan's "autoamputation," took us further away from the baseline temporal rhythms of our species and their innate limitations.

For most of the history of humanity this process, if not completely unrecognized, then was certainly not perceived as a problem. Indeed, it had been a boon if one sees as a positive thing the world of science and modernity and all that it has offered and made possible. The Enlightenment and its correlatives of capitalism and Industrial Revolution took this long historical process to a new and dynamic plane. The rhythms of the clock became the unerring and linear and teleological time that underscored modernity's processes—and again humans thrived within a very specific technological context. In our machine-time, the machine-driven world seemed to be set on a path of steady improvement at a steady pace toward a future that seemed orderable and plannable and controllable. Moreover, the times of our bodies seemed more-or-less in synch with these times, and although all was solid was continually melting into air, this was still considered progress.

At the beginning of the second decade of the twenty-first century, we have arrived at the limits of our temporal relationship with technology. The time of the clock that for two hundred years and more had acted as the mechanical rhythm of our lives, and which we could (more or less) synchronize with in the context of its cognitive demands, is being superseded by what I term a computer-based "network time," a time that is inherently accelerative, and whose speed limits are unknown. Nonetheless, network time has already brought us to a point of desynchronization, to a temporal rupture where we find it increasingly impossible to keep pace with its cognitive demands, and our attempts to do so have spawned new and problematic temporal relationships. The mechanical has been replaced by the digital and the cognitive attention capacities that we have developed as the literacy component of modernity are being displaced by *a chronic cognitive distraction*. Before looking at the pathologies of this chronic distraction in more detail, we need first to understand the temporal logic of capitalism—and how it has been revolutionized.

3

Everything Nowadays is Ultra

The European Enlightenment was, for better or for worse, *the* pivotal-point of modern-world history—indeed it constituted modernity itself. The social forms of the world that we look upon today, in almost every region of the planet, and in almost every aspect of life, can be traced back in some way to the Enlightenment's thinking, its impulses, its verve and assurance—and be viewed as the material application of all these. It was that big a deal. As Terry Eagleton remarked "The story of liberal Enlightenment is one of an exhilarating emancipation which constitutes a legacy beyond price" (2009, 58). But "'emancipation" from what, exactly? Commonly, the answers to such questions are ones that we are aware of and they need not detain us here for long. For instance, emancipation was both political and religious, with the two often constituting the same thing. The Enlightenment was also a revolution of the mind, one made possible through the revolution in print and its widening mechanical reproduction in newspapers, journals, books, pamphlets, and so on. David Hume, for example, contributor to the famed "social contract" debates with Rousseau and others, deliberations over how people should be governed, lost his faith through the act of reading philosophy at university (Buchan 2003, 77). Skepticism, or what Hume himself wryly called "the disease of the learned," directly confronted every facet of life and interrogated every ancient shibboleth and automatic assumption. It opened increasing numbers of minds to see the world anew and to feel confident that through new forms of knowledge the world could be transformed in ways that were to the benefit of people in the here and now—and to future generations also.

Not so often realized is that the mental power of skepticism deriving from the particular arrangements of words on paper led to another form of emancipation: that of the human relationship with time. For most people in pre-industrial European societies, time was understood, courtesy of the church, as infinite, something stretching out into unimaginable eternity, and something belonging wholly to God. You had the gift of your span here on Earth, but one day, and depending upon your personal conduct in this life, you would face your maker who would then decide whether the future stretching out as time without end would be spent in either Heaven or in Hell. A skeptical secularism junked this theologically based terror of time and placed the nature of time into a more rational context that made sense to (and could be easily imagined by) virtually anyone, learned or not. Time was now increasingly being viewed as lived time and how it was spent in lived time—and within Enlightenment temporal emancipation the individual's finite span began to matter more and more. In a growingly material world, time had become imbricated with this materiality and more particularly with its machinic clock time order.

The idea of temporal emancipation, however, needs to be qualified. The secular spectres of reason and logic argued powerfully that time, being a worldly property, must be made use of in the present. Reason and logic also demanded that the time of the world (the clock) and the time of individuals (increasingly ordered by the clock), be used *efficiently*. Max Weber has written perceptively about this in his classic book *The Protestant Ethic and the Spirit of Capitalism* where he linked the new spirit of capitalism with the rationalization of Christian thought that occurred with the Protestant Reformation. Not for the first time Christianity showed itself adjustable to the changing social and political and economic context. And so through Protestantism at least, and crucially in a Protestant country such as Britain, efficient use of time could be wedded to an "ethic" of hard work, punctuality, and frugality (Weber 2003, 58). In his analysis of the aphoristic writings of Benjamin Franklin, Weber shows clearly how the spirit of capitalism was a secular connecting of time with money—and connecting it in the most powerful way possible through not only the appeal to use time in order to enrich oneself by using it "profitably," but also to use it in praise of God. As Weber writes:

> Waste of time is thus the first and in principle the deadliest of sins… Loss of time through sociability, idle talk, luxury, even more sleep than is necessary for health, six to at most eight hours, is worthy of absolute moral condemnation…[Time] is infinitely valuable because every hour lost is lost to labour for the glory of God. (2003, 158)

The secular spirit had surreptitiously donned a metaphysical mask in order to enslave, dominate, and regulate in a new and "modern" way. Theology thus performed another of its doctrinal contortions and many who would have shunned the nascent and thrusting capitalism as barbarous and un-Christian could, with the blessings of the Reformist movements of Calvin and Knox and Müntzer and Luther—and eventually Christian society as a whole—see industry and its many terrible and wrenching social upheavals as almost a (somewhat belated) *gift* from God.

Time counted, literally, like never before. Time, moreover became the abstract motor which created the technical demand for the *actual* motors with which to drive machinery and industry, and these motors, in their turn, drove society at a pace of development such as had never even been dreamt of previously. With time at the very core of the intersecting processes of capitalism, Enlightenment reason—and even the new (modern) appreciation of religious doctrine, we see a dynamic concept of history appearing where material and abstract temporalization becomes part of the broad experience of people. As Reinhardt Koselleck observed, the period that saw the convergence of these social and secular forces, saw also the "temporalisation of history, at the end of which is the period of acceleration we call modernity" (2004, 11). Shortly we will see the precise mechanics of this period of acceleration, and gain an appreciation of the actual driving forces of modern history. But how did this period of acceleration that we now term modernity become manifest in the lives of people? In other words, how did they perceive and experience the new temporalization of life?

> *Frustrated by the rushing flight of time*
>
> —Goethe (1848)

Major philosophers of the Enlightenment period in industrializing Europe did not view the material and social time of life on Earth in necessarily the same way. In the so-called "Scottish Enlightenment," for instance, which had among its number world-changing figures such as David Hume and Adam Ferguson in political science and Adam Smith in political economy, the time of the clock constituted the temporal apex of a rational and modern society, where order, timeliness, predictability, and so on, were establishing the cornerstone upon which the new world of progress was being built. Indeed, Smith, in his *The Wealth of Nations*, famously uncovered a time-based engine for the actual production of this wealth in his observations regarding the fantastic productivity gains that could be made in the so-called "division of labour" in the new-fangled manufactories that were opening, seemingly everywhere, around the last quarter of the eighteenth century (Smith [1776] 2003). This ordered and mechanical perspective contrasted rather sharply with the ideas of some who would come a little later and had had the chance to meditate more on the temporal effects of a rational–industrial society in development. One such figure was the German poet, novelist, playwright, and natural philosopher, Johann Wolfgang von Goethe (1749–1832).

In the first half of the nineteenth century, Germany (or the collection of states that would form Germany in 1870) closely paralleled the British trajectory of industrialization. This was especially so in the building of railways—a development that has been viewed as an infrastructural perquisite for eventual German Unification. What this meant in practice was that Germany, like Britain and like France, was contributing to the vast social and technological upheavals that were making Europe the "powerhouse of the world" (Davies 1997, 759–896). As an artist as well as a "natural philosopher"—the term used before the somewhat desiccated appendage "scientist" came into fashion—Goethe gave his artistry full expression in the Sturm und Drang (Storm and Stress) movement that emerged in the late eighteenth century. This was a movement that set itself explicitly against the overt and dominant rationality that drove Enlightenment thought, such as existed in Britain. The movement was aligned with Romanticism, an artistic movement that also developed in response to industrialization and the processes of rationality. In their rejection of Enlightenment ideas, Sturm und Drang and Romanticism emphasized, through poetry, painting, literature, and music, individual subjectivity and emotionalism as the authentic expressions of the human condition and as the true nature of experience. Emotionalism was given free rein in a heightened sensitivity toward society and nature, and individuals such as Goethe tried to articulate the reality of the world through their "sensitive" art.

The radical transformations of society through industrialization would have been "sensed" as something exciting and progressive by, for example, the powerful strands of British rationalism and empiricism that dominated the leading edge ferment of the new productive processes. However, the anti-Enlightenment "sensitivity" that we see in

Goethe, and also in Britain in the works of Byron and Shelley, saw different processes and felt different emotions. Goethe shows his artistic sensibility toward the actual experience of time in his autobiography where, writing about spending time with his "beloved one," he observes (or feels) that "The presence of the beloved one always shortens time" (2009, 42). This insight, together with further ruminations that we shall come to presently, indicate that for some influential figures of the Enlightenment era, industrialization and the institutionalization of capitalism was having real effects on the processes of social time—not only was life for many people becoming busier with through the hustle and bustle of commerce organized on the growing basis of clock time, but life was also, seemingly, becoming much, much, *faster*.

Fashioned by his particular intellectual and creative disposition, Goethe's senses were susceptible to the deeper lying nuances of change that were part of the meta-projects of industrialization and capitalism that were transforming much of the European economy, culture, and society. Norman Davies describes Goethe as one of the last "universal men" or genuine polymaths who was in touch with a wide range of learning in the arts and sciences. Such breadth of learning has been seen as a particularly Renaissance trait that was being diminished by the one-dimensionality inherent in a new breed of "specialist" that serviced the functional demands of Enlightenment rationality and calculation, and which viewed the clock as a narrow conception of what time is. Davies writes that: "Goethe...was not merely a national bard, he was an Olympian who bestrode almost all intellectual domains. The variety of genres in which he excelled, his *awareness of a rapidly changing world*...gave him a claim to be the last 'universal man'" (Davies 1997, 786) (italics added). We will return to this idea of one-dimensionality, but let us look now at one more example of "sensitivity" in Goethe because it goes to the core of the nature of capitalism and how it is seeded with the logic acceleration, a process that extends beyond the one-speed tick of the clock. In a letter to his friend Carl Friedrich Zelter dated June 6, 1825, Goethe observes ruefully that:

> ...but everything, dear Friend, nowadays is *ultra*, everything perpetually transcendent in thought as in action. No one knows himself any longer, no one understands the element in which he moves and works, no one the subject which he is treating...Young people are excited much too early, and then carried away in the whirl of time. *Wealth* and *rapidity* are what the world admires and what everyone strives to attain. (Coleridge 1887, 246) (italics in original)

Goethe goes on in the same letter to reveal what seems to be his acknowledgment of the passing of an old age into a new one; an age of rapid communications and new temporal experiences that diminish older values and valorize the post-universal man that these were fashioning:

> Railways, quick mails, steamships and every possible kind of facility in the way of communication are what the educated world has in view, that it may over-educate itself, and thereby continue in a state of mediocrity. (...) Properly speaking, this is the century for men with heads on their shoulders, for practical men of quick perceptions, who, because they possess a certain adroitness, feel their superiority to the multitude, even though they themselves may not be gifted in the highest degree.

He concludes his letter to Zelter with a lament for what he senses is an irretrievably fading Golden Age:

> Let us, as far as possible, keep that mind with which we came hither; we, and perhaps a few others, shall be the last of an epoch which will not so soon return again.

Goethe's proto-phenomenological approach to the temporal subtleties and shadings underlying modern rationality and industry *would* return again in the theories of Husserl and Bergson in the early years of the twentieth century. Before that time, though, around the mid-eighteenth century, the "element" in which industrializing man "moved and worked" and which Goethe balefully strove to understand was, somewhat ironically, uncovered by Karl Marx; ironic because Marx used the Enlightenment intellectual tools of political economy, rationality, and the market mechanism for his method—all of which would have been anathema to Goethe's finely tuned Renaissance sensitivities.

All That Is Solid Melts into Air

"Time-Wages" is the title of chapter twenty of Marx's *Capital*. In it he reveals the social processes of Benjamin Franklin's "time is money" aphorism. How can time become money and *vice versa*? We mostly know this to be true in a vague and general sense when we think about our own lives, acting as either an employee or employer in the money economy. The concepts of "if I don't show up for work today, then I'll lose X amount in pay," or at the other end of the spectrum, "if my employees laze around all day and do nothing, then that will cost me money," are easily understood, and the notion is uncontroversial at the day-to-day level. But what actually makes this a durable fact of life, and what does this mean in the broader sense beyond our own individualized temporal experience? What does it mean, in other words, in a *historical–temporal* sense?

To be paid for your work is to be paid for your time. The worker sells her time and the employer buys it. But for this process to function, the worker, the employer, and society more generally, must have a certain conception of what constitutes time. It was Marx who showed that time under capitalism loses its experiential and socially created forms—to become *abstract*. In this it accords with the Newtonian conception of time and its clockwork representation. Moreover, as part of the process of labor and production for market exchange, time in the factory system of capitalism became an *abstract exchange value*—albeit one that had to be differentiated from the use values of the actual commodities being produced. The myriad of things that are produced have use values that are contextually situated and intrinsically different in themselves, things such as a pair of shoes, or an iPod, or a chair. However, if these are to be exchanged for money, then it needs the mediation of a value that is independent of context and universally applicable as an abstract value. *Time is that common value* through which the world of commodities can be evaluated and exchanged (Adam 2004, 38).

In *Grundrisse*, Marx expressed the process thus:

> Every commodity (product or instrument of production) is = to the objectification of a given amount of labour time. Their value, the relation in which they are exchanged against other commodities, or other commodities against them, is = to the quantity of labor time realized in them.

Barbara Adam sums this process up well when she writes that: "Time is the decontextualized, asituational abstract exchange value that allows work to be translated into money...Only as an abstract standardized unit can time become a medium for exchange and a neutral value in the calculation of efficiency and profit" (2004, 38–39). It is in this connection that the "time is money" logic becomes something more than the tacit appreciation of "how the world is," and expresses the hinge-relationship upon which capitalism and thus modernity is built. It provides also the key for understanding why the time of the clock became the organizing principle of modern life, and increasingly so as capitalism spread wider and sunk deeper into economy, culture, and society.

Marx explains the function of time in modern industrial society, but this, we need to remember, is the time of the clock, the time of shift-work and lunch hours, and weekends off, and so on. These are the units of mechanical time that are divisible into slices of time that are uniform (an hour is always sixty minutes) and so can be precisely calculated. It does not explain *acceleration*. The tick of the clock is a single, invariant speed—how can this go faster and faster? The obvious move here is to look at technological development, and the fact that a machine can work faster, and for longer, than can the muscles and the brain of a human. But this begs the question: why then does technology develop? For much of human history technologies developed through accident or, more commonly, through the imperative of diverse human needs—occasionally augmented by the flash of innovative insight. For example, people in ancient societies would have (at some point) noticed that heavy circular stones had properties that flat ones did not—you could move them across the ground far more easily by rolling them. The wheel probably has its origins in our capacity to problem-solve in ways that allow us to act upon our environment. The wheel found its true potential when attached to the horse via a wagon, but it took humans thousands of years to make this connection. The invention of the horse and cart, although revolutionary, remained fundamentally unimproved until relatively recently. The point is that technological development, for most of its history, has been slow, disorganized, piecemeal, context-dependent, and situationally derived from perceived needs and spotted opportunities. Above all, the point is that pace of change could not be measured in any rational way, and did not conform to any rational–temporal logic.

This ad hoc process of technological development was transformed (revolutionized) and systematized with the advent of the Industrial Revolution. Europe began to industrialize, yes, but what was (and still is) the engine of this revolution? In a word—*competition*. The power and dynamism of capitalism stems from the fact that the employer can never stay still, no matter how successful the business, no matter how large the market share, no matter how high-tech the equipment being used. Again the point is obvious, but much that we rarely consider flows directly from this fact: *if a business product or service is seen to be selling well, then others (competitors) will seek to emulate that success.*

The very point of free-market liberalism is that individuals have the right to do this. Of course, when Apple or Sony, for example, brings out a new product, a competitor cannot simply copy it and sell it more cheaply. The challenge is to make a similar product better and at less cost, be it a laptop computer or mobile phone or software application or almost anything at all that people will buy. What businesses *must do* is to *invest capital* in order to explore new ways to make an existing product better or to develop a new product altogether. Superior technology, especially in the manufacturing sector, but also in the delivery of services, is what will give capitalists the temporary edge in market competition (Hassan 2010). Others who strive for this competitive edge will likewise invest in machinery or in the streamlining of productive processes in order to make or supply something faster and more economically. It is this never-ending dynamic of competition that gave the Industrial Revolution what Marx and Engels famously termed the "all that is solid melts into air" vibrancy that ensures that nothing stays still for long. Widespread and socially sanctioned free-market competition is what took technological development from the realm of chance and accident and diverse social context, to place it, like social time, onto the plane of an abstract process where technology develops according to its own relentless logic. To illustrate the point we need only consider the development of atomic weapons in the 1940s. Individuals and societies governed solely by reason would have eschewed such patently terrible weapons by simply contemplating their anticipated (and unanticipated) consequences. However, the deadly convergence of military and economic competition of the time ensured that the emergence of the most destructive energy force ever conceived could not be stopped. As philosopher Jacques Ellul observed in his book *The Technological Society*, "Technique has become autonomous; it has fashioned an omnivorous world, obeys its own laws and has renounced all tradition" (1964, 14). Capitalist competition is what gave technology its autonomy.

Yes, capitalism and the Industrial Revolution—and their corollary of Enlightenment thought—functioned in line with the broad organizational tempo of the clock. And yes, life did speed up in those early days, as illustrated in Goethe's Romantic lamentation to Zelter. However, it must be admitted that what Goethe experienced as "ultra" fast would seem pretty slow to us today. The ordering of life made possible through capitalist rationality and clock time did set a pace and a rhythm of regularity that would have been unprecedented in the early nineteenth century when Goethe looked around and considered the spread of industry. But what Goethe experienced and what generations more would experience, right up until very recently, was not broad-based and open-ended acceleration. This would only come, as we shall see, with the rise of the network society and the emergence of what I have termed "network time." It is important firstly to understand why these forms of technologized times are different and how they have produced different societies with different temporal speeds. The key to understand this is to factor in time's indivisible element—space.

As the Industrial Revolution and the shift to clock time consciousness began to get underway, the growth of this system through the imperatives of competition meant that the logic itself spread in and through geographic space. Again the bald point is evident—but what does it mean if we temporalize the observation? If we do, we realize that, firstly, as capitalism and the consciousness of the clock spread, it did not spread evenly or rapidly or in all directions simultaneously. Moreover, what Australian historian Geoffrey Blainey in another context termed the "tyrany of distance," acted always to "slow" the spread of capitalism and give its growth particular historical and temporal forms. Secondly, capitalism itself tends toward a geographic fixity that has given its spread a form of traction that has entailed a particular historical spread and speed, both of which were contained, managed, and organized within the speed of the clock. Let us look at those two points in their turn.

There has been a good deal of literature that has stressed the impact of communication technologies such as the telegraph and the railways during the nineteenth century as acting to "shrink" time and space in radical ways with purportedly radical social and economic effects (Kern 1983; Whitrow 1988). There is indeed much to be said for the revolutionary force that such communication technologies employed upon the shaping of modern societies. However, as Jeremy Stein argues, the impact of speed upon society has generally been overstated. In his review of the relevant literature he observes that "interpretations of time-space compression typically rely on [the contemporaneous] accounts of privileged observers, and are thereby elitist" (2001, 107). I think it may be fruitful to view Goethe's experience through such a perspective. What Stein is suggesting is that life for most people (for those, say, in Goethe's corner of Germany) would have gone on very much as it did after they saw their first train hurtling past, or noticed the first telegram office opening in town. Social change through new technology was incremental instead of "ultra" fast. It would do so simply because the initial users of trains and telegraphs and steam ships and so on, would have been those in the upper echelons of industrializing society, the "early adopters" who could see utility, advantage, and profit in such technologies in the conduct of their daily business. To obtain a more "nuanced" perspective, Stein maintains, one would be required to research the records of a much broader social strata and interpret that majority's experience of space–time compression. Stein's own research was centered on the late-nineteenth-century Canadian textile town of Cornwall, Ontario, and his interpretation of relevant local documents, such as newspapers, council records, and traveler's accounts, provides a useful corrective to the "elitist" views that often prevail. Stein goes into much of the detail from these records, but to be brief, what he argues is that although the effects of new communications technologies was fundamental and indeed brought great change, the time-line of this change is *much longer* (in typical towns such as Cornwall) than is usually thought to be the case. Space–time compression did indeed occur, Stein finds, but it was "evolutionary not revolutionary" and technological changes in communications were "cumulative and gradual" and although "the effects of changes were widely felt, wealthy social observers were most able to take advantage of them" (2001, 119). In other words, "time-space compression" (if one is allowed a somewhat counterintuitive metaphor) *rippled out* through space to have its effects upon time experience by overcoming tractioning obstacles such as class, geography, culture, politics, and even engrained habit, in ways that constituted a specific and context-dependent *unfolding* of temporal change.

The second issue of geographic "fixity" is also an important one. In his *The Limits to Capital*, a book I note in parenthesis that has been lamentably under-appreciated since it first appeared in 1983, David Harvey provides valuable insights into the nature of the spread of capitalism. Harvey builds upon Marx in the *Grundrisse* and *Capital* to argue a theory of *capital accumulation* within geographic space and through clock time. For Harvey, the accumulation process is the key to understanding capitalism's intrinsic processes, especially its spatial expansion and temporal acceleration. Competition has another effect apart from abstracting time from social-productive processes. From at least the time of Adam Smith it has been recognized that competition produces wealth—or what Marx more blandly phrased as "capital accumulation." No matter what we call it, the process does sound a positive one. Does not it? What could be wrong with the creation of wealth? Well, if like Marx and like Harvey, time and space are factored into the analysis, then a rather large and pernicious contradiction rises into view.

We have seen that capital cannot rest. Spurred by competition capital must, as Marx and Engels phrased it in the *Communist Manifesto* "nestle everywhere, settle everywhere, establish connexions everywhere..." (1975, 38). It is not only competition, however, that provides this motive force, it is the nature of accumulation itself. In *The Limits to Capital*, Harvey shows that as accumulation builds within a certain geographic region, unless it constantly finds profitable outlets, then the problem of "overaccumulation" (of too much unutilized capital) begins to occur and, as a consequence, the rate of profit begins to fall (Harvey 2006 [1983], 412–45). This rule holds for both individual capitalist concerns and for the system as a whole. An excess of material wealth (in the form of too many unsold cars, or food, or books, or whatever) means that capital is unable to find its "realisation" in the form of exchange value, and so profits fall and capital itself is devalued. There are two "solutions" to this problem for capital and its processes of accumulation. The first is spatio-temporal. The second is somewhat more drastic, but as will be seen, both are "solutions" that we are familiar with. In terms of space, capital does what capital has always done when following its inner logic, and that is to expand into geographic space in search of more sources of raw materials, more potential markets, and more reservoirs of cheaper labor. Harvey calls this the "spatial fix" that affords temporary relief to the building of capital toward levels that would begin to affect the rate of profit (2006 [1983], 427). In respect of the temporal, surplus capital is invested into ways and means to enable effective competition, and this as we have seen, has been chiefly and traditionally in innovations in productive processes (through technological fixes) that reduce the cost of labor and accelerate the rate of production. The second "solution" to overaccumulation and the falling rate of profit is: devaluation. This is another understated economistic Marxian phrase, because what it means is bankruptcy, recession, depression, or slump. When this happens, whether at the micro- or macro-level, the effect is the same—capital loses its value and *ipso facto*, the overaccumulation problem is eased or vanishes for a time. Great human suffering is entailed in this "solution" but this tends not to show in the accounting ledger of the system's health.

Of course, geographic expansion and devaluation have been occurring since the beginning of the capitalist system, either on a large-scale or at the level of the business enterprise. And together they have worked to enable capitalism to function through both the good times of expansion and through the periodic crises that can allow accumulation to begin afresh. But the genius of Harvey's book, the insight that is contained in its title, is that there are extrinsic *limits* to this process. The logic of capital, Marx assumed, was digging its own grave in the form of a growing self-consciousness on the part the working classes. This class-consciousness, which he saw would inevitably be politicized, would also herald the communist revolution. Harvey, however, reappraised Marx's analysis from the perspective of the professional geographer that he is—and this led him to a quite different prognosis. Capital's vital need to "nestle everywhere, settle everywhere, establish connexions everywhere..." has geographic limits. There is only so much "everywhere" on our finite planet. For around three centuries, capital could on the macrocosmic scale expand (and suffer periodic bouts of devaluation and contraction) and then expand again, in a kind of two steps forward and one step back progression. However, after the last great expansionary boom, in the decades after the Second World War, the building crises of accumulation touched its spatial "limits" in that there were no longer any unclaimed spaces or easy geographic routes for capital to be profitably channeled. The planet, in other words, was by the 1970s becoming completely colonized by capital and by capitalism's logic. There were important exceptions to this of course, in the form of the Warsaw Pact countries and China, which were outside the normal "circuits" of capital. But more on that shortly. By the 1970s, Japan was becoming a major economic power, with its own highly dynamic and competitive forms of production in "Toyotaism" and "just in time" methods and was making serious inroads into Western markets and increasingly outperforming Western levels of productivity and profitability. Continental Europe was now largely rebuilt after the destruction of the war, and its economies were approaching maturity in terms of their accumulative capacities. The "Tiger" economies of Asia were also rising, as were those of Brazil and Argentina and Mexico. Accordingly, the Anglophone economies of North America, Britain, and Australasia were just more pieces in the almost completed jigsaw picture of pole-to-pole capitalism. In short, capital spanned the globe, with all of it still expanding and building inexorably as it must, and all of it and looking for profitable outlets in a context of diminishing actual geographic territorial space.

This inherent contradiction was already finding expression by the 1960s when rates of profit were falling in the Western economies, and crises of overaccumulation were building in industries such as shipbuilding, manufacturing, engineering, and so on—the mainstays of the postwar Fordist modality of production (Glyn 1990). The building crisis of overaccumulation, moreover, needs to be seen in the context of a postwar *regime of accumulation*, across most of the developed economies, where government management and government participation in the shaping and running of economic life was both significant and widespread (Aglietta 1979). Whilst the so-called "regulation" of the capitalist economies slowed and constrained the "natural" free flow of capital to wherever (and with whatever) it was able to turn a profit, the period of reckoning with traditional capitalism's "limits" within traditional space and time, was unavoidable. The term "traditional" is used deliberately here. Traditional capitalism and traditional conceptions of space and time were no longer adequate to the task of delivering rates of profit and enabling capital to be channeled to fresh fields to enable the process of accumulation to start again. By the late 1970s the space for capital was reaching its limits, and the speed of capital, a machine-based speed that had been governed by the clock since the seventeenth century, was no longer fast enough in the context of growing and intense global competition. The deep economic crises of the decade represented severe difficulties not just for national economies and for individual businesses and for millions of workers. The 1970s represented a watershed for advanced capitalism itself. It had entered a phase where the form of production and accumulation that had its systematizing genesis in the nineteenth century had finally reached its spatial and temporal maturity, and this maturity was now degenerating into sclerosis (Benton 2001). What had developed, one can see in retrospect, was a revolutionary situation, wherein, in an inversion of the old Marxist formula: the ruling classes were no longer *prepared* to go on in the old way, and the ruled classes were no longer *able* to go on in the old way.

Capitalism and Freedom

Britain began its path to industrialization first, and so it seems logical that the British economy would come to maturation—and hence crisis—at the front of the queue. The other major Western economies were not that far behind, but the economic and political array of forces in the UK served to place it (to compel it) to act as pioneer in the seeking of solutions that would lead it to a "post industrial" age. The problems of accumulation that were expressed as falling rates of profit and by the largely uncompetitive state of much of British industry were of course widely recognized by big business, by unions, and by government itself. Indeed, these three institutions were up until that point deeply involved in running the British economy through the so-called "post war consensus" that dictated the shape, scope, and direction of broad economic policy. But with the maturation of the Fordist economy that the political "consensus" created, the 1970s inaugurated a decade of economic turmoil, elements of which had never been experienced previously. For example, the term "stagflation" entered the economic lexicon to describe what was previously thought to be impossible: a stagnating economy that is beset also by inflation. The overaccumulation of capital was at the core of this problem. Militant unionism arose as a response to the overaccumulation/profitability crisis, which forced employers to attack wages and conditions. This served both to drive up social spending and wage demands, which in turn cut into already dwindling profits, thus creating a negative feedback loop (Bello 2006, 1347). Stagflation was the result, and not only in Britain, but across the core industrial economies to a more or less degree. More spectacularly, and even more broadly again, was the "oil shock" crises of 1973 which fed directly into the cost of production for businesses and the cost of living for hundreds of millions of workers. Undergirding these negative processes, and once more not only in Britain, was a rising component of mass unemployment, which reinforced the widespread feeling of crisis, and the growing conviction that something had to be done (Beckett 2009).

The problem was an economic one. However, the "solution" was political, albeit one dressed up as economic theory: neoliberalism. Neoclassical economics—redux theorems that had been doing the rounds in the universities since the end of World War II became salient once more in books such as *The Road to Serfdom* by Friedrich von Hayek which appeared in 1945, and Milton Friedman's *Capitalism and Freedom*, which was first published in 1962. Friedman's book is especially instructive as he explicitly connected the idea of individual freedom with the capitalist system. Individuals could only be free, Friedman maintained, if economic life was free. Markets therefore should not be bureaucratically organized, as this leads inevitably (the

USSR being a case in point) toward tyranny; business should not be overly regulated, as this stunts the entrepreneurial free spirit; direct government activity in economic life should be kept to an absolute minimum—and so on. The book, which made barely a ripple when it was first published, went almost mainstream by the mid-1970s. And so when Friedman was chosen for the Nobel Laureateship in 1976 for his work on economics, it was clear that an idea had found its time.

Freedom. The abstract idea of it was expounded by Friedman, Hayek, and others at some length, however at the level of the individual it tended to remain abstract and elusive. Not so freedom and capital. The freedom of capital through the freedom of markets became the central neoliberal mantra. It was taken up as an explicitly political program first in Britain with the election of Margaret Thatcher's Conservative government in May 1979. Thatcher's government, though Conservative, was not much concerned with conservation. Her neoliberalism was nothing less than the political prosecution of an economic, social, cultural, and technological revolution. The British neoliberal free-market project, one that would spread in time to encompass the whole world to a greater or lesser degree, would consist of two components that oriented around the idea of *flexibility*—the very antithesis of the rigidities and sclerosis that were seen to have characterized post-war consensus capitalism. The first flexibility is one that managers conferred upon themselves in respect of managing capitalism. A major focus of neoliberal argument was the consensus model, which I just touched on, that gave government and organized labor, as well as big businesses, a say in how capital was invested and what it was invested in. In the post-war climate of profit during the 1940s, 1950s, and into the 1960s, there were no major disagreements regarding the shape and direction of capitalism as long as the bottom line remained strong. When the bottom line became decidedly shaky for western capitalism in the 1970s, a period of sharp class struggle ensued, with the question "who is most suited to run business?" being insistently posed by neoliberals such as Friedman. They were arguing that capital was "unfree" (as were its owners) when unions and government had a say in how businesses were organized. The class struggle of the 1970s, moreover, was an unequal affair. It was two against one: employers and government against worker organizations. Over that decade and the one that followed, governments such as the Margaret Thatcher-led British Conservatives, and successive US administrations beginning with the election of Ronald Reagan in

1980, made the deliberate political decision to abrogate their role as active participants in the shaping of national economies. The surface effect of this process has been termed "privatisation," but its political motivation was a much more important issue: it was for governments to do as the neoliberal theorists said that they must, and let the market do its work upon the economy come what may. Those who resisted this process, that is to say, those workers and their organizational bodies in industries that now had to sink or swim, were increasingly met not only by the power of employers to lock-out, sack, intimidate, and more broadly exploit them in the opportunities that arose in the "*new* spirit of capitalism" (Boltanski and Chiapello 2007), but met also by increasingly neoliberalized and neoliberalizing governments who went out of their way to legislate to create what was termed an "attractive business environment" for investment. By the 1990s, the "flexibility" for capitalists to invest and disinvest where and when they saw fit was almost complete. Governments across the world increasingly fell over themselves in a "race to the bottom" to attract capital in the new globalized economy (Tonelson 2002). Such flexibility was the previously undreamt-of power (for CEO's and business executives) to call the shots over the heads of government and organized labor to a degree and to an extent that was unparalleled in the twentieth century. Indeed, reviewing the political and economic conjectures of globalization in 2000, Perry Anderson observed that neoliberalism, as a worldview, had achieved something unique:

> Ideologically, the novelty of the present situation stands out in historical view. It can be put like this. For the first time since the Reformation, there are no longer any significant oppositions—that is, systematic rival outlooks—within the thought-world of the West. (2000, 17)

The second flexibility is one that most people will nowadays recognize in their workplaces and in their wider sphere of living too. It is a *personal* flexibility toward, primarily, the demands of the market functioning in the context of a constant present. It is a flexibility of the mind, the body, and the attitude toward both the nature of work and its ontological meaning. In other words, it is a rationalized and instrumental flexibility whereby the *individual* worker (the collective term matters less and less) is expected to correspond with and synchronize to the unpredictable and fast-flowing economic logic of neoliberal globalization. This flexibilization, of course, stems from the demands of competition, and since the 1970s neoliberal theorists, politicians, and business leaders have repeated the mantra in the form of thinly disguised threats about looming unemployment if the individual does not respond rapidly and adequately to the changing needs of the economy. With the eclipsing power of organized labor unions, the temporal rhythms of labor changed from the predictable and stable, to the contingent and fluxual. What this has meant in practice is a transformation in the times and durations of work. The dominant rhythm of the nine-to-five job, as Juliet Schor (1991) observed, was a thing of the past by even the early 1990s; part-time working and temporary contracts have exploded as individualized workers find themselves unable or unwilling to confront their employers' (and governments') preference for turning labor requirements on or off like a tap. The ideological triumph of neoliberalism has ensured that the need for flexible workers has remained largely and unquestioned imperative, right up to our own time. Indeed, with the global economic crisis that began in 2007, even more "flexibility" in markets and in people was promoted in forums such as Davos in Switzerland, where British prime minister Gordon Brown reminded the assembled members of the G20 countries that: "We should not retreat from the idea that we can solve these [economic] problems and still believe in the idea of an open, free market, flexible, inclusive and sustainable globalization" (VOA News 2009).

It is rarely remarked upon, but the term "flexible" is a deeply temporal one. At the surface level it connotes, and is meant to connote, "efficiency"—which is supposedly a weapon in the constant battle for competitiveness. But what is "efficiency" if not working faster at one's occupation, responding more quickly to "opportunities," and displaying a "quick-wittedness" in everyday economic relations? David Harvey, in his *The Condition of Postmodernity*, phrases its time–space properties well when he writes that: "the more flexible motion of capitalism emphasizes the new, the fleeting, the ephemeral, the fugitive, and the contingent in modern life" (1989, 171). Harvey here indicates that the "motion" of capital has become post-modern, and has evolved out of its post-war Fordist mode into a new mode of "flexible accumulation," as he terms it, where speed and acceleration are the new defining properties of capitalism's latest iteration. In this transition, the time of the clock has lost its position of domination over the life of humans and the industrial economies they have built. Its role as a backdrop to the affairs of people is still important, of course:

trains and buses and aircraft still need to be scheduled according to its strict meter; looser predictabilities still rhythm the tempo of daily life where morning bread is still baked, newspapers and magazines still roll off the presses at pre-set times, classes at school still begin at a certain time of the clock, the museum and the library and the concert hall still open and close at times that may be relied upon.

However, a new temporal world is being created alongside this one, and this brings us, finally in this chapter, to a consideration of what I have elsewhere termed "network time" (Hassan 2009). An understanding of the origin and nature of this new socially constructed temporality is necessary to properly understand the origin and nature of chronic distraction in our own time—and will provide the intellectual and critical tools to seek ways in which the pathologies that stem from our distracted lives may be mitigated or "cured" altogether.

So Perfectly Up-to-Date

Network time is a process that emerges out of the dynamics of the network society. It is the idea of the *network* and the properties of the network, however, that provides the basis for understanding network time as a form of time that is every bit as "real" in its abstractedness than is the time of the clock. Moreover, and like the time of the clock, network time drives humans and human-made systems, and it "conditions" the cognitive process of humans and puts them in a specific relationship to the production, dissemination, and consumption of information and knowledge.

Let us begin by thinking about the nature and properties of networks. The fundamental property of any network, be it based around railways, or television stations, or highways, or computers is that they are vectors for communication: that is to say, they allow people to create and share information across time and space. Indeed, it is the case that networks *create and shape* social time and space, and the particularities of any network are given substance and are defined by the technologies used to create them. I do not yet at this point suggest that technologies alone determine nature of a network but, rather, working in dialectical fashion, we shape the tools that we use and they in turn shape us.

To illustrate the processes of the interaction more clearly, I want to consider three examples of networking through technology to show how space and time are transformed—and how the process of technological determinism becomes *more pronounced* as networked technologies become more tightly networked and increasingly all encompassing.

You will recall from Chapter 2 my observations on the so-called "Republic of Letters" that was the ideational and written expression of the major Enlightenment preoccupations of science, philosophy, and democracy—as they were being conceived and implemented at that time. This constituted the world's first modern communication network in that it worked with universal and secularly oriented themes. The production and dissemination of technical, mercantile, industrial, and philosophical information was the critical function of the network and it is not too much to say that the project of modernity itself depended upon it. The network itself consisted of a tiny stratum of intellectuals, manufacturers, and philosophers—a self-motivated agglomeration that Jürgen Habermas would categorize as the founding elements of the "public sphere" (1989). The influence of the network of letters, of its dynamic of "epistolary exchange," of its production of technical publications, of newspapers, magazines, and books was immense and foundational—but also necessarily slow moving. The "tyranny of distance" and a relatively low level of technical sophistication meant that this network shaped time and space in tentative and partial ways. The time and rhythm of this network was, through its being attached to emergent industry, nascently clock time, but the rhythms were weak and faintly felt by the vast majority who would synchronize with the time–space of clock-driven modernity only gradually. A systematic technological determinism was relatively undeveloped at this time, principally because innovations tended to develop from scratch from the heads of individual tinkerers and experimenters, and not as an extension of a prior vast body of technical knowledge. The fruit of their innovation was therefore not readily connectible to a wider system of technical knowledge and methods—which did not exist to any significant degree in the eighteenth century. People, in short, were *coming to* the time of the clock and slowing building it (or having it built) into their lives. Accordingly, the time of the network—and the time of the modernizing world—was a clock time that had much potential yet to fulfill for the project of modernity.

By the late-nineteenth century the picture has changed dramatically, and a much more comprehensive information network had evolved, one that was much more abstracted, systematic, and technology-based than was the more people-centered Republic of Letters network. Moreover, it was a *global* network of a kind that we more readily recognize today. For example, on August 27, 1883, the volcano at Krakatoa in Java exploded and produced a destructive force that was estimated to be more than thirteen thousand times more powerful than the atom bomb that flattened Hiroshima in 1945. The explosion destroyed almost the entire island and was said to have been clearly audible in Perth, Western Australia. This of course was a world event—but a world event that for the first time was *mediated* as such, with space and time and people being far more susceptible to technological shaping than it had been in the earlier part of the century. Simon Winchester tells us that the ash from the volcano moved along the upper atmosphere jet stream at seventy-three miles per hour, and at this natural speed the ash cloud did not make its appearance in New York until December (2005, 288). However, the *New York Times* was technologically equipped to shrink time and space to such a degree that the explosion was reported by it a few hours after the event itself. A newly laid global network of undersea telegraph cables relayed the first reports being tapped out by a station in nearby Batavia. The *New York Times* of August 27 was thus able to run a small article based on these reports that described the "terrific detonations" from the island of Krakatoa (McNamara 2009). For New York readers, the world had become an ontologically graspable place. And not only for New Yorkers. As Winchester tells it in his book on the subject:

> Fretful and fascinated people around the world, in cities as distant from Java and from one another as Boston and Bombay and Brisbane, all came to know of the event in an instant—and they did so quite simply because this was the world's first major catastrophe to have taken place in the aftermath of the invention of the submarine telegraph. The newspapers were full of it, the descriptions of the happenings made all the more enthralling because they were so perfectly up to date. Words and phrases that had hitherto been utterly unfamiliar—*Java, Sumatra, Sunda Strait, Batavia*—became in one mighty flash of eruptive light part of the common currency of all. (2005, 6)

The "consciousness of the world as a whole" that Roland Robertson (1992, 8) saw as a pre-requisite for present-day globalization, was already developing in the nineteenth century through technological innovation. Technology was literally reaching through geographic space in the form of communication cable networks that pulsed signals of meaning across the world at previously unimaginable speeds. Coding and handling notwithstanding, information could traverse the globe in 1883 in the time-span of minutes. If the Victorians had conquered the space of the world, then so too had its time come under the rational logic of capitalist modernity. Just a year after the Krakatoa global event, another global event with profound temporal consequences took place in Washington, DC, in the USA. It was to here that delegates from twenty-five countries convened to zone the entire planet into a common and agreed meridian time and longitude framework. Greenwich Mean Time or (GMT) was born, and from this point on the world functioned on the basis of a coordinated system of clock time. Not only did this abolish the localized and ancient anomalies of differing times at very close geographic locations (such as between London and Dorchester, which is 129 miles), but it also coordinated in a rational form, entire continents such as the USA, where the coordination of the times of railway companies, for example, helped to produce the unbounded economic efficiencies and the powerful predictabilities that capital desperately needed in that emergent global power (Whitrow 1988, 165).

The "consciousness of the world as a whole" was certainly a major premise underscoring the international agreement to coordinate time on a planetary scale. The technology with which to make this consciousness a material and ontological reality even to a minority of humanity, however, did not yet exist. Winchester saw these global information networks as the means for the creation of what he termed a "brotherhood of knowledge" (2005, 6). Indeed it was, but the brotherhood was a close-knit one, and still dwelled in the realm of the "elite" forms of communication that, as Stein reminded us, has skewed much of our view of the power and scope of early electronic communication such as the telegraph and telephone. Nevertheless, these acted as an important spur to capitalism and its competitive dynamics. The space of the world was opening up, and the time of the world was set upon the logic of instrumental reason that capitalism functioned optimally within. Moreover, the "knowledge" that a global perspective could bring was an immensely powerful tool with which to compete and, as the century turned, perspicacious capitalists began to lead the way in transforming Victorian-age industry and capital—fashioning them into something even more *modern* and recognizable to our present-day senses.

I noted before that artists, people who are often apart from, or at the edge of the mainstream, could sometimes sense society's deeper currents before those who are more fully engaged with its surface manifestations. Virginia Woolf was one such perceptive student. In a celebrated line in her essay "Mr Bennett and Mrs Brown" she observed that:

> On or about December 1910, human character changed. I am not saying that one went out, as one might into a garden, and there saw that a rose had flowered, or that a hen had laid an egg. The change was not sudden and definite like that. But a change there was, nevertheless; and, since one must be arbitrary, let us date it about the year 1910.

Woolf, like Goethe, detected undercurrents of social change—and commented on the change itself. Goethe observed the onset of modernity, whereas Woolf chronicled in her fiction the arrival of *modernism* as an artistic and cultural moment. Modernity was entering its adulthood and was developing at a pace and a speed (and through technological means) that Goethe could have not dreamed of. Woolf wrote her essay in 1924, and so had the added benefit of hindsight to take in the changes, cultural and technological, that had occurred since the new century got underway. For example, in art the Vorticist movement, with which she had personal connections through painters such as Wyndam Lewis and the poet Ezra Pound, came into being around the year 1910. Vorticism celebrated the speed and dynamism of the new machine age and gave expression to it in a radical painting form that attempted to capture speed and motion on canvas (Cork 1976). Vorticism's links to the more widely known Futurism of Filippo Marinetti is perhaps more apposite as this movement gave speed and the machine a fame—and for some an infamy—through a particularly violent and glorifying reading that leaked over into the 1920s Fascist movement in Italy. These references are enough, I think, to accurately contextualize the thinking of Woolf in 1924. Speed, machinery, and the feeling of "ultra" that had Goethe lamenting modernity, was celebrated through a *geometric modernism* that sought to capture in paint and in sculpture, a *network of lines* that echoed the growing (and speeding) information networks that was a capitalist system that had entered upon a truly global age.

What Woolf did not comment on, but what in 1924 her acute cultural antennae could not have failed to miss, was the material dynamic that underpinned the speed of the machine age—and that was Fordism. We have touched on this subject previously, but it is time now to give it a bit more consideration. Woolf's 1910 setting, though arbitrary, was just enough to encompass the Fordist revolution that took place in Dearborn, Michigan two years before. It was there and then that Henry Ford's factories began in a serious and world-changing way to develop and refine the production-line system of (in this case) building automobiles that took Adam Smith's observations on the division of labor from their unsophisticated beginnings in discrete Georgian manufactories, to become the mode of production that would *define* the system capitalism for most of the twentieth century. Ford's revolutionary production lines based upon the conveyor-belt system are by now well known, and the conveyor-belt system—albeit largely automated, and as human-free as possible—today produces everything from microchips to fish fingers, and from shoes to books. What it meant in 1908 was that instead of a group of men contributing to the building of an automobile by adding each stage to a stationary entity, the moving car would pass the standing worker who would add his part to it, identical part to identical position, be it a screw on the hood, or a wheels to the axle. The conveyor-belt is the revolutionary bit. This was a machine technology entimed by the rationality of the clock and the clock-timed world, and set to function at a particular speed—*to which the worker had to synchronize his every action.* This was a shock to the temporal system, one that was identified by another artist, Charlie Chaplin in his 1936 movie *Modern Times.* Chaplin's comedy emphasized the fact that the conveyor-belt never stopped, and the worker had no control over its pace. Indeed, in the context of competitive capitalism, the speed was never fast enough. In Chaplin's scenario, the pressure of competition motivates the factory management to develop an interest in a machine that would feed the workers automatically. The sales pitch for the machine is delivered to the President of the company by a "mechanical salesman" (more efficient that a real person) that speaks through a phonograph record that lauds to the skies:

> A practical device that automatically feeds your men while at work. Don't stop for lunch. Be ahead of your competitor...the feeding machine will eliminate the lunch hour, increase your production, and decrease your overhead.

Chaplin's satire, like all good lampoonery, was based upon an acutely felt reality. Workers could never work quickly enough for the machines they had to use. Nevertheless, the logic of the system dictated that they had to be constantly developed toward the goal of yet more speed and acceleration. Chaplin brings this contradiction out as comic relief, a humorous respite in the cinema from what millions of people experienced every day in their jobs. The cold reality was definitely not funny. Through Frederick Winslow Taylor's massively popular *Principles of Scientific Management* which appeared in 1911, and whose strictures were eagerly implemented by Henry Ford, the goal of extracting the highest degree of temporal rationality from the worker by synchronizing him as much as possible to the rhythms of the machine, became a new branch of time-based "science." Taylor, like most people in management at the time—a period, remember, when Max Weber had reiterated its cultural and economic importance—saw time in capitalism as a value and as something expressed exclusively through the clock. And since it was the clock that governed the production process, it was the precious time of the clock that had to be used most economically—with the worker compelled to fall in behind this logic. Taylor put his case unambiguously, and recommended a "scientific" approach to the work process (meaning the use of measurement, numbers and the stopwatch) with which to eradicate what he termed the "rule-of-thumb method" in order to contribute to "enormous savings in time [by] substituting fast for slow and inefficient motions" in the work flow (1911, 16).

From the 1910s onward, and with a competition-mandated rapidity, Ford and Taylor saw their processes and theories emulated everywhere. Not only was much of US industry "Fordized" by the early 1920s, but in the USSR too Lenin was quick to adopt the capitalist techniques of Ford and Taylor *in toto* in the attempt to "construct socialism" in the fastest possible time. That this was so is testament not only to the full-scale arrival of the machine age, but also the wholesale incorporation of machine-based clock time into the consciousness of an age. The industrialization of clock time had reached its pinnacle with the arrival and global expansion of Fordism. Fordist techniques of mass production, indeed, were the basis of the immensely successful US war effort from 1941 to 1945, and were the principle underlying productive force that enabled the US to emerge from the war with the most powerful economy (and war machine) that the world had ever seen.

The year 1945 saw the beginning of thirty years of the domination of this type of production, a mature phase that David Harvey described as "high Fordism" where it's modality and its temporal rhythms

71

constructed a "total way of life" in the industrial West (Harvey 1989, 135). Dominance by the clock as the fundamental rhythm, not only of industry—but also of society too, was the basis of this "total way of life." The clock entimed mode structured and organized the predictable patterns of work places and working weeks, of shift-work and holidays, of the rhythms of institutions such as schools and hospitals, and in the scheduling of mass media such as radio, television, and so on (Scannell 1988).

The communication networks of "high Fordism" were (and were intended to be) rational and predictable and ordered networks—just like the conveyor-belt system that was at the root of much of socio-economic and cultural life. As we have seen, capital, organized labor and government could coordinate the temporal rhythms of work and life more-or-less successfully because in the post-war context of easy profit and ample time–space expansion of industry, there was a timescape that was able to allow for the clock to govern through a fixed temporality that did not (yet) threaten profitability. But as we have also discussed, the underlying contradiction of accumulation began to run up against *diminishing geographic space* and a clock time rhythm that was no longer fast enough in the growingly hyper-competitive context, a new timescape. What this meant was that the networks of communication based upon a rigidifying Fordist world, were about to become if not obsolete, then very much a second-division player in the emerging world of information technologies.

Historian Eric Hobsbawm's 1994 book *Age of Extremes*, was subtitled "the short twentieth century 1914-1991." His historian's eye for the political turning points of the century led him to identify the outbreak of World War I in 1914 as when the twentieth century began, and the collapse of the Soviet Union in 1991 as marking its end. Taking technology and temporality as my own markers for the beginning and end of "the short twentieth century" leads me to suggest that (and almost aligning with Virginia Woolf), the century actually began in 1908 when Fordism began its colonization of the world to become a "total way of life." The *beginning* of the century's end came rather sooner for me than for Hobsbawm. It terminated gradually, over the decade of the 1970s. Technological (and temporal) revolutions are never quite as dramatic as the march to war that took place all over Europe after August 1914—or as stunning as the almost overnight dissolution of the once mighty Soviet edifice after August 1991. And so the revolution in computing that began in the 1970s was not sudden and stunning such as political transformations frequently are. Information technologies did something else. They cast a kind of technological spell whose influence works like a narcotic. The more we consume, the greater the dependency. It is a technological revolution, but it is also a *permanent one* that has neither end point nor adversary. It is revolution through an autonomous and abstract process to which we cede ever more of our economy, culture, and society. In the ceding of the forms of control (such as they were) in the planned and organized and scheduled society that clock-time Fordism built, autonomous and abstract processes have created a new space (a virtual space) and a new time—the time of the digital network. It is this network time that contains the potential that is making the "ultra" that Goethe felt a tangible reality for *all* of us. This is a post clock-time world where the seeds of acceleration that were planted at the very beginning of the machine age are now beginning to bear an unwholesome fruit.

Non-Rational and Less Scientific Time

The beginning of the book by Eric Hobsbawm that I just cited contains a list of quotes from a list of notable thinkers on what each perceives as the key development or occurrence that, for them, characterized the essence of the "short" twentieth century. Raymond Firth, the New Zealand-born anthropologist, and, I suppose, as an anthropologist, someone more attuned by training to change in culture and cultural sensitivities, wrote that:

> ...technologically, I single out the development of electronics among the most significant developments of the twentieth century; in terms of ideas, the change from a relatively rational and scientific view of things to a non-rational and less scientific one. (Hobsbawm 1994, 2)

Firth here says something rather interesting. On one hand, his quote could fit with a persistent anti-Enlightenment strain that began, as we have seen, with the Enlightenment period itself, with Goethe and his contemporaries. As someone trained in history and human culture, Firth seems to regret the development of "electronics" as a special class of technology that has somehow diminished or superseded or transformed the domination by a more "mechanistic" world. On the other hand, his observation of the slide from a "relatively rational" and science-based world, to one that is "non-rational" and "less scientific" indicates an *affinity* with Enlightenment thought. I discussed this seeming contradiction with a class of graduate students. We agreed that Firth was thinking about computing when he wrote of "electronics." However, one student made the observation that there is nothing more rational and scientific in our world today than computing, and so the statement *was* ultimately contradictory. The point I made in that class, and will argue in the final part of this chapter, is that a *powerful instrumentalism* has shaped the rationality and the science basis of networked computing, rendering this particular form of computing, as Firth suggests, both "non-rational and less scientific." Let me explain.

The networking process that we have looked at through its historical phases, took a radical and *qualitative* as well as quantitative leap to another level in the 1970s. Networkable computers transformed the "Republic of Letters" and the later "brotherhood of knowledge" of information networks into something new and something else altogether—a post-modern digital network. The powerful neoliberalism/ICT revolution conjecture enabled capitalism, through the promotion of thoroughgoing structural deregulation of national capital formations, to break free from the historical–temporal constraints of Fordism. The effect of this conjecture acted somewhat as a palliative for the accumulation problem, the "spatial fix" that capitalism requires in order to function. As Castells observed the fix was partly obtained through the rapid expansion, dating from the early 1980s, of wholly computerized and globalized financial networks with vast amounts of capital being channeled to "information networks in the timeless space of financial flows" (2000, 472). The creation of the networks of financial flows was invariably made possible through the development and deployment of the most advanced computing technologies that were conceived with specific purposes in mind: rapidity, volume, and immense processing power—all on an open-ended scale of development, where the limits to the purposes of computing were/are constrained only by the level of technological sophistication pertaining at any particular time. At this leading commercial edge we see the logic of computing being developed specifically in order to service the demands of autonomous and abstract (and chaotic) market forces (Hassan 2010).

Of course, computing has conquered realms far beyond the networks that connect our planet's financial centers. The age of "ubiquitous computing" that Mark Weiser and John Seely Brown predicted back in 1996 has come to pass. What these authors foresaw as an effect of what they termed the "third wave" of computing, are machines that are "so imbedded, so fitting, so natural, that we use [them] without even thinking about it" (1996). Computing would become so ubiquitous indeed, so part of almost everything we do in work, leisure, learning, and so on, that they are either rendered invisible or made salient as the latest, must-have consumer item. Weiser and Seely Brown were certainly correct in their prognostications, but their writings do not give any indications regarding *why* this would be so. So one is forced to ask: why has a certain kind of computer logic become so phenomenally successful? The answer, I believe, is that computers and computing power and computing applications seem to live up to the ideology of its creators and boosters. As the computer revolution got underway, economy and society discovered that computers *enable*. They not only proved highly productive and efficient in the *automation* of formerly manual or machine-driven processes, such as in the mass production industries, they also enabled productivities and efficiencies in business and industries that were structurally separate from the traditional manufacturing sectors. As Dan Schiller shows in his *Digital Capitalism: Networking the Global Market System* (2000) the *networking of information processes* within businesses and between businesses, placed information production and distribution at the very core of capitalism's logic, and "comprises a sweeping and multifaceted tendency" (xv). This tendency is a feature of capitalism's innate need to expand, but within a whole new sphere of space–time virtuality. Freedom from Fordism gave capital a new lease on life, and a new dimension within which to accumulate. Powerful new dynamics based on information production and a tendency toward intra- and inter-business *collaboration* as well as competition, saw the locking in of a positive feedback loop of "ever-accelerating demand" where networking has the primary effect of encouraging even more networking (Schiller 2000, xv, 20). The effect was immediate and transformational. For example, during the early part of the 1980s, more of the investment dollar in the USA went into computer and related high-technology equipment than went into traditional labor-intensive machinery—indicating a swift overhauling of the Fordist mode within the belly of the beast itself (Kolko 1988, 66). This fed into a rapid process of innovation in computing and their enabling properties that not only revitalized many old industries through automation and the streamlining of production to make them more flexible—but also created wholly new industries, in software, in design, in computer

75

applications, pharmaceuticals, engineering, and in a host of other realms. It is within this ferment of change and opportunity that the world would learn of companies such as Microsoft, Apple, Intel, and the San Francisco Bay Area suburb nicknamed "Silicon Valley" that would become synonymous with the cutting edge of a new way of business and of networking society.

This pattern of a seemingly unstoppable burgeoning technological created the context for a characterization of the network society as being comprised of a *network of networks* whose growth through linking and interlinking was, theoretically, limitless due to its virtual nature. Manuel Castells describes how a virtual capitalism, expressed through these network of networks, disconnects space, time, and the traditionally understood processes of labor from the materiality of everyday life. He writes that: "capital and labour increasingly tend to exist in different spaces and times; the space of flows and the space of places, instant time of computerized networks versus clock time of everyday life" (2000, 475). This disconnect is the expression (or the effect) of the autonomy of computing and its late-modern technological development. It is a development beyond the binary logic of computing, and beyond the quintessence of reason and science that Gottfried Leibniz, the inventor of binary language had in mind in his seventeenth-century theorizing (Hassan 2009). Networks are expressed now in a different kind of logic: a *pragmatic logic*. We have seen in the work of Langdon Winner that artifacts (technologies) are often deliberately encoded with politics. Using similar reasoning, I argue that computers and computer development is encoded with a pragmatism that derives from the market-based politics of neoliberalism, the principle force behind ICT development since the 1970s.

Pragmatism as a philosophical tenet evolved, significantly, in the period of the Enlightenment. Reflecting in many ways the rationalist and empiricist and practical themes of the Anglo-American branch of Enlightenment thought, pragmatism may be characterized as the "primacy of practice" (Blattner 2007, 22). Put more crudely, pragmatism may also be defined as an idea or premise that may be regarded as true if it can be demonstrated (practically) to work satisfactorily. In other words, ideas and philosophies that are not oriented to solve real-world problems may be rejected as mere abstractions that have no relevance to "actual" reality. The pragmatic logic that sustains and legitimizes computing is the undoubted "fact" that they do indeed seem to "work"—or at least have a demonstrable effect on the world that may, or the surface level at least, express "efficient" processing of information in respect of all manner of applications. Pragmatism indeed is contained in the very language of computing in that what is writeable as code is only that which works at the primary binary instructional level of yes–no/on–off/zero and one. But computer pragmatism is *pseudo-pragmatism* in that it is unreflective. Humans are yet to develop a form of consciousness or reflexivity in computer logic sufficient that would allow a "self"-questioning and "self"-interrogation of what it is actually doing, and the real-world effects, short- and long-term, of its information processing. Moreover, the lack of reflexivity is sustained at the higher contextual level in which computing is developed—in the neoliberal milieu where efficiencies in productive processes and the idea that "faster is better" in almost all circumstances. The instrumentally oriented ideology of the market encodes the computer in such a way that its legitimacy is inscribed into its development and use. The fact that it does what it is programmed to do means that it "works" and, therefore, "true"—but only in a strict and narrow sense. This is not the reason nor the science that Raymond Firth thought should govern technological development. What he identified, consciously or not, in the "electronic" revolution that so transformed his twentieth century was an acute instrumentalism—one borne in an instrumental neoliberal culture and destined to play an instrumentalizing role upon that now world-dominant culture. Market logic and its instrumental pseudo-pragmatism *owns* computing in that it now directs its basic conceptions and shapes its developments right up to its (inevitably) market-oriented application across every register of life. Firth rightly saw something that was not quite right with the new "electronics" as far as reason and science were concerned. Market forces and the pragmatism that it engenders have colonized these Enlightenment impulses and rendered them weak and ineffective.

Dan Schiller noted capital's grip over the nature and deployment of computing fairly early on, and also with some prescience. In respect of the network effect of computers, he wrote that:

> Networks are directly generalizing the social and cultural range of the capitalist economy as never before. This is why I refer to the new epoch as one of digital capitalism (...) at stake in this unprecedented transition to neoliberal or market-driven communications are nothing less than the production base and the control structure of an emerging digital capitalism. (2000, 37)

Global networks that deepen and spread and accelerate are the "production base and the control structure" that dominate economy, culture, and society are the basis of a new form of time, a technologically unprecedented form of "network time" (Hassan 2003). Its basis, as we have seen, is capitalist competition—the basis of almost all technological development. However, the special nature of computing, unlike a discrete technology such as an automobile, or a dishwasher, is that they network and are now almost always designed specifically to do so. The networking capability is unlike any other previous form of network. These networks have become an autonomous force in themselves and they act upon the world in ways more powerful and dynamic than Walter Ong could have imagined in his thinking on autonomous technologies. As the key force in the neoliberal-globalization dynamic, not only do networks function autonomously, and in response to abstract market signals, but they also draw humans irresistibly into their logic because there are now fewer alternatives to their magnetizing force. In our daily lives the network touches us—and we it—in more and more ways. The spatial dynamics of this process are clear, and that is why we call it *global*ization: the world now shrinks dramatically for billions of people, from the peasant farmer in Zambia who can use his basic mobile phone to get real-time spot prices for his produce—to the trader on Wall Street who by necessity is connected 24/7, using all manner of devices and applications; for both the networks of digital capitalism are powerfully compelling, if not inescapable.

The temporal dynamics of this process are not so well appreciated, and yet they are just as dramatic. Firstly, as Castells and others have noted, within computer networks temporality *flows*. As space becomes virtualized through networks, then so too does time. In the network space, the rigid time of the clock is rendered marginal or irrelevant. The clock was developed, remember, as a contiguous machine to measure duration as it was experienced locally: from the bell and candle clock of the middle ages, to the zoned clock time that was established to regularized and coordinate and universalize temporal experience in 1883. In the network context, it is no longer so relevant what the clock says where you are physically located, because it will likely say something else where your interlocutor is. Indeed according to Castells, within the network clock time has dissipated into what he terms "timeless time" (1996, 464). However, Castells uses the term "timeless" because he has not fully through his temporal reckoning *beyond* the realm of the clock; he has not, in other words, approached time phenomenologically. It follows in this schema, that if the clock is rendered obsolete, then "time" has in a sense disappeared, because there are no longer the industrial-age temporal coordinates with which to orient oneself in the world. But if we recall and apply Barbara Adam's concept of "timescapes" (2004, 143–45) we get a better picture of the nature of Castells' "timeless time" or the "network time" that I believe to be a better descriptor. The digital network may be autonomous, but people also constitute it as users (consumers and producers of its informational product). And people inevitably bring a bio- and socio-temporality to this technoscape in the form of their own embedded temporalities and the variegated rhythms, patterns, sequences that modulate our offline world. The online, networked world is a radically new technologically and all-encompassing mediation of these embedded times that we externalize and socialize through the creation of network contexts. Being in the network and being connected through it to others, be it one-to-one, or one-to-many, or many-to-many, in business, through social networking, through browsing, moving through chat rooms, talking on the mobile phone, conducting lone research in the endless byways of the network's databases, is to create a new temporal context, or a timescape.

How does this work? Examples are plentiful in our daily-networked lives. But let me illustrate through a personal experience. Recently, I was part of a Skype networked tele-meeting. Participants in this (almost) real-time dialogue were in the UK, the USA, Germany, and Australia. The four of us could hear and see each other and could interact without too much difficulty (only a slight time-lag on line made four-way conversation a challenge in getting used to the "timing" of when to speak). Skype is a free and relatively new and still developing technology. For the four of us, the time–space compression that communication technologies have been delivering since the nineteenth century had reached a new (and commonly available) level. In that clock-time hour that we spent in the network together, the clock itself was irrelevant to our own created timescape—a *network time* scape. Seasons likewise did not matter. The fact that it was high summer in Australia where I was, and the depths of winter in an icy New York for one colleague was only worth a passing comment because we could not share the experience, as one would when meeting face to face. Underlying this network time that we created and shared was the embedded temporalities of our bodies—which are not so easily changed. Tiredness in the early evening in Australia, contrasted with the bright and fresh attitudes of those just starting their day in the Northern hemisphere. The biorhythms of appetites, too, were unavoidably different. Dinnertime and its cultural and traditional patternings were in de-synchronic cohabitation in the network with the differing bodily experiences in early- and mid-morning USA and Europe. These ineradicable times of the body and of nature are important, though, and their fundamentality, as we will see in later chapters, is the core element of the pathology of distraction and disorientation that pervades our world today. Nevertheless, in our global interaction we still all inhabited network time, a time that was utterly unique in its contextual construction. And hundreds of millions of people create their own solitary or shared timescapes every second of every day in a endlessly variegated and multitemporal network of times that burst into life and are terminated in vast and patternless effulgences that correspond primarily to the economic and social demands of the created context itself.

Skype (and doubtless its successors too) may seem to be a triumph of "efficiency," and in instrumental terms it of course is. Not long previously, the fastest means of conducting a four-way conversation would have been through e-mail. And even if we were all on line at the same time, there would have been delays, potential miscommunications, and the "timing" would have been even more difficult in order to stop the pattern of the written conversation becoming muddled. In this techno-logic *actual* letter writing (something that would have been the normal way a generation ago) is now hopelessly obsolete—a fate that e-mail too seems destined to suffer (Lorenz 2007). This is another example of McLuhan's "autoamputation" that was discussed in Chapter 1, where we extend ourselves further and further into the world and away from our bodies and our essences, and burn our technological bridges as we go. However, at the surface level at which most of us operate, we do not imagine that we are burning bridges behind us, but are simply being efficient. And viewed through the pragmatic logic of computing this is constantly validated because *the action seems to work*, and is rendered as an obvious improvement on e-mail and letter writing. Moreover, in the Skype scenario, each of us was required to be at a computer that was attached to cables that connected us to the global network. However, the next and fast-approaching "improvement" (and the latest commercial imperative) is mobile-wireless networks, or 4G, where the same four-way conversation will be enabled to take place when each of us could be on the move, in planes, or in buses or walking down a remote country lane. Advertisements will doubtless portray such 4G scenarios as the very epitome of personal freedom though hyper mobility, where "efficiency" and "productivity" are enhanced yet again through the ability to pack yet another network experience into our increasingly networked lives.

The Skype example is but one example, and is only a single shard of experience in our networked lives where being connected and having fast access to information production and consumption is now considered a fundamental right like food and shelter and protection from physical harm. Common to the totality of these experiences, from the temporal perspective, is that for all the delays in communication, for all the latencies and lags and slow bitrates and network congestion, for all differences in national networks connected at the global level, for all the cultural, economic, and social factors that contribute to an inevitable an ineradicable multitemporality at the network level—*all are oriented toward acceleration.* At every level the encoded logic of pragmatism works toward its instrumental end. At every level, competition drives computer innovation constantly toward perceived efficiency and productivity. And at every level, as a direct consequence, applications, processing speeds, user functionality, network architecture, are getting faster and faster; never are they purposely engineered to go more slowly. What is both startling and overlooked in this dynamic is that for the first time in the history of technology, there are no inherent temporal limits to communicative processes. There is no thought regarding how fast is too fast. Speed is limited only by current levels of technological sophistication, and this is being pushed through the open-ended scale of acceleration by computer engineers whose primary objective—the objective of efficiency set by their corporate employers—is unambiguous.

People are expected, and people try, and people are compelled, to synchronize with the ongoing acceleration of network processes and network time. Compulsion may seem too strong a term when thinking about using Skype, or purchasing a faster laptop or wireless application. But in my illustration none of us declined to use Skype; no one suggested that we use e-mail or write to each other instead. Deadlines were approaching and to suggest anything but the cheapest and fastest and most efficient measure would have been seen as eccentric, if not antisocial. Network time as I have described it, pervades our networked lives. But we have barely scratched the surface of our understanding of what this means. Technological bridges are being burned with hardly a dissenting voice. To question or critique computer innovation that is oriented toward efficiency and speed is to invite ridicule and characterization as a technophobe or Luddite. But until we do seriously question the cause and effects of network-generated speed and the social effects of network time, we will continue to hurtle toward a future world that we have collectively thought very little about—and are still less prepared for.

We are yet to consider the distractive and disorienting effects of network speed and network time. Before we do that, however, I want to spend some time thinking about *what we lose* through speed and acceleration, especially as it pertains to how we produce and consume knowledge and information. Underscoring this temporal investigation is the by-now familiar theory that the time of the clock was fundamental to a former (modern) world that was more or less rational and more or less manageable and formed the basis of the technological reflection of our physical and mental capacities.

4

We Are All
Still Mesopotamian

Mediate Rather than Immediate

So far I have tried to argue that the words that we use to symbolize meaning, the act of writing that fixes these words on paper, and the process of reading those words, emerge from and are expressive of human bio- and eco-temporality. The Mesopotamians who gave us writing, not only used what was at hand in the making of the marks, but they also invented the numbering system based upon sixty that would eventually become the basis for the clock time/machine-driven world. The main point I have attempted to convey is that the prehensile basis for writing and the eye movements of reading are based upon a contiguous physicality (human and environmental) that entimed these processes at their earliest point of development, setting a physical basis for the temporal capacities of the reading and writing process. Put differently, so deeply were words, reading and writing infused with the times of our bodies and the temporality of a contiguous environment in ancient Mesopotamia, that they set intrinsic and ineradicable limits upon how fast this particular process could be conducted before it begins to lose its positive cognitive effects. The point of diminishing return is reached when we begin to not understand adequately what we are reading and writing because we do it too fast, or with not enough attention.

There have of course always been individuals—most of us, sometimes—who are unable to understand properly what they are reading, or really fully know what we are trying to write about. From everyday textual dimwittedness right up to the higher grade of literary pretension, the very human failing in respect of the technological benchmarks of literacy probably came to us from the Mesopotamians too, as part of the technological baggage of knowledge production. We have tried to compensate for this, though, and—aside from the formal education process, with its own rules and conventions—at the cutting edge of intellectual and literary and cultural life, literate societies have developed processes of critique, or counter-argument, or ridicule even, to reassert the rules and conventions and so to try to set the process to right again, onto a more even keel that would make the "progress" of individual and collective literacy (and thus society) more evolutionary and conservative. The fixing of meaning and the upbraiding of the less-than-adequate attempts at the conventionalizing of forms of reading and writing was an important task. It helped "steady" and make more predictable the world that the creation of the uniquely human capacity for literacy was building. Broadly agreed meanings (and their expression) created a form of order. To deviate from the rules and expectations that governed them ran the risk (and this is not to put it too strongly) of the social world spinning out of control into a meaninglessness that would bring the edifices created by literacy crashing down.

Today, under the aegis of the network logic the contiguous bio-temporality of reading and writing—a process that was anyway on the path toward its upper limits with the rise of industrialization and modernity—is now expressed through a *temporal cognitive dissonance* that has become both systemic and systematic. Such cognitive dissonance is not the effect of stupidity or fakery or laxity—and needs to be distinguished from these. The population of the world has never been so educated; with rates of illiteracy halving in the very period this book takes as central, that to say, roughly between 1970 and 2005. However, temporal cognitive dissonance is an inability to adequately relate to the meanings of words—either to take their meanings as formal convention would suggest or, more importantly, to think more deeply about the meanings themselves and how they stand the test of being able to satisfactorily describe the functional reality of our lives and of the social world more broadly. Today, and to an unprecedented degree, we are *unable get properly to grips with words*, written or read, beyond an increasingly superficial level, because we are confronted with the lack of time to do the job properly. And as time-scholar Ida Sabelis has discovered in her sociological research of the effects of social acceleration upon the daily work of CEOs in corporate Holland, this causes things get done badly, or put off indefinitely, or discretely swept under the carpet. Lack of time, Sabelis found, forces us to let things to slip through the cracks; to cross our fingers and hope that our reading of something or our written expression of it will be sufficient to past muster if tested; or we simply leave it to chance that no one will notice our actual lack of understanding (Sabelis 2004). The overall effect is that we are less able to act upon the world in a way that is practically effective, emotionally satisfying, and contributes to the "organizing" of the world through the rational ways that writing and reading had enabled humans to become modern.

Notwithstanding this temporal asynchronicity and the cognitive dissonance that flows from it, the glorious neoliberal ICT revolution that brought humanity to this pass continues unrestricted. Indeed, its continuance is seen as the only way forward in elite policy circles around the world. And in the mainstream of society, it is a revolution that is widely accepted as the positive quintessence of economic efficiency and the basis of a bright, new world. A "knowledge society" has been said to arise from the super-powerful logic that networked computing has put at our fingertips. Michel Foucault argued that "knowledge is power" and this insight constitutes an immensely important standpoint for criticality in almost every sphere of human existence (Foucault 1979, 216). Foucault's fundamental point has been obscured today by the more obscurantist axiom that "knowledge is capital," and that such "capital" is for the first time in human history becoming available to all through computer technologies. As a 2005 UNESCO report titled *Toward Knowledge Societies* puts it:

> The knowledge economy is a particular knowledge-driven stage of capitalist development, based on knowledge, succeeding a phase marked by the accumulation of physical capital. Knowledge thus viewed is in the process of taking the place of the workforce, as Marx had foreseen in the middle of the nineteenth century, and the wealth created is being measured less on the output of work itself, measurable and quantifiable, and more and more on the general level of science and the progress of technology. The knowledge economy underlines organizational and technological complementarities between the expanded possibilities for information codification, storage and transmission offered by the new technologies, the 'human capital' of the workers likely to use these technologies and a 'responsive' organization of the enterprise (thanks to the progress of knowledge management) that makes possible the fullest utilization possible of the potential for productivity. (2005, 45)

All this sounds rather excellent, and the UNESCO staff writer of the Report cleverly manages to link the democratic visions of Marx to the logic of contemporary business practice. But what does it mean?

Well, and in keeping with the Report more broadly, it says nothing that is not in some way related to the economy and the pursuit of technological efficiency. It speaks about people, but only as a function of the economic system, with their "potential for productivity" as the only thing that "human capital" has value for. Computing is key to this concept of knowledge (knowledge that becomes "capital" that is dispensed by "responsive" businesses). But what actually is meant by "knowledge"—and how does high-speed network computing produce it? In my book *The Chronoscopic Society* (2003), I tried to make a clear distinction between knowledge and information and show that the difference is fundamentally a temporal one. Information consists of *data* in its raw form, data that is efficiently converted into digital code (information) through binary language. And binary language as its creator Gottfried Leibniz prophesized, would be mathematical efficiency brought to its highest technical level—and would be able to function as the very epitome of speed through computing. Knowledge, or the acquisition of knowledge, on the other hand, literally *takes time*—the duration and experience of which varies from context to context, from subject-matter to subject-matter, and from individual experience to individual experience. Knowledge, I argued in that book, is related deeply to experience and is something that is validated through experience. Crucially, I tried to convey that at its foundational level there is a powerful element of physical contiguity involved in the acquisition of knowledge. To illustrate my point, I quoted the photographer Peter Gullers (cited in Rochlin 1997, 67–68), who writes on the subject of expert judgment of light in photography:

> When faced with a concrete situation that I have to assess, I observe a number of different factors that affect the quality of light and thus the results of my photography. Is it summer or winter, is it morning or evening? Is the sun breaking through a screen of cloud or am I in semi-shadow under a leafy tree? Are the parts of the subject in deep shadow and the rest in bright sunlight...? In the same way I gather impressions from other situations and other environments. In a new situation, I recall similar situations and environments that I have encountered earlier. They act as comparisons and as association material and my previous perceptions, mistakes and experiences provide the basis for my judgment. It is not only the memories of the actual practice of photography that play a part. The hours spent in the darkroom developing the film, my curiosity about the results, the arduous work of re-creating the reality and graphic worlds of the picture are also among my memories.... All of

the memories and experiences that are stored away over the years only partly penetrate my consciousness when I make a judgment on the light conditions. The thumb and index finger of my right hand turn the camera's exposure knob to a setting that "feels right" while my left hand adjusts the filter ring. This process is almost automatic. (Hassan 2003, 142)

This is knowledge that has been derived through "memories and experiences that are stored away over the years" so to become "almost automatic." Temporality and knowing suffuses the whole quotation, as does the contiguous nature of this knowledge; forms based upon seeing, touching, experimentation—and the sedimentation of these processes to create knowledge in its most unmediated composition. It achieves this to the degree that it becomes *tacit*—part of the individual and his or her physical and cognitive experience. This is deeply personal and individuated knowledge. More *mediated* (or non-direct) forms of knowledge are what largely orient us to the outside world, however. This is knowledge of things that we read about or see on television or hear on radio, or from people we speak with. As Elizabeth Deeds Ermath puts it, this kind of knowledge "is always distanced from direct apprehension, is always mediate rather that immediate" (1998, 34). This mediated knowledge is not tacit in that it does not flow from direct experience, but rather comes from a *provisional* relationship to knowledge that allow us to function in the world. Its provisionality as a truth or fact is an important dimension of the relationship, because as William James observed, provisionality may be viewed as a "collective name for verification processes" (James 1907, 218). In other words, the world is only (and always) provisionally true and real for us, according to the mediated information that we possess about its state. The provisionality of this process is ongoing—and so therefore must its verification processes.

Let us look a bit closer into what is meant by mediated knowledge and how it orients us within the everyday processes of moving through the world. There was a conflict begun in Iraq in 2003, one that lasted for the rest of the decade. It is one where, as I write, there has still to be some kind of conclusion brought to it. I have never been to Iraq but I do believe that its Baathist régime has been toppled from power and that Saddam Hussein is dead (we all saw it on Youtube, didn't we?). I also believe that a large and precisely unknown number of Iraqis died, as did a more knowable number of Allied personnel. These are "facts" that I "know" and they came to me in a mediated and (mostly) electronic form. My knowledge of these events in current affairs, like that of most non-specialist people, is limited and tenuous—even though I probably spend more time on this particular subject than would many. To know more, and to understand the issues more deeply, is of course a temporal issue. I would need to spend more time reading, thinking, talking, writing, and, probably, physically visiting the region several times to experience it "first-hand"—to use that very apt term. But I do not and this is primarily because I do not have the time. So I skim across the surface of what constitutes knowledge concerning this subject through a highly mediated experience of that particular reality. And that is only one reality, one issue, one source of what constitutes my knowledge—and hence my understanding of the world. But still, for me it is provisional, and provisionally real and cannot be any other way. Nonetheless I am also reassured by the fact that "Iraq" as it has been presented to me as a series of facts and realities, is also eminently verifiable if I decided to devote the necessary time to it. Most of us consciously or unconsciously accept this bargain, the bargain of modernity and its mass media literacy that began with the Enlightenment and its project of enquiring into the reality of the world through books and papers with a faith in the power of words set upon paper.

This bio- and eco-temporal basis for understanding the "reality" of the world has become transformed through ICTs. Increasing forms of knowledge—or the expression of the experience of reality—has become *super-mediated* through high-speed networks information. However, a growing amount of this *remains at the level of information* because we have less time to engage with it sufficiently at a deeper level in order to transform it into a form of *knowledge*, something that we have taken the time to get to "know" and to provisionally accept as valid and as representing reality. For much of the information that we are confronted with every minute of every waking day, we have insufficient time to reflect upon its meaning or import at all. It was this cognitive dissonance that the French theorist Jean Baudrillard was illustrating in his much-maligned and misunderstood essay from an earlier conflict in Iraq, the 1991 invasion to oust Saddam's armies from its occupation in Kuwait. Baudrillard titled his essay, which appeared in *The Guardian* and *Libération* "The Gulf War Did Not Take Place." It made the point that through the exponentially burgeoning use of screen-based "information warfare" by the US military, and through the manipulation of computer-driven media outlets, the war had become a "hyperreality," the mediation of a mediation of a mediation, whose essence had been lost, with the physical reality of death and destruction being limited, epistemologically, to dead Iraqis and to those who had to deal with the aftermath of death "first hand." The war and its furtherance were based on US hi-tech satellite intelligence, from video screens, from computer analysis, resulting in "the fusion of the virtual and the real into a third-order of reality" (Baudrillard 2001, 11).

The key role given to the rate and volume and complexity of information production in the network society becomes salient here. "That's too much information" is a popular (and flippant) phrase that people occasionally use when someone reveals a bit more about themselves to you than you really wanted to know. There is nothing frivolous about this term as it relates to our digital lives. "Information overload," or "data trash," or "data smog" are among the epithets used to describe the surfeit of content that pulse and flow through the arterial networks that are the fabric of our digital lives. The fast-growing volume and rate of information production is staggering. For example, engineers at Cisco Systems, the US-based consumer electronic corporation, have calculated that Internet traffic grew from 5 exabytes of data per month in 2007 to 21 exabytes per month in 2010 (Miller 2010). Some perspective might be gained into the actual capacity of an exabyte (the mathematical expression of EB = 1,000,000,000,000,000,000 B = 1018 bytes = 1 billion gigabytes is, to me at any rate, meaningless) when it is considered that in 2009 it was estimated that the store of total digital content was nearly 500 exabytes, which would be the equivalent of a stack of books stretching from the Earth to Pluto, the most distant planet in our solar system—ten times over. Perhaps we can more recognizably appreciate such capacity when we see it as the equivalent of a full to the brim iPod for every second person on the planet (Wray 2009). And this volume is increasing at an exponential rate.

This burgeoning of computer-generated data has been observed at least since the 1970s (e.g., Lyman and Varian 2003; Shenk 1997; Toffler 1970). A common thread in such works is that a solution to information overload is to be found at the level of the individual. It is argued that we need to be more selective in terms of the information we consume (and produce). So we should turn the computer off more often; write and read e-mail less frequently; leave the mobile phone at home sometimes; have "device free weekends," and so on (Eriksen 1999; Gleick 2000). What such advice presumes, though, is that we have more-or-less full control over our digital lives and that we are free to switch off whenever we like. This "selective ignorance" allegedly enables us to enjoy the tranquillity of what author Tim Ferriss calls a "low information diet" (Ferriss 2010). A moment's reflection, however, would indicate that these are not realistic options for the vast majority of the billions of people who are a part of the network society. As we saw previously, the network society involves a "network effect" (Hassan 2008) where we are essentially compelled to produce and consume ever-growing amounts of information. In our jobs and in our education and in our leisure pursuits, we have to engage more and more with ICTs and their multifarious applications because this is now a vital and unavoidable aspect of what might now be considered a normal life.

The network effect does not convey compulsion as an overt and menacing feature. Compulsion is subtle and it is psychological. Like shopping, it is a "need" that is created for us as an intrinsic element of late-capitalism, a need that spans social and economic life (indeed networks connect these spheres into a singular realm). And so we regularly become more expert in this or that facet of computing because our employers (without consulting us) have just installed new software or new hardware in order to make us work more "efficiently"; we find ourselves one day with a next-level IPhone because everyone else seems to have one; and we may well find ourselves registering for Facebook because, again, everyone else seems to be doing it. We tend to skim along the surface of this experience, and may find it pleasurable at this level. However, and again like shopping, at the more deeply subjective level, if we think about it and are truthful to ourselves, the network effect can be felt as compulsion and a part of a never ending and never fulfilling process of a kind of digital slavery.

Most of us either do not have the time for such considerations—or would prefer not to face the deep-lying reality of digital domination. Better that the network effect and its compulsion is obscured for us by a more comfortable *rhetoric of information*—a discourse that expresses what Scott Lash (2002, 26) terms the "logic of information" that has superseded the Fordist "logic of manufacturing." This informational imperative finds growing political expression and momentum at the multilateral level where calls are made to make access and connectability a fundamental and universal right. Couched in the language of "rights," the network effect and its compulsory nature begin to disappear. For example, at the UN-sponsored World Summit of the Information Society in Tunis in 2005 it was proposed that: "we recognize the Internet to be a global public good related to the concept of the common heritage of humanity and access to it is in the public interest, and must be provided as a global public commitment to equality" (Spang-Hanssen 2006).

This untested assertion (and thus the compulsion of the network effect) has been put into practice at almost every level and in every part of the world, notwithstanding any local political, economic, and social conditions that may pertain. We see evidence of this in the work of Nicholas Negroponte, ICT hyper-booster, founder of MIT Media Lab, and author of such books as *Being Digital* (1995). In 2005, Negroponte set up the not-for-profit organization called One Laptop per Child (OLPC), whose mission is to distribute for free a simple and modified and connectible laptop computer to "create educational opportunities for the world's poorest children" (OLPC website 2010). It would seem on the face of it that in terms of the education of the most disadvantaged, this must be a good thing, surely? The first question to be asked is why must it be through the means of laptop computers and not, say, through more traditional means such as exercise books, and novels and comics, and thesauruses and dictionaries, and pencils and other material objects that do not depend upon a connection to the network? The point, from the Government of Rwanda's perspective, which is distributing 100,000 of the estimated 1.4 million laptops that are already in use in 35 countries such as Haiti and Afghanistan, is simple: it is to enable them to participate in twenty-first-century economic competition at its leading edge of social and technological acceleration. The aim is not to foster a generation of individuals who are educated to a degree and extent that they are able to have the beginnings of ontological awareness of themselves and their place in the world. Neither is it to exploit learning as the basis for a durable and democratic political entity, such as sub-Saharan Africa fundamentally needs. As Peter Beaumont observes, the overriding rationale is to realize "...Rwanda's ambition to turn itself into a knowledge-based economy [where] the government hopes to train 50,000 computer programmers within the next decade...a scheme whose aim is not to catch up with neighbors such as Kenya, but to leapfrog them within a generation" (Beaumont 2010, 26). If successful, Rwandan society is to be launched into a virtual global economy. There are no McLuhanesque technological bridges to be burned in this trajectory—the "development gap" is to be leapfrogged and Rwandans will land directly into the logic of the computer and computer-based competition where the worth of the individual will be assessed on how "efficiently" he or she synchronizes with the fast-flowing information torrents of neoliberal globalization.

Given the comprehensiveness of the global "logic of information" and the dynamic of capitalist-competition-driven speed that propels it—and given the fact that our relationship to the physical act of reading and writing and making sense of what we do through these processes have not changed, *and has barely been examined in the context of the network society*—the stakes could not be higher. Implicated in this are not just our own chronically distracted subjectivity, and our growing inability to cope with the demands of the information society. The way that we developed the practice of reading and writing and the temporal rhythms that we encoded into in our ancient societies, are also the very basis upon which modern civilizations are constructed. Our categories of meaning and understanding, the temporalities of past, present, and future, the relevance of Enlightenment reason and of the politics of democracy that it developed as the basis for a just form of human organization, are all implicated in and flow from these physical acts. We need now to consider more carefully *what it is exactly* that flows, temporally, from the physical processes of reading and writing. We need then to go on to consider that as a consequence of the new "logic of information" we (our brains and their cognitive capacities) have not evolved at the same rate. In short, we need to realize that reading and writing, the earliest and most important of our civilizational tools, are no longer adequate for us to function adequately in the network society.

Amazon or an Apple?

The *New Yorker* magazine of April 26, 2010, carried an article by Ken Auletta titled, rather unoriginally, "Publish or Perish." The article was interesting, however, on a number of levels. First, it relates the commonly held perception (or presumption) that the physical book form is slowly dying. Publishers of books and newspapers and magazines see only crises ahead as sales slow or dip and margins shrink—across all these forms—because increasing numbers of readers are moving across to "free" content online. Their rationale is straightforward: Why buy a book in a store, or pick up the morning paper, when the same thing is often accessible at no cost just few mouse-clicks away—and where the choice is vastly more diverse than anything you could get your hands on locally? The network effect is luring countless numbers of customers to websites where they do not have to pay a cent for what they previously had to buy. Google, for example, is feverishly scanning millions of titles and putting them online for either selective reading or for full access to out of copyright titles, and newspapers and magazines have been putting their content on the Internet for free for a decade and more. Just as worrying for publishers is the fact that a whole generation has now grown up with the expectation that "free stuff" is largely what the Internet is about. A second issue that the *New Yorker* article reflects is that the so-called "e-book" will hopefully resuscitate the fortunes, and secure the futures, of the major publishers. The logic is that by *moving along with* the millions who are migrating to the Internet to satisfy and recalibrate their reading habits, publishers will be able to revive the revenue streams that have been drying up for years. The bulk of Auletta's article then goes on to discuss the technological means that are hoped to "save the book business" with an evaluation of the Amazon-produced Kindle hand-held reader, and the 2010-launched Apple iPad, and how very high-stake corporate survival strategies are being played out through these (and doubtless future competing) digital technologies (Auletta 2010).

The most important issue lies in the unstated sub-text of the article: for all the high-stakes that are being played for by the global heavy-weight publishers such as Hachette, Simon & Schuster, Penguin, HarperCollins, *New York Times*, News International, and others, there is very little being said about the concerns of authors and journalists (established and new)—and nothing at all said about the *nature of the content*. What is being fought over, in other words, by publishers and by high-technology companies is information, and information in is most functional digital form, existing as a commodity. Content as information, or information as content—it's all the same in the digital context—and is all that counts. The overarching priority, then, is to develop what Auletta terms the "most efficient and multifunctional" technology to make content/information pay (2010, 47). Robert Darnton, an author and librarian who laments this instrumentalizing process, especially as it pertains to books, is under no illusions that there can be any way to stop the dyke from being flooded, no way back to a pre-digital past. He writes in his *The Case for Books* that "whatever the future may be, it will be digital" (2009, xv). Of that there is no question. But what are we losing sight of in this unavoidability? Darnton and this author see the informationalization of knowledge (and thus its dissolution) as a key effect. Darnton, however, sees "knowledge" as still "embodied" in texts, irrespective of whether they are in servers or in bookshops, with the issues of access and balance as those that we need to concern ourselves with (2009, xvi). This however is too easy, and too unreflective of the power of networked computing. This does not address the bio- and eco-temporality of both reading and writing, and the incipient destruction of this relationship through an uncompromising digitalization process.

The Time Sense of Typographic Man

There is something deeply powerful about our relationship with words. Walter Ong saw writing (marks made upon papyrus or paper) as constituting a technology so extraordinary that we do not any longer see it is such (Ong 1992, 293). We see writing as simply part of what it is to be human, something so profound that we cannot imagine a reality that is separate from the one that it had made. This intimacy is also physical, tactile, and sensual. Children, even before they are formally schooled, seem to have an innate disposition that draws them to books. I still recall the sense of awe I felt when walking past my then one-year-old son's suspiciously quiet room one day and seeing him sitting in the middle of the floor, cross-legged with a book on his lap, slowly and rhythmically flipping over page after page of what were to him incomprehensible words and pictures. Nonetheless I could see from his body language, from the tilt of his head and in the deliberateness in the turning of the pages, that he was immersed in his own pre-literate world, his own timescape—thinking who knows what—but definitely beginning to be encultured into the age-old physical and sensual and temporal relationship with the acts of reading and writing. In a similar vein, very few literate older children and adults are not almost automatically slowed to another physical pace and simultaneously enter another cognitive space–time when coming across a bookshop. In my hometown there is a shopping mall that has, in a slightly disconcerting retailing effect, a Borders Bookshop that is set in a kind of "open plan" context amid cafes and shops and restaurants. The way it is set out means that you can enter the shop without even knowing it (leaving with a tagged book is another matter, of course). However, the transformation from "inside" the bookshop to "outside" is more noticeable in its space–time dimensions. The timescape of the bookshop is slower and quieter. In the presence of filled bookshelves people, consciously or unconsciously, changed temporal gear and enter the inner-centered realm of browsing and reading. This is encouraged and readers are able to sit for as long as they want on the easy chairs and sofas provided. Soothing muzak hangs ponderously in an atmosphere that is redolent with the smell of new books that is set to such a pitch of unobtrusiveness that the cynic might think it a scent manufactured. This contrasts sharply with the timescape contexts of only a few meters away where shrieks of exited cinemagoers blend with the chattering of teenagers in cafes, which competes with the earnest conversations of distractible shoppers over the merits of this skirt with that top, or that shirt with those trousers. The Borders Bookshop experience is simply a particularly late-modern extension of the effect of the rather older tradition of the Public Library, that Victorian shrine to a mass literacy culture. Here, readers and writers enter a particularly modernist and Enlightenment-derived space that is consciously set apart from the hubbub and rhythms of daily life. Library visitors become disconnected in ways not seen anywhere else. They are engaged, more so than in the commercial bookshop, in the solitary and private acts of reading and writing, acts performed properly and fruitfully when alone, or in a relatively quiet and slow-paced context. Distraction is explicitly discouraged by signs and by vigilant staff who will keep the timescape as conducive as possible to the optimal physical and environmental requirement—a slowness and a quietness that we just know, through experience, to be necessary.

Books and writing act upon us physically and cognitively because they reflect much of what we are. From the time of the invention of the clay tablet with cuneiform marks upon it, we humans encoded the creation with the rhythms of our elemental body and mind and environment. Because it mirrors our corporeal proportions and capacities, we design books to be within a certain range of sizes, not too heavy, or too large, and with fonts that are pleasing to the eye and help ease the strain of the process of reading upon the eye. Long association with reading means that to hold a book—to encompass its in-built portability—feels as natural as wearing clothes. If walking with a book we easily forget that it is in our hand and has become a literal extension of the body. The book contains part of our process of becoming in terms of the information, ideas, customs, and knowledge that it contains and we will incorporate to become an aspect of our attitude to the world. New books have a specific smell which is also temporal in that it can instill a feeling of anticipation and a future orientation (of things to come). Old books have their own very different and very specific smell and color. Gone is the pristine white of the page, and a more muted and aged shade replaces it; with the sweet-sour smell being the odor of long years on a shelf. They may contain their own history, with the fold of previous readers made in the corners of pages paused or forever stopped at. Their margins may contain their own personal narratives in the notes where the pauses have been more specific and reflective of people often unknown, possibly long dead, that leave behind evidence of a moment of revelation, or exasperation or clarity or incomprehension. The printed word on paper is as close to human as it is possible for a technology to be. It is palpable in its materiality, and exudes life, lives, and cultures, and the bio- and eco-rhythms that stretch back all the way back to the time of those innovative peoples who lived between the Tigris and Euphrates rivers.

The *act* of writing is inseparable from bodily capacities in respect of speed and time. To write clearly, we are told from the age of five, is to write slowly, to *take your time*, in order that it be legible enough for others to read. To write too quickly is to scrawl, to write *irregularly*, and in a way that is difficult to read because the right time has not been devoted to it. The technology of the stylus or quill or pen, the literal extension of the hand acting as our extension into the world contained, or was encoded with, the originary times and rhythms implanted by the Mesopotamians.

Typographic Man was born with the broad enculturation of the encoding process through a growing literacy. McLuhan in his *Gutenberg Galaxy* describes how typographic culture was expressed in the temporal rhythms that metered and punctuated and paced literate society comprised of people who read and wrote with the same physical means and technological tools. He lets speak William Cobbett, English pamphleteer and journalist who published in 1795, *A Years' Residence in America*, where he observed that:

> They [American farmers] have all been *readers* from their youth up; and there are few subjects upon which they cannot converse with you, whether of a political or a scientific nature. At any rate they always hear with patience. I don't know when I ever heard a native American interrupt another man while he was speaking. There *sedateness* and *coolness* and *deliberate* manner in which they say and do every thing, and the *slowness* and reserve with which they express themselves; these are very wrongly estimated, when they are taken for marks of a *want of feeling*. (emphasis in Cobbett's original)

The shared literacy that Cobbett noticed has a common source—the physical media itself, the printed words affixed upon paper and held in the hand of the singular reader. Again, because we are so deeply inured to the technology of writing and to its ubiquitous printed form, it is very difficult to recognize the importance of this technology and its initial *temporal* "restructuring" of our thought processes in the far distant past. With the fixing of words on paper, thought became exteriorized and free-floating extensions of the author's ideas. But as words and sentences and chapters and books, they remained unchanging and unchangeable—locked down, so to speak, between the covers and titles that marked their beginnings and end. The book, however, is mute, silent, with the words absolutely *still* and void, as if in a vacuum. We can only see in retrospect, and in comparison with the advent of the electronic age, the temporal significance of this. As Walter Ong maintains in his *Interfaces of the Word*: "writing [and reading] is itself a closed system: a written text exists on its own, physically separate from any speaker or hearer.... Print creates a world even more spectacularly contained: every *a* in a font type is exactly like every other; every copy of an edition matches every other" (1977, 305). If, as we saw in Chapter 1, the experience of time can be identified as through change and movement (Tabboni 2001, 7), then the temporality of the writing (and the reading of the writing) remain relatively frozen, reflecting a formerly alive and moving timescape of the author's thoughts being transposed to paper and thence to fixity and closure.

The closure of the printed text and the closure of the thought-processes that its reading enacts are not, of course, total. Stating the obvious, Ong balances his closed-text thesis with the reminder to any reader that "writing and [reading] print also open and liberate. They give access not only to information otherwise inaccessible but also make possible new thought processes" (Ong 1977, 305). Put differently, and put temporally, the openness and liberatory potential of writing and reading is actual movement and change and hence encodes the processes with their own temporal rhythms. Writing and reading necessarily connect other ideas and other books and synthesize new information with new perspectives and orientations to the world, be they social, legal, technical, philosophical, or literary. The interaction of the innate and mutually inhering closure and openness of writing and reading creates a kind of traction. Temporally speaking, it reflects the material world of typographic culture, its forms of technological development, or what Regis Debray saw as the material processes through

97

which ideas were transmitted—the networks of communication "that enable thought to have social existence" (2007, 5). The specific nature of these material processes—from the dawn of civilization to the advent of the age of the machine—were bio- and eco-temporal. These were oriented, to be sure, toward acceleration through competition and innovation and were increasing rationalized by the time of the clock to give it a sustaining and ordered temporality, but they always remained more-or-less within the physical and bio-temporal capacities of human culture. The typographic culture of the pre-machine age had its own temporality that was not much different from that of the Mesopotamians. Growing literacy did bring a widening of a specific set of temporalities through our relationship with the technology of writing and the process of reading, but just as importantly, it *made more uniform* a culture and relationship with time and knowledge that had been in existence for thousands of years.

Of primary importance however, is that the "pedagogical juggernaut" (Ong 1983) that created a literate typographic culture brought us from an ancient world that was dominated by orality and rhetoric—with its inevitable imprecisions of communication, and its propensity toward a *radical openness*, where voices intermingle in potential chaos, and disputation—to a world of modernity, of a sense ratio that would be dominated by the visuality of reading and writing and by the thought processes of logic. As Ong writes in his *Orality and Literacy*, formal logic or a critical reasoning that seeks to understand "how we know what we know" had by the sixteenth century begin to supplant the culture of orality and rhetoric in Europe. Ong argues that logic has a "chirographic base" that was "the invention of Greek culture after it had interiorized the technology of alphabetic writing, and so made a permanent part of its noetic resources the kind of thinking alphabet thinking made possible" (1982, 51–52). The "chirographic base" of the Greek influence on modernity is often overlooked. It was this "base" and its rhythms of bio- and eco-temporality that gave us—gave the *philosophes* of the Enlightenment—the logic of democracy and critical reasoning that are still (formally at least) the institutional and epistemological underpinnings of the globalized twenty-first century.

Irreducibly Temporal

Here I want to explore the function of *narrative* and *canonicity* as the primary bases through which textual knowledge is created, codified, and disseminated in society—deep-rooted social processes that have enabled individuals and societies to get a fix on the world and to navigate their way though its complexities. These functions—or processes—are nothing if not temporal and durational, with their existence and their effectiveness dependent upon a much longer, as opposed to shorter, timeframe. This temporality, importantly, is also a kind of traction in that it is a form of time that tends toward the consolidation of information, ideas, and knowledge. The time or the duration of the process, moreover, is not the abstract time of the clock, but the human time of experience, and the contextual times of the social timescapes that humans create. Through narratives, in other words, we tell ourselves the stories that give the world meaning; and these can become part of the canon—the textual resource, the books containing the ideas (and the narratives)—that have shaped Western civilization since at least the time of the Enlightenment. It is my argument here that their formation into "grand narratives" and "the Western canon" took place over a *long time*, and their stories and strictures still largely govern how we see our society and derive meaning and attribute many forms of knowledge and construct reality within it. However, just as it took time for these institutions to develop and concretize, so too does it take time for society to properly engage with them and their range and complexity. More importantly, however, it takes time for us as individuals and as members of society to understand these sufficiently to be able to critically engage with them in order to reinforce them or change them or reject them altogether. Let us look briefly at the conceptions of narrative and canon in their turn, before assessing the consequences of our not being able to engage with them today on an adequate temporal basis.

The absolute foundationality of narrative as a mode of being in the world was put rather unambiguously by Barbara Hardy who wrote in an 1968 essay that: "we dream in narrative, day-dream in narrative, remember, anticipate, hope, despair, believe, doubt, plan, revise, criticise, construct, gossip, learn, hate and love by narrative." Hardy goes on to note that: "In order to really live, we make up stories about ourselves and others, about the personal as well as about the social past and future" (Hardy 1968, 5). In the same vein, Jerome Bruner argues that the power of narratives and narrative comprehension within the human psyche, acts as a "...form of not only representing but of *constituting* reality" (Bruner 1991, 5). Bruner notes also that the force of narrative upon the psyche, and the human receptivity to narrative power, acting as an orienting, cohering, and validating force, begins in early childhood. "There is compelling evidence to indicate" he writes, "that narrative comprehension is among the *earliest powers of mind* to appear in the young child and the most widely used forms of organizing human experience"(Bruner 1991, 9). That our receptivity to narrative is deep-set and ancient, suggests that these "earliest powers of the mind" are bound up with our initial relationship with writing and its technologies. And so just as the act of writing and the reading of the written word enabled the formation of consciousness, from a bicameral to unicameral state, as Julian Jeynes argued—and the interior development of our "own" voice, as suggested by Walter Ong—then so too did narrative become technologized (as distinct from being purely oral) and encoded with the bio- and eco-temporalities of the Mesopotamian innovation. More, Bruner, in his "The Narrative Construction of Reality" tells us that narratives (and the reality they construct) are "irreducibly temporal" (1991, 5). It follows from what I have been arguing that the irreducible temporality that Bruner speaks of can be identified as comprised of those same temporalities that are encoded in the originary means that gave narrative its technologized form. In short, the narratives that we tell and hear and live by undoubtedly have their origins in the oral cultures of preliterate civilization. However, once the word had been technologized and temporalized, the narrative construction of reality took a technologized and temporalized form also.

The linking and sharing and networking of narratives obviously serve to expand their reach and their social power. The narrative thus becomes a *meta-narrative*, which, according to Stephens and McCallum, may be described as "a global or totalising cultural narrative schema which orders and explains knowledge and experience" (1998, 6).

Moreover, the reach and power of the meta-narrative—as well as being a process "whereby materials from disparate sources are rendered coherent and unified" (Stephens and McCallum, 1998, 130)—contributes also to a form of *traction* where meaning (through the circulation of printed narratives) gain a certain *stability* that acts to give narrative a normativity and precision that it could never attain through purely oral transmission. The *long durée* is the temporality of the meta-narrative. It enables the sedimentation of narratives to form into intergenerational stories that are disseminated through the technology of the printed word. These produce the cultural and ideational signposts that societies steer by, and the members and institutions of society look to these as the ready reckoners for meaning and orientation and sense of place in the cosmos.

In his *Archaeology of Knowledge*, Michel Foucault sees this temporalizing process as the essence of history, one where "history is that which transforms documents into monuments" (1972, 8). Documents that have become totalizing monuments were the backdrop that gave the social world a stable center that would more-or-less hold. The universal religions of the world, those of Islam, Christianity, and Judaism are word- and book-centered, and have comprised the psychic and spiritual narratives that have shaped the lives of countless millions of individuals for centuries; the totalizing monuments of science (word-based and methodologized as well as verified through documents) have offered since the sixteenth century at least, a rival perspective, or alternative meta-narrative to the metaphysical; and modernity produced its own meta-narratives that we have already looked at, and whose effects reverberate still in the form of the politics of democracy, of the Greek-derived philosophies of reason, justice, and ethics, and so on.

Another way of describing the documents-to-monuments transformation through time is as a process of *canonicity*. The formation of the canon in social and cultural life can be seen as the power dynamic of the narrative process, with the canon reflecting the elite judgment upon cultural knowledge and cultural production in its textual forms. The canon is said to be reflective of what is authentic and valid in terms of human experience and human self-representation. In its ideal type, the canon is a literally a list of "works that constitute a tradition and convey a set of shared values" (Lauter 1991, 249). "Tradition" is a key term here, because canonicity as a process and the formation of canons are diachronic concepts. That is to say, they relate primarily to texts and ideas and ways of being and doing that emanate from the past.

The ideas of "tradition" and a past orientation regarding how the past is read—the "shared set of values" that Lauter sees as a narrative effect—are constructed through specific relations of power. As we saw in Chapter 1, Russian society is currently engaged in a power struggle over its past, a struggle for the formation (or reformation) of the canon that narrates that country's past—and by extension its present and future also. Being a reflection of power contestation means that the canon is not necessarily carved indelibly into granite. Things change. Books and their ideas can come to be included in the canon whilst others may fade from relevance. Some of this change may be fairly minor and peripheral to the core of the canon itself, such as in literature, where being *en vogue* may matter more than a straightforward reflection of a power interest. Writers of literature who may be a major influence at one time, such as, say, the quintessentially Victorian Ford Maddox Ford—at his zenith in the first two decades of the twentieth century—is little read today outside the dwindling departments of comparative literature (McDonough 2002). Contrast this with the more acutely power-related canonicity of the economist John Maynard Keynes. The catastrophic economic slump of the 1930s propelled Keynes' ideas to the forefront of economic thinking across the world, and his theories of "managed capitalism" became the economic axiom in many major Western democracies up until the 1970s. However, as noted before, it was around the 1970s that the long-neglected (but conveniently market friendly) ideas of von Hayek and Friedman displaced Keynes in the canon to become the new principles for economic management. And more recently in the wake of the global economic crisis of the 2008–2010, the free-marketeers started to fall out of favor, with Keynes' work enjoying something of a revival—though not yet to canonical status (Judt 2010, 198–206).

Notwithstanding the traffic in and out of the list, the process of canonicity is essentially slow moving and very conservative—conservative in the literal and classical sense of its political meaning in that it seeks to conserve what *is* and move only with caution and only as a response to manage deeper social, economic, and political change. What this has meant is that a solid foundation of texts and ideas that gave humanity a specific form of ontological coherence has been laid down. Nineteenth-century cultural arbiter Matthew Arnold who sought to canonize such knowledge saw his mission as "knowing and spreading the best that has been reached in the world—an object not to be gained without books and reading..." (1960, 163). The stories that we tell ourselves through books, reading, and writing, became the basis for which most of us, down through the generations, took to be the reality of the world itself. Being a reflection of power, as just noted, means that the stories through which we make sense of our world are always subject (at least in theory) to challenge, modification, and change. With the rise of capitalism, of modernity and the influence of the Enlightenment, though, the narratives that accompanied this trajectory, and the textual canon that congealed around it had measure of constancy. Reason, progress, material prosperity, the all-conquering power of science—and even the meta-narratives of Christian thought—would comprise the slow-building and slow-changing core of knowledge and values that explained to us what it was to be human in the modernizing world.

The contradiction that besets this neat state of affairs, however, is of course capitalism. The imperatives of competition and capital accumulation are the seeds of acceleration that were planted at the heart of the project of capitalism at the beginnings of the Industrial Revolution. Mechanism really began to dominate capitalism in the nineteenth century, when steam power, then electrical and combustive power, set the processes of competition and accumulation onto the plane of what Daniel Bell saw as a "new rationality" that was an "abrupt break from the rhythms of work in the past" (1973, 224). Through a broad-based and competition-driven logic, technology was becoming, as Ong put it, "autonomous" from the more contiguous thought processes and knowledge-creating dynamics that had pertained since the time of the invention of writing. As the autonomy of the machine grew more powerful it began to work back upon the society that initially created it. Hans Magnus Enzensberger, a German thinker in the tradition of Adorno—and identified by John Simon as one of the "renaissance men (or women) who are in short supply these days" (1982, vii) was equipped with enough of the cultural and artistic acuity of Goethe, or of Woolf, to see what this machine-driven manifestation meant for human thought and human consciousness. Enzensberger began his 1982 essay "The Industrialisation of the Mind" with a quote from Marx's *The German Ideology* which says: "What is going on in our minds has always been, and always will be, a product of society" (1982, 2). He goes on to say that this is only a very recent insight, one that arose with industrial society. Before that the shaping of minds through reaching or indoctrination by the elites was taken for granted and was contiguous and fairly unproblematic—if not necessarily fair or democratic. As Enzensberger (1982, 2) observes:

> Only when the processes that shape our minds became opaque, enigmatic, inscrutable [Ong would say 'autonomous'] for the common man, only with the advent of industrialisation, did the question of how our minds are shaped arise in earnest.

The "industrialisation of the mind" came about through direct exposure to the panoply of technologies that constitute the whole way of life that built modernity and the industrial society. A primary consequence, in Enzensberger's view, was a process that served to "expand and train our consciousness—in order to exploit it" (1982, 10). A machine culture evolved though the related competition-accumulation imperatives where the quest for a certain kind of efficiency (one gained through an unreflective resort to temporal acceleration) infiltrated every facet of life. No realm of life was immune from the accelerative effect of a competitive machine logic—including the process of writing itself.

From Arguments to Aphorisms

By mechanizing the process of writing we not only increase the speed in which writing can be done, but we also transform the forms of information and knowledge that we transpose onto paper. In other words, machination, when it came in the form of the typewriter, it changed, or as Walter Ong put it, "restructured," the way in which we both thought and gave extensionality to ideas (1992). Typographic Man underwent a mechanization of the mind, as a result of the radical disconnection that began with what we will see is the *inevitability* of the introduction of machine-writing processes. The dynamic of restructuring, however, was subtle and would have been almost imperceptible at the level of the individual. Nevertheless, we do have some evidence of just this kind of restructuring process at the individual level—and we have it from the example of one of the nineteenth century's most influential thinkers.

In 1882, just before he sat down to write *Thus Spoke Zarathustra*, arguably his most significant work, Friedrich Nietzsche went out and bought himself a typewriter. It was the latest Malling Hansen model, for which he paid 375 Reichsmarks. As Friedrich Kittler, notes, the fact that Nietzsche's eyes were rapidly failing was the reason behind what would have been a fairly radical purchase. However, after a week of practicing with the somewhat tricky and temperamental type keys, he was able to write with a seeming reinvigoration that "the eyes no longer have to do their work" (Kittler 1999, 202). This was something of an event. The widely read philosopher was known to have had to quit his teaching job because of his eyesight, and the *Berliner Tageblatt* now wondered what the new device meant for his intellectual production, and mused whether "...we can hence expect a book along the lines of his last ones." Kittler gives his verdict on that particular subject:

Indeed: Nietzsche, as proud of the publication of his mechanization as any philosopher, changed *from arguments to aphorisms, from thoughts to puns, from rhetoric to telegram style.* That is precisely what is meant by [McLuhan's] sentence that our writing tools are also working on our thoughts. Malling Hansen's writing ball, with its operating difficulties, made Nietzsche into a laconic [and he] shed his first attribute in order to merge with his second. (203) (italics added)

Here we see an identification of the fine-grained transformation wrought by the mechanization of writing. Nietzsche's "restructured" thoughts through the use of the machine give issue to restructured and more mechanized ideas in machine-written form. With the invention of the typewriter, we see the invention of what Kittler terms *écriture automatique.* On the wider scale we can see also that the typewriter (its invention) was not a discrete innovation or accidental discovery—but the inevitable result of the imperatives of the heightening logic of a growing and accelerating modernity that required more and more speed in all its processes. The dialectic feeds back into modernization process *in toto*, and "telegraphic" thinking gives rise to "telegraphic" society in a tightening feedback loop that will eventually deliver us the electronic computer. But the effect was more than an instrumentalization and incipient banalization of thought: it was also a *quickening of thought* that synchronizes with the acceleration in the speed of writing. Kittler quotes Otto Burghagen, who wrote the first analysis of the typewriter in 1898, and observed:

> ...the significant *savings of time*, which endear the machine to the merchant. With its help one can complete office work in a third of the time it would take with the pen, for with each strike of the key the machine produces a complete letter, while the pen has to undergo about five strokes in order to produce a letter.... In the time it takes the pen to put a dot on the 'I' or make the 'u' sign, the machine produces two complete letters. The striking of the keys follows in succession with great speed, especially when one writes with all fingers; then one can count five to ten keyboard hits per second! (190) (emphasis in original)

With the advent of typewriting, this apparently "innocuous device" as Kittler (1999, 183) describes it, a fundamental technological gap had been jumped and there was no way back. The invention and ubiquitous use of electronic computer-based writing would take another century, and much else in economy and society would have to change, but the prehensile-based relationship with tools for writing had been broken, and the human extension into the world had become subordinate to a free-floating and proto-autonomous machine. The logic of speed and efficiency had severed this age-old relationship and with this act the bio- and eco-temporalities that has suffused writing and reading would inexorably dwindle, as would the dominance of handwriting and the practice of cursive script. Where an amount of consideration was encoded in the handwriting process (in the form and legibility and speed of the sentence construction process) machine writing had placed this originary skill and its bio-temporality on the road to extinction.

It would take almost another century of growing speed and efficiency within the technological processes of capitalism before a substantive break with machine-based industrialization would occur. During that phase, the time of the clock and the time-world it produced would reign supreme. Our thinking, writing, and knowledge-producing processes—from the written word to *écriture automatique*, would spread geographically (and increase temporally) within the context of what was in its essence a Victorian model of capitalism. The space needed for this model began inexorably to run out, and the speed of this model—as competition became ever more acute—was increasingly insufficient. By the 1970s, when the crunch finally came, typographic man was unprepared for the autonomous computer-driven shift to a new level, to a new form of network, a digital network where speed had broken free from the constraints of the clock, and where our relationship with the technologized word, written and read, had entered an new, intense, and intensely fraught stage.

5

The Chronic Distraction of Everyday Life

Prologue to Distraction: The Logic of Manufacturing Gives Way to the Logic of Information

In the many ways that defined the decade of the 1970s, the fact that information and knowledge were to play a more central role in life was becoming an increasingly palpable one. By that time electronic automation, large-scale computing, industrial-sized data processing, and so on, were rapidly springing to life from the drawing boards of post-war computer visionaries such as Vannevar Bush and J.C.R Licklider. Such ideas were being augmented and made tangible by the vast institutional research drive within the computer science networks in American universities and in the secret military laboratories—a collaboration that would eventually develop into the commercial Internet. Spurred by Cold War imperatives and by the insatiable needs of industrial productivity, an information-dominated society was beginning to take on the characteristics that we more readily recognize today (Edwards 1995). For example, in the increasingly aggressive business realm, the Fiat automobile company famously presaged the shape of the world to come with its introduction, in 1977, of the world's first robot-manufactured car, the "Strada," that was promoted with the equally prescient catch-phrase "hand built by robots." And just a couple of years previously, on the West Coast of the USA, Bill Gates and Steve Jobs were busy founding the companies that they confidently foresaw would capitalize not only on the coming widespread commercialization of computing, but on the insertion of computer logic into the consumer core of everyday life at the level of the individual.

Information and knowledge were what made the new post-Fordist economy possible. In the quest to increase its spaces of operation, the classical labor-centered value-creating processes of capital had, through the imperatives of accumulation that we have already discussed, moved beyond the realms of formal production in factories, in offices, and in the production of services. Labor had taken on another, almost magical aspect. It had become "immaterial" and was embodied in the value-creating processes of information and knowledge. As Michael Hardt and Antonio Negri put it in their 2005 book *Multitude*:

> Not only have computers been integrated into all kinds of production but more generally communication mechanisms, information, knowledges...are transforming traditional productive practices... (182)

Indeed, sociology and social theory had watched the straws blowing in the wind somewhat earlier and several noted theorists had already offered their own reflective prognostications. Daniel Bell, for example, in his 1973 *The Coming of the Post-Industrial Society* saw computing and information and knowledge as forming the very nucleus of the way we would soon live. Bell's "post-industrial society" would be a society where the knowledge-based production of services would preponderate over the Fordist production of material commodities. Knowledge, in this view, would be of a special kind, however. It would be a *technical knowledge* created through what he termed "intellectual technology" and the task of this technology would be to organize the growing complexity of the world. Such ordering, he argued, would be "possible only with a tool of intellectual technology, the computer" (1973, 29–30). Bell's post-industrial society would be a "classless" one—at least in a way that counterposed Marx's idea of the class-based industrial society based upon capitalist production of material commodities. The most important strata in a society that is service-based, would be occupied by an elite of technically proficient functionaries, a "technical class" of "knowledge workers" who would shape, organize, and direct the "knowledge society" (1973, 214–16). This, for Bell is a largely positive social development—provided politics took on the leading role, to create a situation where there is a "politicisation of science, [and where] the sociological problems of the organization of work by science teams all become central policy issues" (1973, 117–18).

Alvin Toffler interpreted the portents rather differently. An immediate bestseller, his 1970 *Future Shock* seemed to catch the incipient zeitgeist forming at the threshold of social change, where the social, economic, and political complacency of the 1950s had met its antithesis in a 1960s decade of dreams and dissent that was now petering out. Like the broader western culture whose unease was nourished by growing threat of nuclear war, or by the dawning realization of ecological destruction, Toffler perceived technological development as racing headlong and unrestrictedly toward what he termed a "super-industrialism" (1970, 23). The "shock" in the title of the book, was the shock of disorientation that people would feel through the rapid rate of change that super-industrialism would bring. Super-industrialism generated an increasingly fast-moving and atomized society where information flows dictate the pace of technological change. As early as the early 1970s, Toffler could see the importance of the new temporal rhythms where "down time cost more in lost output than ever before. Delay is increasingly costly [and so] information must flow faster than ever before..." (1970, 139). Speed and technologically driven acceleration is a prescient and key feature of *Future Shock*, and Toffler lays his central thesis out unambiguously at the beginning of the book where he claims that:

> The acceleration of change in our time is, itself, an elemental force. This accelerative thrust has personal and psychological, as well as sociological consequences. [...] Unless man quickly learns to control the rate of change in his personal affairs as well as in society at large, we are doomed to a massive adaptational breakdown. (1970, 2)

Both Bell and Toffler prophesied the rise of information as signaling the end of one way of industrial life and heralding another. Bell, however, made the common-enough category error of conflating information with knowledge. In fairness, in 1973 he would not yet be able to fully appreciate what effect computer-based information would have upon the acquisition and use of knowledge. Rather more culpably, however, Bell thought that a technocratic elite (albeit one that he hoped would be democratically controlled) posed no real problems for either individual or society. This was a dangerous complacency and indicative of Bell's unclouded faith in the positive power of technocracy. The rise of a commanding technocratic elite carried the real risk of upsetting the critical balance between *veritas logica* and *veritas aesthetica* (between science and art) that prominent nineteenth-century philosophers such as Alexander Baumgarten saw as necessary for a fuller perception of reality (Hadot, 154–255). Such an imbalance would see the construction a homogenizing universe built and led by all-powerful strata of engineers and scientists. Life lived through such a machine ethic would be pitched to the highest degree of instrumentalism, and the role of art, and the perceptions of other ways of being and seeing that *veritas aesthetica* can bring would be in danger of dwindling—if not disappearing.

Toffler was rather less insouciant (and more accurate) in his "social forecasting" (as Bell termed his project). He perceived computer-generated *information itself* as having a much more instrumentalized role, and cognitive overload as a growing problem for economy, culture, and society. Writing in the 1970s when most of humanity would have no real conception of what computers were, much less have them integrated into every facet of life, Toffler's own "social forecasting" nonetheless found a echo deep in the socio-psychological structures of that world. It was a world that resonated with an immanent fear and feeling of helplessness regarding what accelerated technological change would bring. Toffler himself claims coinage for the term "future shock" with which to describe the "shattering stress that we induce in people by subjecting them to too much change in too short a time" (1970, 2). One could argue that a "shattering stress" is possibly overblown in the register of rhetoric for a comparatively sleepy 1970s. However, this was no mere authorial license. Toffler had taken his cue from a wide range of professional opinion, including psychiatrists, doctors, engineers, and educators. He also—in a none-too-subtle promotion of the importance of his work—adds that he had called upon the opinion of eminent and relevant Nobel Prize winners. Indeed, he cites several of them in his book, including Sir George Thompson, who was awarded the prize for physics in 1937, and whose 1955 book *The Foreseeable Future* asked the perennial question, to which Toffler could acutely relate: "Will this rate of material progress, which seems to be steadily accelerating, continue faster and faster, will it level off to a steady and much slower advance, or will [society] end in a catastrophe and a dark age?" (vii). Another Laureate that Toffler would cite—though one who had to wait until 1978 to be summoned to Oslo—was Herbert Simon. He was awarded the Noble Prize for economics, and specifically "for his pioneering research into the decision-making process within economic organizations" (http://Nobelprize.org). Significantly, Simon was also an eminent cognitive psychologist and computer artificial intelligence (AI) pioneer. For his work in these fields Simon was awarded another prize, the 1975 Turing Prize, for making "basic contributions to artificial intelligence, the psychology of human cognition, and list processing" (http://Britannia.org). Simon's work has clear correlates with Toffler's (although he dismissed *Future Shock* as being light on facts) (see Crowther-Heyck 2005, 286). Nonetheless, just a year after the publication of Toffler's book, Simon bluntly stated the problem of rapid change through information technologies—and the fundamental nature of their effects upon people:

> What information consumes is rather obvious: it consumes the attention of its recipients. Hence, a wealth of information creates a poverty of attention and a need to allocate that attention efficiently among the overabundance of information sources that might consume it. (Simon 1971, 40–41)

The problem of the speed and volume of information has grown immeasurably since 1971. What Toffler and Bell, and also what Simon and Thomson were concerned with in their differing ways has indeed been a perennially identified problem—that is: how do humans cope with the accelerating convergence of information and technological change? What has been missing thus far is a *temporal perspective* on capitalism, a social process that has, in its space–time crises, brought about a largely unrecognized crisis in the processes of reading and writing and cognition. Unless we accept that these are predicated on deep-lying bio- and eco-temporalities that beat at the heart of the individual (literally) and in human society more broadly, and have remained basically unchanged since the dawn of writing in Mesopotamia, then we will fail to understand the full effects of the twenty-first-century network society.

Having outlined the nature of technological change within industrial society, and having argued a theory for the processes underlying the explosion of information through a constantly accelerating computer rhythm into every register of life, it is time now to consider, from the fundamental perspective of temporality, what Simon identified as a "poverty of attention," and what I term a "chronic distraction." And as we shall see, the temporal perspective suggests a present and an ongoing future that consists of far more than simply being overwhelmed by words written and read—it opens up as problematic the very basis of which our societies nominally function.

1,802,330,457 and Rising

That the lives of hundreds of millions of people across the world today are filled with a growingly *dense* and *intense* interaction of networked applications and processes is a fact that is both banal and extraordinary at the same time. Banal because we barely reflect upon the increasing ways that we exist as nodes in this network, and banal because the age of ubiquitous computing that was predicted a generation ago has now come to pass. Banal because children are born into the network society, and adults have become habituated to it as a persistent and insistent part of life. Banal to the extent that no one any longer looks twice at people engaged in Bluetooth-enabled mobile phone conversation, whereas a decade ago one would have thought them schizophrenic. And banal that no one any longer considers it as significant, as they might have done during the tech-boom of the late-1990s, that "The Internet will change everything and everyone." Today, mobile communications and the network just *are*. They form an increasingly indispensable part of normal life. Take aspects of it away and we feel its loss; adding more of it to what we do seems completely natural. Indeed, the digital network is more than natural; it is viewed increasingly as vital. A CEO of a UK services company noted on BBC radio, that when individuals tighten their belts in response to unemployment, or recession, the first thing they tend to cut are those things that are seen as luxuries, or extravagancies. Fifteen years ago, the executive noted, the mobile phone would have been one of the first things curtailed in order to save money; today, he asserted, the *last* thing an individual would sacrifice is his or her mobile phone, so central a role does it play in being part of economy and society. To not be connected in times of economic difficulty is now regarded as a significant drawback (BBC 2010).

The very banality of the networked life, however, is a major aspect of its power, part of its hold over us. Like the two-party system of government, such as in the US, or the UK, or Australia, where each gets its turn in power, this passes for democracy and choice because it's a banal power. Because it has become so banal, we do not (because we do not have the time) to reflect upon it in ways that might question the validity and appropriateness of this kind of politics.

And yet the networked life is *extraordinary*. When one has the chance to look up from the constant preoccupations of work and family and friends and constant distraction, and then pauses to reflect, a few of the business and society-oriented clichés of a Bill Gates or a Nicholas Negroponte in the middle of the 1990s do actually raise some very important issues. For example, his relentlessly sunny business focus aside, Gates was correct when he prophesied in 1996, a time when the commercial Internet was still in its infancy and mobile phones still fairly exotic, that: "Once this new era is in full swing, you won't leave your network connection behind at the office or in the classroom. Your connection will be more that just an appliance.... It will be your passport to a new "mediated" way of life" (1996, 3). Gates, of course, was thinking of the purportedly seamless business efficiency of being connected to the growing network in such an "always on" way. For his part, Nicholas Negroponte, Founder of MIT Media Lab, was more philosophical (but just as positive) in his prognostications. He does get ahead of himself a bit by describing (1995) as the dawn of the "post-information age" where networks will mean that "smart computing" will make us unique nodes that will be treated as individuals and not as part of a demographic; and where computers will be able to "understand [such] individuals with the same degree of subtlety (or more than) we can expect from other human beings" (1995, 165). Today the notion of our being masters to the digital slave is, in the twenty-first-century age of Web 2.0 marketing and the "locked functionality" of consumer computer technologies, somewhat debatable (see Zittrain 2007). Where Negroponte stands on more solid ground is with his idea—one contained in the title of his book, *Being Digital*—that we are becoming *merged* with data, and are creating a world wherein digital "bits" mix with human "atoms" in the ocean of networked communication. As Negroponte sees it, we *are* the network and "each generation will become more digital than the preceding one" (1995, 231).

Standing on the shoulders of giants such as Bell and Toffler, both Gates and Negroponte were correct in their prediction that computer-based information would move to centerstage in the development of economy and society. Except for Toffler, all were more-or-less sanguine; and none really considered temporality (again except for Toffler, but only in the sense that society is "accelerating") in a way that would allow us to get to the bottom of the problematic of computer-based information under the auspices of neoliberal capitalism.

The extraordinary information society that we live in today renders humanity a super-massive networked entity. The meaning of "network" has been transformed far beyond the relatively sedate and plodding but nonetheless deep-thinking network that was the "Republic of Letters" that we based much Enlightenment reason upon—and which we (wherever we are able to stop to think about it) still base our understanding of the contemporary world upon. We are networked in a new way through transformative technologies with instrumentalized ends that are based upon the fast-flowing information that draws much of its nature, shape, and content from the imperatives of capitalist competition. Information, as opposed to knowledge, is the currency of the network society, because it is produced at speed to be consumed (digested) at speed. The "Republic of Letters" consisted of an infinitesimally small number of individuals compared to the inhabitants of the network society, but the *philosophers* knew the importance of time and were able to take their proper measure of it for the intellectual and practical tasks at hand. We, on the other hand, have lost the appreciation of the nature of time, and in its machine-driven instrumentalized mode we have precious little of it to spare anyway.

What is the scale of the human information network? The population of the planet is estimated today to be around 6.7 billion. Well over 26 percent of that number or, more precisely, 1,802,330,457 of us are classed in a survey as "Internet Users." This number is up from a mere 360,985,492 a decade ago, and corresponds to an almost 400 percent increase (IWS 2010). Distribution here, as with any resource, is uneven and inequitable, but every region is a growing part of the "network effect" of sprawling and growing connectivity. The expansion of the network effect is given different rationales in different parts of the world, a rationale that is dependent upon specific economic contexts. And so, for example, a wealthy country such as Finland can loftily pronounce, as it did in 2010, that high-speed broadband is now to be considered a "basic right" for every Finn (AFP 2010). At the other end of the scale, the government of Rwanda experiences the network effect *as aid* as it recognizes the logic of the Washington Consensus and accepts second-division laptops for its children in order for them to compete with their Kenyan neighbors for the distinction of being the cheapest programmers in the continent. Either way, in developed or developing countries, almost 2 billion people are mostly willing nodes in an unimaginable density of connections that is set upon a growth trend that is going in one direction only.

The Internet is only a singular, though important, element of our networked life. Indeed, the first phase of Internet communication as expressed through the practice of sitting at a computer at home or in the office or in a café, is fast fading into the background. We can see an example of this transformation when it is realized that the reign of the mighty desktop personal computer that shaped the 1980s and 1990s is now rapidly coming to an end. The demand to be "always on" led directly to the development of new wireless Internet technologies that are making the tethered desktop increasingly redundant. Mobile laptops, it need hardly be said, are the new means for going online. In 2008 it was reported that global laptop sales had eclipsed those of desktops—and did so four years faster that the experts had predicted (Mathis 2008). The wireless technologies that brought us the mobile phone have converged to give us mobile Internet, the new and more "efficient" means of communication. Now we can use the laptop as a phone and the phone as an Internet-enabled computer that allows us to move with increasing fluidly through virtual space—and to do this almost anywhere in physical space. Considering future trends, the Pew Internet Project's *Future of the Internet Report* predicts the continuance of a "path of innovation in gadgets and online applications" that is "incredibly fast"—leading to a market-propelled consolidation that will foster the "major and mass adoption" of the most "useful" (i.e., the most "efficient") of these across the whole of society (Anderson 2010, 39–40). As the ease of uptake and connection increases, then so too does the volume of information seem set to expand in exponential fashion. Pew's *Report* gives an account from the evidence of the 895 "experts and stakeholders" that it consulted, suggesting that this is generally seen as a good thing. It makes two points in particular that are relevant to our narrative. First is a response to a much-discussed essay from 2008 by Nicholas Carr in the *Atlantic Monthly* titled "Is Google Making Us Stoopid?" In it Carr makes precisely the same argument as this book in that:

> The kind of deep reading that a sequence of printed pages promotes is valuable not just for the knowledge we acquire from the author's words but for the intellectual vibrations those words set off within our own minds. In the quiet spaces opened up by the sustained, undistracted reading of a book, or by any other act of contemplation, for that matter, we make our own associations, draw our own inferences and analogies, foster our own ideas. Deep reading…is indistinguishable from deep thinking. (2008, 37)

The *Report's* "experts and stakeholders" overwhelmingly rejected this unpleasant prospect and fully 76 percent of them agreed with the opposite and optimistic view that "people's use of the Internet has enhanced human intelligence; as people are allowed unprecedented access to more information they become smarter and make better choices…" (Anderson 2010, 8)

The second point that emerged from the response to Carr's premise is that 65 percent of the "experts and stakeholders" supported the Pew proposition that "reading, writing, and the rendering of knowledge will be improved." The *Report* did caution, however, that a substantial minority (32 percent) believed that by 2020 "it will be clear that the Internet has diminished and endangered reading and writing, and the rendering of knowledge" (Anderson 2010, 3). There is, it seems, at least some degree of consensus within elite thinking about what the explosion of computing is doing to the ways in which we produce, consume, and utilize information. The majority remain positive about ubiquitous computing and tend to reflect the mainstream media and industry propaganda regarding their purported meta utility that views them as, to borrow an acid phrase from Theodore Roszak: "a solution in search of problems" (1986, 51)

Let us look more closely at Carr's thesis. Carr developed his Google essay into a book, published in 2010, called *The Shallows*. Here, Carr paints even himself as a victim of a rampaging information society, where the quiet places of contemplation and deep thinking have been occupied by a restless beehive of hyperactive "users" who cannot stay still or bear to disconnect themselves from the Internet; indeed (and this is an important insight) in the developed world it is not even necessary to be connected any more. He writes:

> ...what the net seems to be doing is chipping away my capacity for concentration and contemplation. Whether I'm online or not, my mind now expects to take in information the way the net distributes it: in a swiftly moving stream of particles. Once I was a scuba diver in the sea of words. Now I zip along the surface like a guy on a Jet Ski. (2010, 7)

This is a clever use of metaphor to describe what is a real problem. *The Shallows* is an important book and it deserves to generate much more debate than the Pew Report's selective passages allowed for. Perhaps Carr's most important achievement is in his use of the data from cognitive psychology to show how the brain actually changes in response to the ways it is trained to process information. Concentrated thinking about a particular subject, he maintains, actually strengthens the synaptic connections in our brains, thereby making them capable of more deep and concentrated thinking. If however, we "zip along the surface" of inattention and distraction, the synaptic connections that shape the ways in which we think become weaker—and so our thinking, as the title of the book suggests, becomes shallower and less able to hold to any subject to any great depth or length. The danger in this dialectic between information volume, speed, and human cognitive capacity is that the worse it gets, the less we realize what it is we are losing. What happens is that we undergo a kind of network society-induced dementia, where as individuals and as a society we cannot see the problem due to the effects of the problem itself. Carr is to be congratulated here in his efforts to bring the issue to at least some level of public awareness.

The Shallows is analog in many ways to this book. It shares similar fears and sees similar effects from the application of unrestricted computing. But this is a good part of the book's problem—and its fatal limitation. It calls our attention to an urgent issue, and then describes it, over and over, in all its manifestations. Apart for the insights from cognitive psychology, *The Shallows* is a book loaded with description of effects that leaves no room for a critique that would allow one to speculate (at least) on what the *causes* of these might be. Fundamentally there is no critique of capitalism, the system that is the creaking and cracking base that supports the fragile superstructures of modern and post-modern society. Some biography may be apposite here: Carr is an ex-Editor of *Harvard Business Review*, an influential (and non-peer reviewed) journal that is unencumbered with a reputation for searching critiques of the nature of capital, or for reflections on upon plausible alternatives to its hegemony. The Index of Carr's book has two listings under "capitalism." Both are in-passing references, with the term utilized merely as a functional descriptor for the equally unproblematic concept of "business." The most important omission, given the subject of the book, is a critique of time, or the human relationship with the technologies of time. Tantalizingly, Carr does exhibit an awareness and sensitivity toward the constructed nature of clock time and how our bodies and brains and societies became synchronized with the Newtonian clockwork universe (50). However, he does not develop this description to the point of critique. And nor could he. Without a conception of how capitalism and the time of the clock are profoundly interconnected, the key element behind the problem of distraction, inattention, and the "shallowing" of our intellect must either remain hidden, weirdly inexplicable, or simply inadmissible as evidence.

A Confusion of Impressions

Distraction is a common, though commonly sublimated experience. When we do stop to consider what our life on line consists of, we can readily recognize patterns of work and cognition that are less than what is mandated as "efficient." Who of us with an instilled protestant work ethic—or even with a deadline looming threateningly—does not feel the pang of guilt when suddenly finding oneself down a byway of the Internet and realizing that you had been distracted (again) without realizing it? Another twenty-five precious minutes have just evaporated. Starting off with the intention of reading an article at work or at home, or following up on a news story you heard on the radio earlier, or even checking the train departures for the trip you need to make tomorrow, without deliberate and conscious intent, you soon begin to click through sites on enamel paint colors that match the train set you used to have as a kid, then through to Ebay to search to see if you can still buy those Airfix model Spitfires that you remember you always painted badly with the same kind of paint, and on through to a clip of the flight of a Spitfire on Youtube, your eyes then wander to the bottom of the screen and you notice that the music playing on the clip is by Elgar, and responding to the self-addressed question "what's the name of that tune again?", you click through and discover it is "Nimrod" part from "Enigma Variations" conducted here by Sir Colin Davis and played by the London Symphony Orchestra which you can buy from iTunes for $13.99; and as you continue to half look and half listen, you notice the comments section on the screen and read that someone has posted: "Written during a time of overwhelming pride for the greatest Empire the world has ever seen. Makes me nostalgic for a time I never even experienced." You ponder the meaning of this for a while; think briefly whether it is illogical in its temporal reckoning, and wonder for a second or two more about the imputed significance of the capitalization of the word "EMPIRE," and then muse idly what it means that nearly a million people have already watched this clip.

The experience of flitting between websites is almost seamless (or so it appears at the "surface" of the network connection), because the Internet is engineered to be so in the interests of "efficiency" and speed. But the hyper-connected and hyper-efficient technology masks what Corey Doctorow (2009) calls an "endless click-trance" where the individual is barely aware that he or she is veering wildly from the intent and logical path of the initial thought. And so a practically oriented thought about information needed for a train departure time leads through model airplanes to old war movies to Elgar—with (almost always) the added the risk of making an impulsive purchase at the end of it. Far from being a seamless process, "seamless" as Bill Gates might have conceived it, as in being laser-directed and "frictionless" in getting exactly what one wants or needs, the process is, in stark contrast, fractured, directionless, unstable, and more often than not leaves the user frustrated, yet more pressed for time—and possibly $13.99 poorer. Writing in the *New York Magazine* in 2009, Sam Anderson, in an article called "In Defense of Distraction" puts the essence of the "confusion of impressions" (the dictionary definition for distraction) far better than I can. Underneath a Photoshopped image of a man designed to convey the sense of someone "fractured" of falling apart through "information overload" in front of the computer screen, Anderson begins his critique of the "doomsayers" with an eloquent description of what it is they contend:

> I'm going to pause here, right at the beginning of my riveting article about attention, and ask you to please get all of your precious 21st-century distractions out of your system now. Check the score of the Mets game; text your sister that pun you just thought of about her roommate's new pet lizard ("iguana hold yr hand LOL get it like Beatles"); refresh your work e-mail, your home e-mail, your school e-mail; upload pictures of yourself reading this paragraph to your 'me reading magazine articles' Flickr photostream; and alert the fellow citizens of whatever Twittertopia you happen to frequent that you will be suspending your digital presence for the next twenty minutes or so (I know that seems drastic: Tell them you're having an appendectomy or something and are about to lose consciousness). Good. Now: Count your breaths. Close your eyes. Do whatever it takes to get all of your neurons lined up in one direction. Above all, resist the urge to fixate on the picture, right over there, of that weird scrambled guy typing. Do not speculate on his ethnicity (German-Venezuelan?) or his back-story (Witness Protection Program?) or the size of his monitor. Go ahead and cover him with your hand if you need to. There. Doesn't that feel better? Now it's just you and me, tucked like fourteenth-century Zen masters into this sweet little nook of pure mental focus. (Seriously, stop looking at him. I'm over here.)

Anderson knows what distraction feels like, and anyone with a modicum of Internet experience, a job and a (at least virtual) social life will also recognize elements of themselves within this little vignette.

And like Doctorow's "click-trance" the immanent logic of the Internet creates a zigzagging pathway that is potentially "endless." The point Anderson makes is although this is real life for hundreds of millions of people, and that "Information rains down faster and thicker every day" and there is no "retreat to a quieter time" any longer, the question is "how successfully we can adapt" as individuals to the imperatives of information overload. Doctorow himself writes a similar essay that was published in *Locus Magazine*, also in 2009. Titled "Writing in the Age of Distraction," he too acknowledges an immense problem: we all need to write, be it professionally or in blogs or texting or social networking. Writing is the currency of communication more than ever before, but to engage with it we need also to engage with the network and the growing array of devices and applications that adds to the at-tractive–distractive modality of information. We are constantly at that liminal space on the Internet where we can be "distracted and some-times overwhelmed by the myriad distractions that lie one click away" (Doctorow 2009). Distraction comes with the territory, and Doctorow echoes Anderson in that although we are always in danger of being "frazzled and info-whelmed," we would better get used to it, because there is no going back. Getting used to it, or adapting to the new real-ity is, for Doctorow as with Anderson, a personal project. And so he advocates a "balancing things out" strategy, where a sustained bout of self-control and discipline in front of the screen will act as a check to the lures of distraction that the networked life brings. With bullet-point briskness Doctorow outlines six strategies for anti-distraction. These are fairly straightforward work habits and consist of such things as developing a "short, regular work schedule" where pre-set targets are achieved in reading and writing. He also, again quite logically, advocates a conscious control over the technologies that you use, such as turning off many of the distracting elements of the networked computer, such as e-mail alerts, and "anything [such as RSS alerts, Skype rings, etc] that requires you to wait for a response" (2009).

Now these authors speak in prudent tones. They realize that we live in an age of chronic distraction and that something must be done about it. However, they project from a purely neoliberal context, where it is *the individual* who must take responsibility for what is instead a *social phenomenon*. And notwithstanding the rhetoric of self-control and individual responsibility in the confronting of a social problem, by their advocating that we adapt or work with the reality of chronic dis-traction, they place the individual in a place of relative powerlessness.

Anderson's call to "adapt" to the reality of information overload and the acceleration of the network society—is nothing less than a puny human attempt to synchronize to a powerful and system-generated time–space compression that knows no speed limit. And Doctorow's bullet-point approach to neoliberal self-control and self-realization is similarly flawed. For the individual in real world to seek to limit his or her time online is to skirt with social and economic disaster. Not being connected to the network means opportunities lost, crucial connections not being made, the "offer" of a job or opportunity going elsewhere. In any case, to switch off the mobile phone, or laptop computer, or e-mail, or voicemail, etc., is to have their connections to you build up only to be dealt with at another time, by which time it may well be too late for that job or opportunity.... Such individualist "solutions" essentially leave one powerless in the face of technological giganticism. Of course some people may be as disciplined and as controlled as required in these scenarios. But life is not like that, and we are still made of the same crooked wood that Kant recognized in the eighteenth century. Life is messy and most of us fall short of the standard of perfectibility. In either case, to set your face to the screen as an individual is to be a slave to the screen under the delusion of personal control. The network will not wait for you, and if you cannot keep up with the production and consumption of information at faster and faster rates and increasing volumes, then what Adorno (2005, 114) termed a "frantic optimism" begins to infiltrate. "Frantic" because one's life moves so fast, and "frantic" because at another level of consciousness, we all know what happens in late-capitalism to those who cannot keep up—they can be relegated to the dark offline world that is now increasingly reserved for the poor, the unemployed, the old and the sick, and the stubbornly technophobic who are destined to populate the margins of society.

To finish this chapter I want to move to look at what I see as the reality of chronic distraction within the networked life. I want to measure its "pathologies" against what are taken to be the grounding values (those grand narratives) that supposedly still orient the individual and the collective toward what it means to be a citizen of the world—those of democracy, of liberty, and of Reason.

I took a speed-reading course and read War and Peace in twenty minutes. It involves Russia.

—*Woody Allen*

121

Woody Allen perhaps expresses a deeper truth than he knew, and his humor speaks to a malaise that today goes far beyond the satiric potential in spurious self-improvement fads. We skate on the surface of knowledge because the time-squeeze gives us no choice. Consider for example: Why is it that the workings of the economy of a country, or of the world—admittedly a growingly complex thing—is a near-total mystery to many if not most of us? Possibly, in the shame of our ignorance, an unawareness that persists notwithstanding the millions of words devoted to economic issues every day in the print and electronic media, we console ourselves with the idea that at least there are experts who know what they are doing; professional and politically neutral economists who understand these things and who can make policy recommendations to politicians who will be briefed on the nature of the problem and the options for fixing it. Right? Well, not really. Economic pundits regularly and sometimes spectacularly get it wrong; indeed often it appears as though it is only the law of statistical probability that ensures that some are proved "right" in their prognostications anyway.

We saw this in the global economic crisis that began in 2008. Panicked stock markets and teetering banking houses signaled the dénouement for the property and asset and banking bubble that had been inflating across the world since the late-1990s. Calamity struck suddenly and with a ferocious severity; and so quickly did it hit that almost no one saw it coming. What an appreciation of the nature of time in capitalism tells us is that the growing speed of the post-modern global economy now *ensures* that crises will spring up unawares. The same accelerative logic ensures also that regulatory oversight—or even institutional pondering of underlying risk factors—will be either non-existent, too little, or too late. Moreover, if the political economy of speed was a factor in the sharp and shuddering downturn of the global economy in 2008, speed was also a factor in the frantic methods employed to stave off total catastrophe. A lack of *knowledge* within an ocean of economic information became apparent as the crisis was playing out. In September of that year, as the situation seemed to be spiraling out of control, the U.S. Senate considered the first of its "stimulus packages" for its stricken economy. The prevalent feeling was that it *only had a weekend* (before the stock exchange reopened) to fix the problem. Senator Lindsay Graham, a Republican representing South Carolina, and present at the crisis meetings declared to a Fox News journalist afterwards that: "The process that's led to this bill stinks. There is no negotiating going on here! Nobody is negotiating! We're making this up as we go" (Graham 2009). When markets are waiting impatiently for signals, and when individuals are not in possession of all the facts nor the necessary time to comprehend them, then "making it up" is all there is to do.

Stories such as these make it evident that we are all seriously out of time with the economic rhythms of our digitally and market-powered networked society. This macroeconomic narrative is bleak enough, and the yawning extent our non-comprehension of "how the world works" can always be pushed down into the recesses of our consciousness, leaving it to hope that either someone knows what they are doing, or that we can all just muddle along in some half-baked way. In the micro-realm of the individual, though, at the space and time where our own life meets the real world, the effects of speed and distraction, and our inability to synchronize with the imperatives of "digital capitalism" (Schiller 2000) are not so easy to sublimate. Here I will discuss just a few, which nonetheless are symptomatic of the distractive malaise.

It should come as no surprise that the great functional social and economic "skill" of our networked life, multitasking, should be derived from computer science. The term was coined initially to describe the ability of computers to "parallel process"—to perform more than one operation at a time. The attraction for those who use computers is obvious. As we have seen, the logic of computing allows for a great deal of flexibility in the operations in which it is programmed to perform. Its flexibility, indeed, in the post-Fordist era, was the computer's single-most important benefit to the capitalist. To automate as many workplace processes as possible is to drive toward the competitive Nirvana of high-speed manufacturing at progressively lower input costs. Of course it was never going to be possible to automate every process, and in fact people have been required to become computer "users" (mere adjuncts to a machine) to an extent that would have been unimaginable in, say, the early 1960s when automation was being discussed, and the dreams of people being freed by automation from the drudgeries of most forms of work was seen to augur a coming "leisure society" (Dumazedier 1967; Malcolm 1962). But "users" we almost all have become, and as such are expected to synchronize with or adapt to the computer's logic. And so multitasking, as Oriel Sullivan put it, is the individuals' necessary response "to the burden of multiple obligations" (2007, 8). If computers multitask, then so must we.

123

In the realm of neoliberal competition, the ideology argues that it is that the ability to multitask is a skill to put at a premium. And in the heady mid-1990s no less than Bill Gates was held up as the model to aspire to. In a cringingly hagiographic article in *Time* magazine from that period Gates is described as a "frightening blend of brilliance, drive, competitiveness" which make him (in a phrase that fits neatly with the thesis of this book): "the Edison and Ford of our age. A technologist turned entrepreneur, he embodies the digital era" (Isaacson 1997). Revealingly, Gates' colleagues, or so *Time* informs us, regularly heap the highest possible praise on him by referring to him in computer metaphors: "Wander the Microsoft grounds, press the Bill button in conversation and hear it described in computer terms: he has 'incredible processing power' and 'unlimited bandwidth,' an agility at 'parallel processing' and 'multitasking'" (Isaacson 1997). Over a decade later, the value of the multitasker is no less appreciated in business and in life more broadly. We are expected to be multitaskers in the home as well as at work—with the Internet as the tool to make us efficient and productive individuals and workers (Kenyon 2008, 283–319). We have seen how individuals such as Anderson and Doctorow advocate a kind of *regimented multitasking* as a way to cancel out the chaotic allure of network distraction—controlling distraction by channeling it into what they see as productive and efficient processes of work and play through the application of discipline and will. From the neoliberal perspective, then, to multitask represents not a "burden" or "multiple obligations" but simply an efficient and flexible and *successful way* (e.g., the Gates example) of interfacing with the networked society.

However, outside the world of business studies, and beyond the literature of computer magazines to the general hegemonic neoliberal ethos that these inform, there exists a growing body of empirical and clinical evidence that shows that network-mandated multitasking is making us less-efficient workers, poorer learners, and more distracted and less-focused individuals. There is a deep-seated psycho-sociological element involved here. Bill Gates, as we saw, is noted for his alleged multitasking prowess—and it tends to be an unquestioned assumption that he must in fact possess this (and that it is fantastically positive gift), given the success of Microsoft. Gates himself will doubtless have a self-confidence that many would like to replicate at work; and more than a few would indeed approach their work and other dimensions of their networked life with such a motivated attitude. Now there is nothing wrong with feeling that you are able to take on the world and everything that it can throw at you. However, in terms of cognition, there is a problem with (literally) such a way of thinking. Clifford Nass, a Stanford psychologist, conducted clinical testing on the issue of how multitaskers perceive themselves to be as productive individuals—and how their capabilities measure up to their self-perceptions. In an article for the *Chronicle of Higher Education*, writer David Glenn cites Nass' work to make the point that "heavy multitaskers are often extremely confident in their abilities" (Glenn 2010). This feeling, Glenn observes, can arise from the process of multitasking itself, where if the brain is being stimulated to perform several tasks at once there is the illusion that you must be doing them well. He quotes Nass himself as saying that "There's evidence that those people are actually worse at multitasking than most people" (Glenn 2010). The test involved "self-described multitaskers" who actually did "much worse on cognitive and memory tasks that involved distraction" than those who said they worked better by focusing on individual tasks (Glenn 2010).

This is supported by research reported in *Scientific American*, this time concerning new work in neuroscience, which found that by using functional magnetic resonance imaging (fMRI) scanning, the brain's medial frontal cortex can be stimulated to higher processing when motivated by a (monetary) reward. Scientists Sylvain Charron and Etienne Koechlin from the French National Institute for Health and Medical Research found that the part of the brain that is active during multitasking behavior, the frontopolar cortex seems to "organize pending goals while the brain completes another task." What is significant in a sociological sense is that even in a response to monetary reward (the baseline motivation for individuals in capitalist society) our brains cannot actually "execute two distinct tasks" (Harmon 2010). The article quotes Paul Dux, a psychologist from Australia, who agrees with the finding of the French research, but adds that although the brain may be capable of being trained to organize and prioritize multiple tasks, "there are still large dual-task costs" when people choose (or are compelled) to switch between tasks, which leads, he cautions, to "non-efficient multitasking" (Harmon 2010). Like simultaneously driving and talking on a mobile phone, we think we can do it, but road accident statistics (and growing legislative action) show that it is inherently dangerous thing to attempt. It is of course no small irony that multitasking turns out to be "non-efficient"—and speaks volumes of the ideology of neoliberalism which asserts that economic efficiency (speed) is all, and our acting as human computers is the best way to attain this Nirvanic state.

More Like This…

In a digital world that is allegedly brimful of diversity and opportunity, it is sometimes sobering to be reminded that when asked "what do people mostly do when connected to the networked society?" The answer is that we mainly *search for information*. For example, the distractions that I discussed in the little vignettes above are instances of our constant flitting from site to site and from one network context to another, which are all oriented toward information seeking and gathering and consuming (reading). Other times we find ourselves *processing* information in the form of writing, or uploading, coding, etc., which adds up to the totality of the networked process. During the early years of its development it was the *search engine* that drove and shaped the web and the Internet to its popularized form. These applications came and went in many forms, such as Lycos, Infoseek, and Alta Vista, which all appeared in the early 1990s to find their niches or commercial graves in the digital sphere. However, it was Google, launched in 1998, which not only became the dominant search engine, but also transformed the relationship that most of its users have with information and with the networked information society. Alexander Halavais calls our networked society a "search engine society." His eponymous book shows how corporations such as Google (overwhelmingly Google) are set up to distract users by catering to every whim or thought that comes into one's head whilst online, and does this, crucially, through the portal of a "sparse home page" that "epitomizes simplicity" (2008, 18). Underneath this aesthetically pleasing interface, however, there lurks a closely guarded secret. It consists of code, or software in the form of an algorithm called PageRank, after one of Google's founders, Larry Page. The technicalities of the PageRank algorithm are complex, but suffice it to say, is that they direct input queries to popular sites that ostensibly correspond to a "match" for that query. Each time a user is directed to a particular site its "page ranking" is increased, making it more likely to be at the top of the list of results when someone else inputs a similar query. One could say that this shows that, to use the cliché, "success breeds success," and that the more people who seek certain information, then the more relevant are the results likely to be. However, the results in fact reflect the logic of the algorithm as opposed to any intrinsic qualities of the "match," or a response that matches what the query really is seeking. It does so, moreover, in a way that is organized into patterns of searching that tends to eliminate spontaneity or the unanticipated or the truly random in what the results list delivers. Google's algorithm does this, of course, in order to sell the commercially useful patterns in these searches to its advertiser clients.

Clearly, Google is rather more than the ubiquitous search box that is planted temptingly and distractingly in the upper corners of almost every browser on the planet—ready and willing to connect to any random thought. Google search functions now incorporate such applications as Google Books, where new and out of copyright books may be read in part or in full; Google Images and Google Video will trawl the Internet for pictures and vision that "match" the input query; and Google Scholar, which "stands on the shoulders of giants" as its tag states, will aggregate academic texts and citations in a range of formats and across a wide disciplinary sphere. Blogs, Groups, Maps, Gmail, Reader, and a growing number of functions sprawl Google's influence far and wide to become central element in the construction of what has been termed the "society of the query." This is a radically transformed society, in respect of its relationship with texts, time, reading, and writing. It is, as David Gugerli phrases it: "a society which has to be understood in terms of the *permanent fluctuation of its conditions and relations, of its writing and reading*, of its calculations and decisions, and indeed, of its practices of search and query" (Gugerli 2009) (my emphasis). Gugerli's summation is suffused with all the ingredients of network-induced distraction—speed above all. It carries with it the notion that to "query" and question is to be constantly outwardly directed, to be in a cognitive state of "permanent fluctuation" between tasks, and in random pathways of inquiry. In its temporal manifestation this is to necessarily limit the time needed for introspection, for pauses, for deeper reading and thinking, and contemplation—to militate against all those human practices that engender knowledge from the raw material that is information.

This is an effect of what might be called "Google logic" (Cubitt, Hassan, and Volkmer 2010), a logic that expresses perfectly the nature of neoliberal capitalism and how it has changed the ways we relate to information and knowledge. Like the economic system it so accurately reflects, Google, being utterly advertising-dependent, is neoliberal to the heart of its algorithmic code. And like neoliberal capitalism, it is built upon the unrestricted application of computers and views computers as a solution for every problem—be it in productivity, or education, or social interaction, or entertainment. Google logic also expresses a very neoliberal talent for human exploitation. We see this in its exploitation of users to earn its billions from advertising, which is generated through its perceived capacity to deliver vast numbers of potential consumers to its clients' sites. Users get Google and its myriad applications for "free," but this comes at the cost of their own time that they *spend* on it—*for free*. Taken together and seen from the perspective of society as a whole, the nexus comprises a massive realm of *waste*—both of the time of users and of the material waste, that is many millions of unplanned and unintended and (possibly) unwanted and unnecessary purchases. Lastly (but not exhaustively) Google logic reflects the inner tendencies of capital toward both speed and domination. Growing speed, as we saw earlier, is what makes capitalism tick, and what gives capitalists their temporary edge over the competition. Google is no different in this respect. The business magazine *Fast Company* noted this tendency in the company in a 2003 article—even if it was unable to explain why this is so. In a routinely reverential piece on the "search for the growth secrets of one of the world's most exciting young companies," staffer Keith H. Hammonds admiringly observed that "[Google engineers] pursue a seemingly gratuitous quest for speed: Four years ago, the average search took approximately 3 seconds. Now it's down to about 0.2 seconds. And since 0.2 is more than zero, it's not quite fast enough" (Hammonds 2003). There is of course nothing gratuitous about being the quickest; it's the *sine qua non* for staying at the front of the pack, and the argument clincher when trying to sell its users to advertisers.

This edge, coupled with being "filled with cutting-edge ideas" is both cause and consequence of Google's domination—and is another intractable element of capitalism's logic of monopolization (Sweezy and Baran 1966). Google expresses this through its incredible speed of evolution. From its launch in 1998 it has risen to become the multibillion dollar-valued preeminent portal to the web. Google is designed to distract. Because it is dependent upon advertising for its revenues, it must perpetually attract more and more users through its speed and simplicity of function—and it must constantly attract them in ever-increasing numbers to satisfy its sponsors. In the ocean of information in which most of us swim, we need to navigate (or at least think that we are navigating) to the sources that we need, and the sources that are most applicable to our wants—be they in work, or leisure, or in education. But the need to "own" the eyes of its users means that Google must lure them back again and again. It must also direct them to their other suite of seemingly noncommercial (or tangentially commercial) platforms and applications such as Google Earth in order to create a dominating Google presence for users. It must keep them constantly on the move (algorithmically directed) in cyberspace, tempting them with offers of "more like this" or "recommended for you" (on Youtube). Web 2.0 technologies thus gives Google the capacity to conduct a *faux* dialogue with you and me, keeping the Internet close to the center of our lives—keeping you always moving and interacting and spending.

It could be countered that these are just the age-old tactics of business, updated for the networked society, and if you are disciplined and focused, then the Internet and Google can still be used to work for our individual and collective benefit. After all, is not Google free and gives us access to the immense reservoir of information that can enrich our lives? Well, yes and no. Google is indeed free, but the access to all that information needs to be qualified (as above), and the distractive effect of Google must be laid alongside another, potentially more serious epistemological effect. But let us look first of all at the kinds of numbers involved in Google's search engine society. In December of 2009 Google performed 87.8 billion searches out of a global total of around 131 billion. The Google number was up 58 percent from the previous December, which gives another indication of the growth of both Google and its popularity with users. Another way of looking at this is to see Google as performing over a *trillion* searches per year (Sullivan 2010). Whichever way you calculate it, this represents millions of people who are constantly searching, querying, idly browsing, or otherwise being led down the byways and highways of the sum of digital human knowledge. Most of these users, one could reasonably argue, would imagine that they are swimming in the whole ocean of available information, and as having "the world at their fingertips"—to quote a phrase from a review by computer scientist Jon Kleinberg on two books on Google in the magazine *Nature* (2006). Google does not care to disabuse us of this particular assumption. However, in his essay "The Deep Web," Michael K. Bergman explained the task he undertook to gauge the size of the Internet in terms of the information that it holds in its myriad interconnected databases—and how much of this search engines such as Google actually trawl to service our queries. He writes that "Public information on the deep Web is currently

400 to 550 times larger than the commonly defined World Wide Web." Bergman goes on to refer to research that suggests that:

> The search engines with the largest number of Web pages indexed (such as Google or Northern Light) each index no more than sixteen per cent of the surface Web. Since they are missing the deep Web when they use such search engines, Internet searchers are therefore searching only 0.03% — or one in 3,000 — of the pages available to them today. (Bergman 2001)

Bergman wrote his essay in 2001, and given the all-pervading immensity and diversity and power of Google, it is reasonable to think that it might have overcome its immature capacity that allows for fishing only in the shallow waters of the information sea. But no. In 2009 The *Guardian* newspaper interviewed Anand Rajaraman, co-founder of a new generation of "post-Google" search engine companies. Rajaraman observed that "Many many users think that when they search on Google they're getting all the web pages." He continued that:

> I think it's a very small fraction of the deep web that search engines are bringing to the surface. I don't know, to be honest, what fraction. No one has a really good estimate of how big the deep web is. Five hundred times as big as the surface web is the only estimate I know. (Beckett 2009)

Bergman's idea of the "deep web" and the later expert opinion regarding our continuing inability to search it in anywhere near its totality, raises serious questions that extend beyond those that are related to our increasingly distracted relationship to information. First is that through search engines such as Google, our organization and diversity of information and knowledge is based upon a narrow band of what is available—even narrower than that if the bias of the PageRank algorithm is factored in. Our networked world is thus marked by a paucity of real choice regarding what we can see, hear, and interact with, and that narrowing choice is itself marked by a commercially oriented instrumentalization. The second issue is temporal. Our historically based conception of what constitutes knowledge is that it is something that is relatively "fixed" in time and space. This is to say it resides within the pages our newspapers, journals, books, encyclopedias, etc., and this becomes *historically situated* through the continued existence of the fixed media and the myriad social and cultural contexts in which they are found—in people's houses, in libraries, in stores, and so on. This store of knowledge, a literature, a canon, technical, philosophical, and so on, can (and is) retrieved and re-read, differently understood and reinterpreted through whatever new context can impinge upon its reappearance as the basis of new discourses.

Online "knowledge," however, becomes in practice a form of *dynamic information* and we see this clearly in the function of Google. Google's dynamism is viewed unproblematically as an "efficient" way to retrieve information, and as we have seen the faster Google runs the better users and advertisers like it. But as Hellsten et al. observe, the close to real-time speed of search engine retrieval coupled with a process of constant updating, means that the "structure of received information erodes over time" and generates "a particular experience of the 'present'" (Hellsten, Leydesdorff, and Wouters 2006, 901–2). In simple terms, if you put a specific query into Google today, and do the same a month from now, you get two different lists. This has longer historical consequences, and to illustrate this the present writer conducted a simple experiment. At the time of writing, an oil spill in the Gulf of Mexico from the BP-operated Deep Water Horizon rig is described commonly as the greatest ecological disaster in history. There was another corporate catastrophe that rivals this, however, at least in terms of its human toll, and this was the gas leak from the Union Carbide plant in Bhopal, India, in 1985. In the historical literature there would be no argument regarding the (continuing) significance of Bhopal. Nevertheless, when "BP Oil Spill" is typed in to the Google search box, it delivers sixty-five million results. Type in "Union Carbide Bhopal" you get just over a million. The logic suggests that "relevance" diminishes over time, and correspondingly, that Google's memory is increasingly short term. Such pathologies, coupled with our chronically distracted state in the network more broadly makes for a radically diminished relationship with information, knowledge, and the subjective experience of time.

A New Engagement with Reading, Writing, and Communicating

It was reported in the *Christian Science Monitor* of August 2010 that the social-media platform Twitter had logged its twenty billionth tweet (or message) (Shaer 2010). Twitter is a microblogging site that was launched in 2006 and is estimated to have 190 million users producing 65 million tweets per day (Schoenfeld 2010). A chief characteristic of Twitter is its technologically constrained brevity: tweets are limited to 140 characters. The *Monitor* article reported that the twenty billionth tweet came from Japan and translated as: "So that the barrage might come back later all at once." Which could mean many things or nothing at all—except that it undeniably means that we are expressing ourselves differently today. The brevity of the transmission mirrors exactly the brevity of the moment. We can say what we want within the 140-character limit, and so can mangle and shorten and be infinitely creative within its capacity. That it is massively popular means that it must have a functional utility in the networked society—and we must also find it satisfying at some level of comprehension.

Mobile phone texting, which has been in mass use for fifteen years and more, has primed us for the current age of the tweet. Texting was shaped by economics (voice calls could be expensive) and it could be time-consuming, and so users adapted—we changed (were compelled to abbreviate) our writing in response to an economic and technological change. People now use texting in every conceivable context, and for younger people especially it constitutes an indispensable mode of social interaction. Texting very quickly had pedagogical effects for young people too. In 2006 New Zealand education officials began to allow high-school students to use "text-speak" in their exams. Education officials decreed that "credit (for the exam) will be given if the answer 'clearly shows the required understanding,' even if it contains text-speak" (USA Today 2006).

If we are writing in a way that is radically different than at any time in history, then so too are we reading differently. It was in the year 2010 the Amazon.com CEO Jeff Bezos announced a "tipping point" in our relationship with the reading of the written word: the sale of digital books (texts downloaded to your e-reader) had outsold the quantity of hardbacks on its website for the first time. Amazon said that it was selling 180 e-books for every 100 hardbacks (Tweney 2010). The motive force behind the upward e-book sales curve is the (Amazon-made) Kindle e-reader. A look at the Kindle website today (August 18, 2010) informs that the device has actually sold out temporarily, "Due to strong customer demand." The Tweney article from the *Wired* article just cited, stated (in July of 2010) that "sales of [Amazon's] Kindle e-book reader have tripled since it cut the price from $260 to $190," to the extent that they cannot match demand. Of course, and no doubt quite soon, Kindles will be in plentiful, if not in oversupply in the stores as the market reacts to demand. But the scale of demand says something about our appetite for the digital form of text, and suggests that we are acquiring a taste for its digital immateriality, for its "efficiency," and even for its speed. As the Kindle website blurbs: "Books in 60 Seconds—Download books anytime, anywhere" and "20% Faster Page Turns" (Amazon.com 2010).

This new engagement with reading and writing, however, is fundamentally underscored by social acceleration and the attendant time-squeeze that grips our lives. As David Harvey noted of his observations on the effect of time–space compression, that we "are forced to alter, sometimes in quite radical ways, how we represent the world to ourselves" (1989, 240). The dearth of time and the tyranny of distraction and the demands of the neoliberal existence obliges us then to text instead of writing by hand, or to even write more fully in digital text. Twitter and its like are doubtless fads that will be superseded by something else, but their popularity is itself an expression of a *forced representation*, a mirror of the world as how it is today, and how we are compelled in growing numbers to be part of this logic. The purchase of a Kindle or any of its analogs is at root an expression of a generalized synchronizing with the networked economy. The purchase is justified through an instrumental logic where downloading a book is reckoned to save us from wasting time in a bookshop, and its "60 Seconds Download" means that we save even more time by not having to wait for the hardcopy to be sent all the way by airmail from Amazon in Seattle. What does this new engagement with reading and writing and communicating mean?

We saw in Chapter 3, and particularly in the work of Dan Schiller, that the Internet's commercialization is more than a mere adjunct effect of a wider techno-social logic; it is its very *raison d'etre*. The network society more broadly, indeed, is driven by the innovations of the market, and by the flexibility that ICTs bring to capitalism in order to satisfy its never-ceasing competitive requirements. Moreover, if commodified and commercially oriented information are the lifeblood of the network society, then *words* are its DNA.

Luckily we still have historians who make it their vocation to incorporate the longer view into their analysis of the world. We see a relevant instance of the *longue durée* in some of the last and deeply reflective writings of Tony Judt. In an essay for the *New York Review of Books*, Judt published "Words" which was a lament on the "disrepair" that he saw language and words had fallen into. For Judt, the "increasingly commercial bias" of networked communication, and digital communication more generally through the Internet, "brings an impoverishment of its own" (2010, 37). He noted of this that when "words lose their integrity, then so do the ideas they express." For Judt, this is an effect of "the privatizing [of] language no less than we have privatized so much else" (2010, 37). This is a deeply fundamental point that we have too little understood. We forget that written words are (and always have been) *tools*; technologies that we construct and which in turn, as Ong and McLuhan suggest, have their reconstructive effect upon the ways in which we think and act. If they have increasingly become privatized in that they are oriented toward brevity, toward instrumental ends, toward the needs of business and entertainment, and toward high-speed and superficial social network-ing, then it follows that words have not only become privatized—*they become commodities too.* And functioning as commodities we are thus increasingly becoming alienated from words as reflections of our thoughts and as expressions of the fundamental meanings that gave structure to the whole of that which western civilization has been built upon. Words "are all we have" argues Judt, and this is the fundamental truth of it all. If we no longer own them, then it is not too much to say that we own our destiny, both individual and collective, even less.

Again, Marx is instructive here. In Chapter 3 we saw how Marx analyzed commodity production and showed that it was, at its root, a deeply temporal function. A principle *effect* of this process, Marx also showed, is one of *alienation* where under the particular context of capitalist production, the worker is separated from the object of his or her productive work, which has become a commodity (Marx 1982, 716). Similarly, in the network society information constitutes capi-talism's *forces of production*, the "material" that underlies the system of production and which produces (by means of the user-worker) the commodities that the system was set up to produce—which is more information with specific commercial utility that is oriented toward the production of yet more commoditized information, and so it goes on. The logic is circular and self-motivating and the worker-user (as producer) stands apart from it because, as Marx put it:

> ...before he enters the process, his own labour has already been alienated [*entfremdet*] from him, appropriated by the capitalist, and incorporated with capital, it now, in the course of the process, constantly objectifies itself so that it becomes a product alien to him [*fremder Produkt*]. (1982, 716)

The network, in other words, functions primarily as a vast economy, a gigantic production site, whereupon to enter it is to leave behind his or her subjective self in order to produce what Marx termed "objective wealth" (1982, 716). Dan Schiller, in his *How to Think About Information*, makes a similar argument that states that information in its digital form is a commodity like any other. Through our production of information (and becoming increasingly dependent upon it in its digital and networked forms), we become separated from its social, democratic, and historical potential because when we enter the network, we enter it as we would a factory or an office, precisely because these once-separated realms—separated from culture, from the social and private spheres—have now become intractably blurred. The term "information worker" or "knowledge worker" now takes on a rather different meaning from the merely technical ascription given to it by Daniel Bell in the mid-1970s (Bell 1976, 14–33, 374). Today, the process of the assemblage of words into the necessary (or mandated) forms constitutes the *intellectual labor* power that drives the whole process. This is a transformation of the theory and practice of "labour" as it has come to us from the Industrial Revolution and from Marx's analysis of it as the basis of human exploitation under capitalism. As Michael Hardt and Antonio Negri put it in their book *Multitude*, "In the final decades of the twentieth century, industrial labour lost its hegemony and in its stead emerged 'immaterial labour', that is, labour that creates immaterial products, such as knowledge, communication, information..." (2006, 108). They go on to insist that the labor that produces the immateriality (the "ideas, symbols, codes, texts, linguistic figures, images and other such products") is itself still stubbornly material: "what is immaterial is *its product*" (108–9) (emphasis in original). It is the immateriality of material production processes that makes the exploitation and alienation in the process so much more difficult both to define—and resist. Whereas the site of exploitation in the process of industrial material labor is relatively easy to define: i.e., workers often produce commodities that they cannot themselves afford and have no control over what happens to them after they have produced them. Producing (and consuming) information in the context of the whole of the networked society, however, seems far too complex and diverse to analyze through a single Marx-derived frame. Nevertheless, if we do identify the whole of the networked society as the site of exploitation and alienation, through the changed relationship with information and with time, then that fact that all this activity, no matter what its provenance or endpoint, contributes to an exploitative system that is organized and evolves principally to suit the projects and imperatives of the neoliberal capitalist system that gave life to it in the first place. And so being an "information worker" in an office or at home or at college, with a beautiful computer and a super-fast network where one can blog, and e-mail and Skype and write for publication, and so on, can seem to be creative and autonomous process—when in fact this would be to lose sight of the position of the individual in a vast and furiously fast realm of immaterial production that comes from the age-old wellspring of material labor power that has energized capital for three hundred and more years.

In this wider context of the exploitation and alienation of producing individuals, nothing very much has changed. Humans—individuated and atomized as they are today—are vulnerable to the predations of a system whose inner logic has not substantively changed since the eighteenth century (Beck and Beck-Gernsheim, 2002, 33). Time (and distraction) is acutely bound up with this process. In terms of the temporal aspect, the new relationship with network time is having its disorienting and disempowering effect. In her book *Time* (2004), Barbara Adam considers what she terms the "human-technology-science-economy-equity-environment constellation" that is unique in human history to capitalism, and where "people become the weakest link when the timeframes of action are compressed to zero and where effects expand to eternity" (134).

As the "weakest link" in this bio-technological chain of logic, the user (consumer and producer) of information becomes susceptible to its code-written ordering. And so we are distracted more readily because the network is engineered for just such an effect. Under the constant assault of information bombardment, a continual flitting from website to website and from application to application becomes the default coping strategy in a world where we are psychically conflicted by the allurements of a global economy at our fingertips, and by the economic pressure to try to keep up at our jobs and in our social and cultural lives. Continually preoccupied by active and persistent information in all its networked diversity leaves us little time for reflection and pause; little time to stop and consider our increasingly inattentive condition, either as an individual or as a member of an at least notional class of exploited information workers. Moreover, our present-centeredness diminishes our natural and eons-old affinity for narratives as a prime modality for subjectively constructing our world. As Ron Purser observed of this diminution:

> ...narrative sequence implodes into a concern and fixation with the real-time instant. What used to comprise a narrative history—sense making based on knowledge of the past, present and future—contracts into the buzz of a flickering present. (2001, 13)

With these cumulative and ongoing cognitive, subjective, experiential, and narratological assaults upon what it is to be human and literate and rational in the social world, we find ourselves, at the beginning of the twenty-first century, in a unprecedented situation in respect of the "constellation" that Adam sees as the vital timescape context of our age. The individual is atomized and collectivized as he or she has always been under capitalism: atomized still as the alienated and exploited cog inside the vast machine—and collectivized by the objective class position. Atomization remains, but the objective and material class position whereby one is able, at least in theory, to recognize this position as being part of a collective class—is vanishing, as is the subjective capacity to experience this recognition as real and as relevant to their situation. The most important point is that information (immaterial and digital) as the prime mover for the post-modern economy has made more intractable the real-life conditions of what is now post-industrial life. Here the time-squeeze affects almost all to a more or less degree, and the logic of speed and efficiency through computing has robbed all of the spaces and times for actual or potential autonomy. This applies to the corporate CEO and City money trader, just as much as it does for the billions who toil in front of screens in administrative and information processing tasks in offices and in homes in every corner of the networked world.

A persistent and chronic distractive state is both the cause and consequence of this political economy of speed. As an individual and collective pathology, it prevents us from seeing precisely how we have been transcended by a particular logic written into a particular technology. Words, as Judt tells us, are indeed all that we have. But the more that we produce them within this particular logic, then the more we lose any capacity for control over them in order to make them work in ways that are beneficial and empowering for us all.

137

6

Canon

In his book *Reality Hunger: A Manifesto*, David Shields attempts to rationalize and articulate the dying of the novel as the traditional and quintessentially modernist mirror of life, of lives led, and of the contemporary condition of modern society per se. The eclipse of the novel is a good thing, he maintains, and indeed his *Manifesto* seeks to bring its demise along quicker. He wants to replace a form that he feels to be retrograde and exhausted and a distortion, with a kind of writing that more accurately reflects the actual "reality" of the world. In short, the traditional novel that has come to us from at least the eighteenth century, with its linear and narrative form, is literally outmoded—at least for Shields. Interviewed on what he feels to be the motivation for his "manifesto," Shields told an interviewer that the novel form:

> ...strikes me as antediluvian texts that are essentially still working in the Flaubertian novel mode. In no way do they convey what it feels like to live in the 21st century. Like most novels, they are essentially works of nostalgic entertainment. (O'Hagan 2010, 36)

Without actually explaining what is wrong with "nostalgic entertainment," Shields goes on to argue for a literary form to displace the narrative one; a form that eschews plot and narrative and reflects the "real" which is an "unprocessed, unfiltered, uncensored and unprofessional" writing (O'Hagan 2010, 36). This he maintains is a more truthful representation of the reality that we allegedly hunger for, the actual reality of dissonance and fracture and the lack of a cohering center in our post-modern existence, an existence where the novel of the modern period clings tenaciously to a world that has outgrown and outpaced it.

Reality Hunger itself is necessarily non-narrative and consists of a listed series of aphorisms that agglomerate as terse and impatient provocations against the novel. Alighting on Jonathan Frantzen's best-selling book *The Corrections* as symptomatic of the problem with the form, Shields writes that:

> I couldn't read that book if my life depended on it. It might be a 'good' novel or it might be a 'bad' novel, but something has happened to my imagination, which can no longer yield to the earnest embrace of the novelistic form (Shields 2010).

Blockbusters like Frantzen's (and the sales of novels *in toto*) nevertheless attest to our continuing habit for the narrative form of reading and writing. For Shields, this blindness to the actual reality of the world means that we miss out on fruitful and fulfilling engagement with what really is the essence of our post-modernity. Shields argues that "to write serious books, you must be ready to break the forms" (589). To do this truthfully the writer and the reader must be ready to confront and engage with "Randomness, openness to accident and serendipity, spontaneity" (3) and embrace the idea that "never again will a single story be told as though it were the only one" (617). On the surface, lines such as these, taken (and written) as scattered aphorisms, are seemingly reasonable and could be held up quite easily as the standard approach of the artist, and as the precondition of making the new from the transcending of the no longer functional. But what is Shields actually advocating in *Reality Hunger*?

The novel, despite being the centerpiece of Shields' rage and frustration is in fact only the surface expression of a deeper issue—our relationship with words and writing. Narratives, as we have seen, are at the very core of how literate societies, and before that aural societies, constructed their worlds. Writing is the tool, the technology, or technique that made this world real. We do not "yield" to narratives as Shields argues; rather, narratives are expressions of the ways in which human consciousness is constituted. Readers buy Franzten in numbers that completely put into shade the works of anti-narrativists such as James Joyce and his *Ulysses*. Joyce, of course, has been and continues to be enormously influential—but overwhelmingly within literary circles, whereas standard novels are the storytelling nourishment that satisfies the psychologically based *narrative hunger* that millions across the world experience every day.

Shields' argument for a more truthful relation of the randomness and dissonance of post-modern society, seen in this sense, is problematic on at least two levels. First, Shields sets great store in the need for a new artistic form, and sees himself as part of what he would doubtless be happy to be labeled as an *avant-garde*. However, the fact that he seeks to mirror the chaos and disjuncture of the post-modern world in order to be more faithful to it is both reactionary and passive. By simply being truthful to the material processes of the world through reflecting them in our writing is to leave aside any prospect of agency or possibility of political change. To put it somewhat crudely, John Steinbeck's *Grapes of Wrath*, or Arthur Koestler's *Darkness at Noon*, or Alexander Solzhenitsyn's *One Day in the Life of Ivan Denisovitch*, have had a far more progressive influence on the shaping of the real world than has Joyce's *Finnegan's Wake*. The list of consciousness stirring novelists is long, and from it one could cite, just off the top of the head, luminaries such as Aldous Huxley, George Orwell, and (even) the execrable political novels of Ayn Rand.

Second, by making our relationship with words so passive, we neutralize them as tools for political and ethical change. To abandon the narrative form would make books that express a rage at the world and its injustices impossible to write and therefore make progressive and democratic transformation equally unattainable. Shields' kaleidoscope of aphorisms calls itself a "manifesto." But a manifesto is a political program—an ordered and structured and rational and reasoned basis for promoting reconstruction. *Reality Hunger*, in reality, acts as the very antithesis of this, and the "artistic movement" that Shields seeks to bring to life, would be the first one in history that did not exercise autonomy over the tools of their creative process—their words.

It is clear from much that has been written so far in this book that we are indeed on the path toward powerlessness and passivity in the face of fast-moving dynamics of economy and society that are expressed in the "randomness" that Shields identifies. Deep in our psyche we are being daily bombarded by the post-modern onslaught of information. The questions we need to ask are: what is the cause of this disempowerment? And what can we do about it? We have discussed in some detail the temporal aspects of writing and reading and how the temporal transformations of late-capitalism have reacted negatively upon the very core of the relationship we have with this most fundamental of tools, the "technologized word." It is time, however, to look at the process from a slightly different angle, from the social–psychological aspect of our relationship with technology—a view that gives the temporal dimension added clarity and analytic power.

Instinct and Information

Arnold Gehlen's 1980 book *Man in the Age of Technology* (the German original was published in 1957 to widespread acclaim) is in one respect an odd book to continue my argument on the foundational aspects of modernity that are being dissipated through speed and a transformed (post-modern) capitalism. Gehlen was rather hostile to modernity, partly in a way that is rather pointless (because modernity has affected us so deeply for over three hundred years), and partly in a way that is insightful in its appreciation of what modernity gave us (or left us with). Gehlen's usefulness lies in his thinking of and linking of social anthropology (or what is known in Germany as philosophical anthropology) with the effects of modern technology. In other words, he gives us the social anthropologist's insight into the raw, archaic state of humankind and how its "nature" has been changed through "technique" and the "advance of industrialization" (Gehlen 1980, 1).

Gehlen reaches deep into not only our ancient past, but also into the biology of human development for his philosophical and anthropological grounding. He argues that we humans are unique in that we have evolved to be born in a particularly helpless state, and that the most important factors in our development occur after we are born. We are born "unfinished" so to speak (Gehlen 1980, ix). Critically, and unlike other mammals, however, Gehlen maintains that we are born with "instinctual deprivation." That is to say, stuck as we are in our "unfinished" state, we lack the inherent coding that drives the lamb immediately to its mother's teats, or the sea turtle to the sea from its nest on the beach. In nature, mammals are (more or less) adapted to suit their particular environments, whereas humans live and thrive in every variant of nature, from high altitudes and cold, to sea level hot deserts, tropical jungles, and temperate savannahs. The difference is that humans are *driven to create and lead* a diverse life rather than evolve to live organically within a narrow environmental setting. This is so because we "(Thakkar, 2010)" lack the perceptual filter that comes from instinct and which allows the mammal to ignore stimuli that are not vital to its environment and respond only to what it must in order to survive.

This lack of instinct would seem to be an immense problem for our species. To have a less than developed instinct is to be thrown into the world as "unfinished." It would leave us prone to a devastating sensory overload because we cannot automatically filter out unnecessary stimuli—all the information that is not directly relevant to our survival and learning to lead a life. Jonny Thakkar has analyzed Gehlen's work and argues that our instinctual deprivation would cause: "an unbearable cognitive overload...were it not for our habits and routines; these substitute for instincts by reducing the world's intrinsic complexity, enabling us to see what is salient in a given situation and freeing us from the burden of continual decision making" (2010, 2). Thakkar (through Gehlen) goes on to say that the key to our cognitive survival were precisely those "habits and routines" which became forms of human institutions—a vital consciousness forming cultural phenomenon. We are what we have become through our human capacity for institution building. However, as Thakkar continues, "if these institutions should collapse we would lose our mooring. *We would be at sea in a storm of information*" (2010, 2) (my emphasis).

For Gehlen himself it is the orientation toward institutions that gives respite to the senses and allows man to reflect upon his world and enables him to develop the regular habits and customs from which would arise, from very early in the history of our species, forms of culture. Culture was the bedrock upon which humans could build and "stabilize the world's rhythms by smoothing out irregularities and exceptional occurrences" (Gehlen 1980, 12). This allowed humans to move beyond base survival and early death and toward the building of tools, including writing, which would develop both the reflective consciousness, and the civilizational meta-institutions whose appearance in antiquity, "betrays a semi-instinctual need for stability in the environment" (Gehlen 1980, 13).

Gehlen's essentially anti-modernist stance does not mean that he thinks technology to be somehow alien to our species. It is a non-controversial point for Gehlen to make that technology is fundamental to the organizing of the world into stable forms. Technology, or "technique" as he puts it, "is as old as man himself" (2). However, Gehlen seeks to subject this relationship, the relationship (that "discloses man's mode of dealing with Nature," as Marx saw it) to a more critical, philosophical–anthropological gaze. He distinguishes three different forms of technique adoption that act as "organic substitutions." These are: replacement techniques, strengthening techniques, and facilitation techniques. He observes that:

> Amongst the oldest artifacts we find weapons, which are not given to man in the form of organs; fire should also be thought of in this con-

nection, having come into use for both security and warmth. From the beginning this principle of organ substitution operated along with that for organ strengthening: The stone grabbed to hit with is much more effective than the bare fist. Thus, next to *replacement techniques* that allow us to perform beyond the potentials of our organs, we find *strengthening techniques* that extended the performance of our bodily equipment—the hammer, the microscope, and the telephone reinforces natural abilities. Finally there are *facilitation techniques* operating to relieve the burden upon organs, to disengage them, and finally to save effort—as when use of a wheeled vehicle replaces the dragging of weights by hand (3).

The example of the wheel as combining all three dimensions of the relationship is intentional. It signals both the power potential and the limits to this power insofar as human control over technique is concerned. This achievement, as Gehlen notes, is both "life-fostering and at the same time life destroying" (5). Such an "organic" dialectic between nature and tool-creating cultures held the stability of institutions on more or less a knife-edge of development for thousands of years. The tool–nature relationship was "organic" in the literal sense for Gehlen. He writes that "the replacement of the organic by the inorganic constitutes one of the most significant outcomes of the development of culture" (5). There were two sub-elements to this "replacement." One was that artificial materials were developed to replace those organically produced; and non-organic forms of energy began to replace organic energy. In terms of the first, "the development of metallurgy constitutes a cultural threshold of the first magnitude" (5). As late as the Middle Ages, Gehlen states, almost everything that was built (bridges, vehicles, houses, and so on) was constructed from wood and stone. Metallurgical breakthroughs eventually leading to mass-produced steel would change the world and construct the foundations of the Industrial Revolution. In terms of energy, the basis of industry and modernity was fueled through oil and coal. These are of course the legacies of ancient organic life, but our use of them enabled energy sources to be developed that allowed humans to slip the ties of being dependent upon sources that needed to be renewed from year to year. Gehlen sees in this the beginning of our departure from the environmental temporalities that had accompanied humankind down the ages:

> As long as wood remained the most significant fuel material, and the work of domestic animals the most important source of energy, the advance of material culture…met a limit of a non-technical

kind that rested upon the slow tempo of organic growth and re-production. (6)

To develop this logic along the lines of my own argument, we can see that Gehlen views the approaching modernity as representing a sort of liminal space for humans and their relationships with the temporalities of their biological constitutions and the rhythms of their environments. Machines began to become both thinkable and possible through artificial materials and "non-natural" forms of energy and would set the ancient organico-temporal relationship upon a revolutionary and rational path. For Gehlen, the issue was not the development of the machine per se, but the profound structural changes in the institutions of economic, political, and scientific life that would make *systems of machines* possible. This change was, in other words, the beginning of the Enlightenment, where science wedded to capitalism created the motivation for scientific experiments that would isolate natural phenomena through experimentation, and would open nature to the scientific gaze and thence to render discoveries amenable to technical application—a breakthrough whereupon "technique derived the breathtaking tempo of its advance" as cause and consequence of a much wider institutional transformation (9).

An unintended effect of industrialism was that it began to dissolve the stabilizing foundations, the cultural institutions, upon which humans built both consciousness and the capacity to lead the fully organic life into which the species was thrown and had evolved to survive in. Life, as it became materially more prosperous (or at least materially different) and as ancient cultures and ways of life were drawn into the orbit of abstracted and developing technological systems, became correspondingly more complex and the social context for new and increased informational stimuli became increasingly unavoidable. According to Gehlen, modernity and the unstoppable technological development that it brought signaled the beginning of the end of our biological bargain with nature. No longer would we be so easily able to compensate for our "instinctual deficiencies" by "identifying nature's properties and laws in order to exploit them and control their interaction" (Gehlen 1980, 4). Henceforth, our institutions would lose their deep and stable rootedness into the life of humans and become more malleable and contingent. And as Thakkar notes of this transformation, "institutions that are optional cannot sufficiently reduce complexity—they take too few of our choices away—and so we are once more subject to overload. We develop over-complicated inner lives and existential crises..." (2010, NPN). Gehlen argued that modernity and industry brought with it "randomly changing circumstances" (52) which constantly undermined institution building and preserving. In such a world, "any belief in constant principles of orientation is in danger of being denied that minimum of external confirmation without which it cannot survive" (53).

It has been my contention that as humans we have capacities of cognition, the intellectual ability to develop and acquire reason, and use reason to construct and make sense of our material world. I have argued also that this capacity has a temporal watermark that is indelible in that at its very core it is rooted in the temporalities of our biological make-up, and in the "non-technical," as Gehlen puts it, rhythms and tempos and cycles of nature. From our earliest phase of development of this cognitive and temporal capacity to act upon the world, we were always stretching these capacities and, at the same time, eating into our reserves. We see in Gehlen that modernity and its "rational" approach to technological development began to effect what was for thousands of years, a fairly stable relationship with nature, with the cultural institutions that we built, and with the speed of the temporalities that these contained. The rise of modernity and industry did signal a systematic challenge to our inherent temporal capacities, but nevertheless these capacities did still have sufficient reserves to be drawn upon which constituted the basis of the new (modern) cultural institutions that would themselves be more or less stable and more or less able to act as guide and orientation that would keep information overload and existential crises at bay.

In order to understand and try to recuperate something our present situation, we need to look back to the basis of modernity, to where (for Gehlen) it all went wrong. For me, in contrast to Gehlen, the *Enlightenment is all we have*. We have look to Enlightenment thought—as opposed to ancient and now long-dead and irrecoverable cultural institutions—to try to regain control over our inner complexity and receive the "external confirmation" that we require to place our cognitive and temporal capacities on a more sustainable basis.

Given that we live in an information society, and that prior to that the world as it developed was based upon (at its deepest level) the information technology of the written word, then it is to the *stabilization of the written word*, both printed and electronic, that we must look to as the source of cognitive recuperation and relief from the informational stimuli of our post-modern condition. Modernity created its own information stabilizer, a cultural institution within which assemblages of the written word and the ideas contained therein, contain the meta-narratives that acted as the guides for action and for contemplation and reflection. We call it the *canon*, and it is to this that we need to look in order to appreciate and recuperate and reactivate what Enlightenment has given us.

Ideology and the Canon

The general conception of the constitution of what has been portentously termed "the western canon" is today very far from what Victorian high cultural guru Matthew Arnold, in his *Culture and Anarchy*, famously saw as embodying "the best that has been said and thought in the world." The canon, as we shall see, is today considered (when it is considered at all) to be a tool of the elites and more particularly of white imperial oppression. Moreover, those who dare to advocate it these days find themselves frequently pilloried for promoting a form of cultural imperialism over those who are said to be in need of culture and ideas because they are incapable of generating them themselves. So what has happened? Why has the once-uncontroversial notion that one set of ideas may have more merit than another and may possibly contribute to what Herbert Marcuse (1977, x) saw as a social and cultural "standard that remains constant" become so anathema—to the point that we barely have the debates any longer?

To answer this question we need to go back a generation, to the time of widespread economic and political upheaval that was the transition from Fordism to flexible accumulation that we discussed in Chapter 3. Since that time (around the turn of the 1980s) and the "culture wars" in the Anglophone campuses over the nature and function of the curricula in schools and universities, the "western canon" has had a very bad time of it. This malaise has developed to such an extent that to speak positively today of a canon of works that should be read and debated as being important in their own terms is almost to break a taboo (McCain 2006). Often there were good reasons for the critique of the canon, which I will come to shortly, but the debates themselves were almost always ideologically driven (Searle 1990). In the main the disputes that were generated occurred between a broadly Left and Right politics that had their roots, boringly and shallowly, in the domestic contemporary party politics of the Anglophone countries such as the USA, Britain, and Australasia. Debates—if they could so be characterized—were colored by the 1980s monochromes of "political correctness," a mode of thought that was itself a consequence of the political retreat of the Left from its more traditional spheres of political economy, political ideology, and a general critique of capitalism. The identification and rejection of the canon and its works formed a part of the Left's continuing preoccupation with issues of culture and identity in the wake of its abnegation of 1960s and 1970s political militancy (Judt 2010, chap. 14). For the new Left of the culture wars the canon was a standing affront to ideas of diversity and pluralism in thought and action, and was excoriated as little more than the ideological hegemony of the ideas of "dead white males." The canon was, for the Left, a sizable and ever-expanding list that could include anyone from Shakespeare to Gibbon, and from Plato to Joyce. Taken together, these constituted the ossifying material for what Mary Louise Pratt termed "a narrowly specific cultural capital that will be the normative *referent* for everyone, but will remain the *property* of a small and powerful caste that is linguistically and ethnically unified" (cited in Searle 1990). There is of course more than a grain of truth contained in this statement, one further defined by Pratt as the effect of "the West's relentless imperial expansion" which ruthlessly promoted the growth and institutionalization of a certain class of ideas that did not allow space for other voices and other perspectives such as those of women, blacks, and the subaltern more broadly.

The identification of the role of ideology meant that there could on occasion be a well-aimed and influential critique of how a canon may operate insidiously within society. For example, Edward Said's pioneering *Orientalism* (1979) drew back the curtain on two hundred years and more of the West's creation of the "Orient" as an idea, and a set of discourses that were used in order to dominate non-European peoples, societies, and cultures. Said's work identified concepts, typologies, and discourses that were canonicized in an English, French, and German philology that encompassed (among other things) sweeping racial theorems, broad theological assumptions about Islam, and a general condescending treatment of the territories and peoples East of the Levant as culturally inferior.

The problem, though, is that Said's nuanced approach tended to be overrun by a broad-based attack (such as Pratt's) on the western canon per se as hierarchical, oppressive, and elitist. The main consequence of this was that in its culture war zeal the Left threw out the canonical baby with the cultural bathwater—leaving no room for a truly critical approach that could accommodate the possibility of at least some universal benefit arising from the cultural institutionalization of certain ideas. That this rigid interpretation coincided with the rise of the influence of post-modern theory in the universities was itself no coincidence. A literary and cultural post-modern theorizing emerged out of the abandonment of the politics of practice that I just noted. The politics that this sort of post-modern theorizing expressed was of an abstract and inward and fetishistically textual kind, especially in the disciplines of English and Literary Studies. More significantly, this fed into a wider "depoliticization of the public sphere," as Boris Frankel has argued, where politics became hegemonized by issues of identity and meaning and culture—but in specific ways that were disconnected from the real and material concerns of the vast majority who were outside the universities and the opinion-shaping media (Frankel 1992, 15).

Again it should be stressed that many of the issues taken up in the post-modern culture wars were both important and overdue. The logic of what Pratt and her ilk would write is of a kind that many post-modernists (and many others on the Left) would readily agree with: there needed to be "space" in the textual universe for the subaltern Other, for those essayists and theorists and novelists such as Frantz Fanon or Gayatri Chakravorty Spivak or Gabriel García Márquez, people from the margins who could nonetheless illuminate aspects of the totality of the human condition. A positive outcome from this is that many invisible people and silenced voices were now beginning to be seen and heard, and with influences that began to be felt in the world. But the post-modern context of the arguments that helped bring the subaltern to life also nurtured a *political apathy* in terms of the possibilities for a truly transformational politics. It was a relative indifference to deep and substantive social and political change that would characterize the entire post-modern project. What this meant was that whilst we could admire and accept the works of, say, Donna Haraway or Val Plumwood—the economic and political steamroller of neoliberalism trampled its way across the world, bringing major reversals to many of the gains that had been made in the developed world and beyond since the end of the Second World War (Derrida 1993, 12).

The post-modern context tended to be constituted under the sway of philosophers such as Jacques Derrida and theorists such as Jean François Lyotard (see Norris 1992). To take Derrida first: he advocated a very influential text-based politics of "deconstruction," where the famously misunderstood aphorism "there is nothing outside the text," tended to be taken as an argument for an infinite relativism. As Norris shows, however, interpreters of Derrida's work "fail to grasp" the actual meaning of his work and instead imbued in it an "anything goes" hermeneutic that "cheerfully pronounces an end to the regime of reality, truth, and Enlightenment critique" (1992, 18). The influence of this "large scale distorting mechanism" (Norris 1992, 19) of misinterpretation generated and helped to sustain a post-modern relativism within the realms of meaning and politics that left little impulse for an actual and materially oriented politics of social change. Indeed, the post-modern relativism that influenced the academy and armed the culture war soldier against the canon of "dead white males" generally saw no reason to engage in a practical politics anyway, because the modernist politics of socialism, or conservatism, or indeed any politics with a organized program per se, were a part of the problem for the post-modernists. Here the cues came from Lyotard who argued in his *The Post-modern Condition* that the politics of the modern period were the politics of the "metanarrative," the BIG stories that overarch culture and society and ground it in a specific and universal ontology. This was, according to Lyotard and his acolytes, a form of "totalitarianism" that had to be combated at the micro -level of meaning in order to avoid applying one free-floating "phrase-regimen" to a universal application (Lyotard 1979).

From this perspective the canon was seen as irredeemably hierarchical and totalizing. It was a textual foisting of the reality of an elite upon the masses, not in order to educate them, but to exert power over them. The problem for the post-modernists, though, is that hierarchy and "truth" had to be combated through its own relativistic worldview. This meant that post-modernism explicitly eschewed the only kind of politics of change that our world (as it is currently structured) is able to accommodate: a structured and hierarchical and programmatic politics that is based upon core "truths" and "values" that form a metanarrative of orientation through which to make sense of the world—which is the only possible basis for changing it in a meaningful way. It was ironic that the post-modern Left in the culture wars chose to take a totalizing perspective vis-a-vis the western canon in order to dismantle the allegedly totalizing view of a "small and powerful caste." This logic of double negative had the effect of painting the post-modern Left into a corner in terms of its ability to develop a critique of the western canon in ways that might view certain aspects of it as socially and politically positive.

But what then of the Right? What of the traditionally conservative wing of liberal democratic politics and opinion that would seem to be more naturally aligned to the idea of a canon?

In 1994 Harold Bloom published *The Western Canon*, which, as its jacket blurb states: "argues eloquently and brilliantly against the politicization of literature." And here we see, or so it would seem, what is a reasoned and rational rejoinder to the culture war post-modernists who had arisen, and armed with a mission, set out to eradicate the noxious legacies of "dead white males." Unfortunately, however, *The Western Canon* is primarily a list of what Bloom thinks the canon *should consist of*; a roll call of those uplifting and valuable texts that *he thinks* must be read and studied in schools and universities. Bloom lists twenty-six of them, from Dante to Beckett, and these were chosen by him for their "sublimity and their representative nature" (1994, 1–2). And Bloom, by way of the "eloquent and brilliant" argument the blurb primes us for, justifies who is in and who is not, by his noting in these works their "strangeness" and "originality" that "makes the author and the works canonical" (3). After this unpromising start, Bloom merely proceeds to go through his list. His book thus misses the point entirely. Instead of being a reasoned answer to the "politicization" of literature, or a brilliant case for the indispensability of the canon (as we were told it would be), the book emerged into public view as a large and lumbering target for the post-modern snipers waiting in their university perches to pick off his choices at will. I will say more on why the book misses the mark shortly.

What Bloom *did* achieve was a heightening of the "politicization" that it purportedly sought to avoid. Its main fault is that it was a book about what *should* be taught, not *why* it should be taught. In this it was an echo of Roger Kimball's *Tenured Radicals: How Politics Has Corrupted Higher Education* (1990). In this book Kimball directed his ire at the 1960s counter culturalists, those sundry Leftists who he saw moving into their comfortable tenured jobs in "protected purlieus" and were now setting about changing the university to align with their own ideological worldviews. From their unsackable positions, Kimball argues, all that was good and nourishing and important—from the conservative perspective, that is—was now being demolished by those afflicted by what he sees as a "juvenile cultural relativism" (2008, xxxiii). Indeed in the book's third edition, in 2008, Kimball argues that notwithstanding the positive trend of Right wing television in the shape of Fox News, and the broadening reach of a new generation of Right wing talkback radio hosts, things have actually gotten worse, and the tenured radicals are today more deeply entrenched than ever, busily hypnotizing millions of gullible American students with "relativist" courses on popular culture, transgender, ethic studies, gay and lesbian studies, and so on (2008, xv).

Now this is all good knockabout stuff, polemical and impassioned—but, and as with Bloom, it has nothing to do with the canon, canonicity, or the formation of the canon. Kimball simply meets Left politics with Right politics. And Bloom is content to tack up his list as a response to perceived threat of relativism and anti-canon Left. This is all fine as far as it goes. But the fact that these contretemps did not gain much purchase beyond the universities and a narrow media and literary elite, says much about the wider appeal and the perceived relevance of trench warfare inside the institutions of higher learning. And yet it all did matter (and still matters) very much. This is because what tends to become the ruling ideas of any society are those that emerge from its elite formations: *ergo* the university educated take with them their worldviews into business, into media, into government institutions, and into all the other realms of opinion forming and shaping. This trickles down, often imperceptibly, to congeal as the unquestioned assumptions that govern the thinking and attitudes of a majority. From this logic, there emerged two separate processes, from the Right and the Left, which has left the *idea* of the canon as something moribund and almost dead.

Firstly, from the radical economic Right of the 1970s, as we have already seen, there was the evolving dominance of neoliberal ideas. This was fundamentally the promulgation of pure political economy, with no interest in ideas other than those with practical application as drivers of a more efficient economy. In such an economy, the university, like any other business or institution, would need to synchronize with the imperatives of the marketplace. And so it has transpired. Today, questions over the social and cultural relevance of Dante or Vico as against Arundati Roy or *The Simpsons*, pale into insignificance for the student with mounting tuition bills to pay, and for the professor with classes to fill. Vocationalism, and not inquiry for its own sake, is the new watchword in the academy. The new "academic capitalism" means that neoliberalism, as the new face of twenty-first-century conservatism, has little or no interest in what the universities actually teach, canonical or not—so long as they are responding flexibly and efficiently to market signals (Slaughter and Leslie 1997).

Secondly, the culture warriors of the Left have by and large moved on from the battles over the canon. Academics and students today are largely unconcerned with such issues, or they if they are, they tend to accept that the western canon does indeed represent dead, elite, imperialist thinking. And in any case for students it is more fun to "deconstruct" episodes of *South Park*, than attempt to actually understand what Edward Said or Jacques Derrida were trying to tell their parents about the importance of ideas and of texts. Teachers, for their part—unless they form part of the globe-trotting professoriate who move easily from Harvard to television, and from the Op-Ed page to the hugely popular blog—fight mainly for their jobs, fight overwork and the pressure to publish, and fight to make themselves and their courses appear relevant to the real world, or more accurately, what appears as relevant to the agendas of university management. And so amid what is now a generation-long politicization of the form and function of the canon, very few now take the trouble to think and argue about what the canon is, or could be, and what relevance it might have for our society of speed and distraction. Still less, indeed, has this been done from the perspective of time.

The Point and the Time of the Canon

As dispassionately and objectively as I can, I want to argue for the recognition of the importance of the western canon and the need for a revival of the process of canonicity from a perspective that is beyond Left and Right politics (if such a dichotomy can be meaningly said to exist any more anyway). We can begin by dispensing with the pseudo-question "what is the canon?" as being one (if put like this) that is always inherently political, and gives rise only to lists and resentments to be thrown at one another. A more pertinent question would be "what does the processes of canonicity do?" "And what might the canon be capable of?" To answer these we need to move to the recognition that ideas (written ideas in the form of books that have circulated and have been read and debated) are able to form into the background consciousness of a culture and give shape and substance to that culture. Taken as an agglomeration, the canon is able to become institutionalizing and stabilizing (in Gehlen's sense of these terms) and to become the textual and ideational cues for the values and mores and ethics that comprise the very bedrock of our sense of being in the world.

An example of this would be the Bible, and Christian doctrine more generally, from where the term "canon" originally emerged. The Bible and its stories, its metanarratives and the belief systems that they engendered, have obviously had a functional value in that they formed long-lasting and relatively unchanging ways of holding cultures and societies together through shared orientations and shared faculties for meaning-interpretation. Moreover, Islam and Judaism, being similarly text-based and book-bound worldviews have also acted as central pillars in the development of institutions of civilizational coherence for a thousand years and more. It does not matter what one may think of religion. The effect of the canonical status of religious doctrine have been palpable and real, and have worked as a stabilizer in that their texts have been accepted as a not only a moral and ethical code or law, but also as a reason for existence in the world. To move the example to what is perhaps a logical development of the effect of religious canon, we can say that for a short time at least the Marxist–Leninist–Maoist canon(s), ideas that were based upon nothing but the belief in the written word as expressing the literal meaning of the world (think of the millions of kids who flourished copies of Mao's "Little Red Book" in the 1960s and 1970s), meant that institutionalized ideas and worldviews could endure for millions of people over the span of several generations. In the case communism of course, its relative "stability" was vouchsafed by repression, or worse, particularly for those for whom the canon was something to be interpreted and debated.

It is clear that to do away with the idea of the canon as the cultural warriors have done, or to forget it altogether as the neoliberal-dominated Right have done, or to leave it in suspended animation as either a long-ago academic battleground, or an irrelevancy for the majority, is potentially catastrophic. In a very real sense this is to do away with the perceptual building blocks that we need to construct and to strengthen our instinct deficiencies and the ability, individual and collective, to stave off our susceptibility overstimulation and confusion. The demise of the idea of the canon says something about an effect of our current age of distraction. And so in our network society of high-speed digital flows of information, the need for an appreciation of what the canon is for and what it can achieve has never been so urgent.

One of those who first revealed the functioning of the western canon, as we have seen, was Edward Said. His *Orientalism* was a rallying cry for a long-suppressed subaltern theory and practice that has now burgeoned far beyond the dreams of anyone in the 1970s when the book was written. Thanks in part to Said's widely influential effect, novelists such as Salman Rushdie and theorist/activists such as, say, Vandana Shiva, creators of non-western ideas and non-western writings, have percolated up to make space for themselves in the global consciousness: part of an incipient global canon, if you like, that has force and stability and is part of the formative bases of a more diverse cultural institutionalization. Indeed, this was Said's overlooked argument: by revealing the hegemony of the western canon, he did not *ipso facto* argue that canonicity itself was necessarily negative—his target for critique was a potentially infinitely expanding but nevertheless specifically focused "set of texts authors and ideas that make up the *Orientalist canon*" (1979, 4) (emphasis mine).

Elsewhere in his work, Said makes the case for a more positive function for a canon of ideas. His point is that the institutions and cultural stabilizing forces that the canon make possible should not be scrapped, as the post-modernists argue. Rather, they should be held up as institutions of cultural stability—and held up again to constant analysis and debate to produce what he terms in his *Culture and Imperialism*, a "critical literature" (1994, 54). This would be a canon that is solid and dynamic at the same time, endowing an always-provisional relevance to its works (1994, 54). Its solidity would ensure that it is not easily removed or ignored, and its looming presence in our culture would constitute the basis for our duty as citizens to have some common knowledge of it and its rationale (more on this in the next section). Its dynamism would prescribe a democratic and open and constantly critical analysis of the texts and ideas that we use as the basis for our institutional grounding in the world, in politics, in ethics, in economy, and so on. This would mean that some would become redundant or marginal, whilst others (fresh ideas and new works) could be provisionally admitted. The canon should not therefore repose and calcify in what Said termed a "venerable petrification" (1983, 143) or become some sort of holy realm or rarified space for high-level debate. Instead it must be the material for publically accessible discourse that all could enter into and help shape should they choose to do so.

Susan J. Hekman elaborates on the need for a dynamic and re-interpretive relationship with the canon and its formation. In her collection *Feminist Interpretations of Michel Foucault*, she makes the case specifically for a feminist approach, but her logic has universal application. In the Introduction to the collection of essays she has assembled, Hekman constructs its overarching theme and context:

> The process of canon transformation will require the recovery of 'lost' texts and a careful examination of the reasons such voices have been silenced. Along with the process of uncovering women's philosophical history, we must also begin to analyse the impact of gender ideologies upon the process of canonization. The process of recover and examination must occur in conjunction with careful attention to the concept of a canon of authorized texts. Are we to dispense with the notion of a tradition of excellence embodied in a canon of authorized texts? Or, rather than abandon the whole idea of a canon, do we instead encourage a reconstruction of these texts to inform a common culture? (1996, ix)

Whilst we are interpreting Foucault (through Hekman), I note that I cited him previously as writing that "history is that which transforms documents into monuments" (1972, 8). History, of course, deals with temporality in that it deals with the past. This brings us to the most indispensible feature of a canon, *which is its temporality*. Time, or the *longue duree* is what qualifies a text for entry into a canon, be it politics, or literary studies, or cultural interpretations of what the character of Homer Simpson represents—although a canon formation around the latter might need to wait a few more years yet. The aphorism "it stands the test of time" is apposite here. Time is not only a prerequisite for canonicity; it is also what gives it durability, legitimacy, and institutionalization. Without critical scrutiny, canonical works can easily become the expressions of elite power. Time can then give them the aura of infallibility or unquestionability. Such works are effectively ideas that are held in place through the repression or exclusion of others. Notwithstanding the positive and negative effects of the canon, the fact still remains, *canonicity works*—it works on the mind of the individual, it works on *dispositif* of institutions, on cultures, and on world-orientations.

Social acceleration, however, is fatal to the functioning of the canon, be it a canon in the service of elite purposes or democratic ones. This does not mean that the canon and its works must be set in stone—to become the "monuments" of power that Foucault warns of. Since the beginning of the period of Enlightenment especially, the world and its technological, social, cultural, economic, and political processes have been marked by dynamism. To look to immovable ideas as our epistemological anchors in a rapidly changing world simply would not work, because the cognitive dissonance would be so great. Canonical ideas and canonical works must reflect our social dynamism, but in a way—and at a pace—that fosters (or at least does not endanger) relative stability. And so just as works and ideas should not be "admitted" to the canon immediately, neither should they be "evicted" arbitrarily and with equal rapidity. This has occurred in our recent past, in a time where ideas were far more hotly disputed than they are today. We saw it, for example, in the USSR in the 1930s where suddenly Leon Trotsky vanished from the Marxist-revolutionary canon. It was apparent also in early Nazi Germany where bonfires were made of the writings of Jews and communists and democrats. Such abuses of canonicity, however, served mainly to illuminate the structures of dictatorship and its intuitive realization that monopoly over knowledge and information (what constitutes the canon) are vital for the maintenance of power. However, the dynamics of an ideal-type process of canonicity, in a world where it functions as Said, Hekman, and others envisaged that it should, is a dialectical and temporal one, between the canon and the people (the culture) that it informs. Let us unpack this process.

When thinking about the canon of major works of literature and works of political economy, philosophy, and so on, we are struck first of all by the fact that it comes to us from the past. This is not to say that it is dead or inert—but that it is diachronic, something that is inherited, and that this diachronicity has its own temporal depth that can range over the short, medium, or long term. These differing temporal depths are the complex variable that gives the process of canon formation its life. How might this work? Well it can be posited that the works of, say, William Shakespeare and J. K. Rowling may be said to be part of a western literary canon. Similarly, the writings of Thomas Hobbes, for example, would be a part of the canon of western political philosophy, alongside a rather more contemporary theorist such as John Rawls. The former in each comparison reside in the deeper temporal depth (the *longue duree*) whereas the latter are only just beginning (and tentatively in the case of Rowling) to enter the consciousness that helps direct our cultural orientations. Time is what gives them eventual canonical status, and time is what causes them eventually to endure. But this is not a one-way process. The canon and its content must always be provisional. And so this would mean that even Shakespeare might someday fall into obscurity and irrelevancy. And conversely, it may be possible (and necessary) that the now semi-obscure works of someone such as Hobbes will be resurrected and analyzed and ventilated across a much wider domain in order to gauge his significance for our own time.

Works may drop out of the canon through lack of relevance. For instance, hardly anyone reads Hilaire Belloc or G. K. Chesterton anymore, but these writers were immensely popular and influential around the turn of the nineteenth century. Alternatively works may steadily gain in prestige and authority over the years. One can easily see this in novelists such as E. M. Forster and D. H. Lawrence, who were living contemporaries of Belloc and Chesterton. Moreover, old works may be discovered, such as the *Epic of Gilgamesh*, and new technologies open up the possibility for whole new forms of canon, be it film (French New Wave), music (jazz, rock n' roll), architecture (neo-classicism, modernism), and so on. These canonical shifts are detectible to only those who take the trouble to look. Post-modernism and the apathy that it has spread in respect of the idea of the canon mean that the canon continues to exist but that its engagement with a democratic public sphere public is close to non-existent. Once again, canonicity works, but for it to work as a positive set of orientations for culture and society it would have to function on the basis that it is the public that must determine the content and depth and span of the canon, and it is the canon that will in turn determine the broad orientations of the public culture.

Just as important as this temporal analysis of the canon, are the temporal rhythms that stem from the dynamics of the technologies involved in canon formation itself. Here I recall previous arguments on the entimement of technologies themselves that we saw in Chapter 2, coupled with what Regis Debray called the "material forms" that give ideas their existence (2007, 5). The "material forms" that constituted the ideas that gave us the world as we know it today, and the underlying basis of Enlightenment and modernity is, of course, the book. It is the circulation of the written word on paper that formed what Debray saw as the principle "communicative networks" that brought ideas toward their material reality (2007, 5). From this insight we can say that without paper-based communicative technologies there would have been no technological basis for a functioning canon—and without a functioning canon (brought to the world through the network of the "Republic of Letters") there would have been no Enlightenment (and no modernity and capitalism as we know it). In the Enlightenment-based canon formation, the fixing of ideas in time and space on paper preserved their order of words (if not the interpretation of them). These were disseminated and circulated by eighteenth- and nineteenth-century technologies (as we have also seen) that were still paced and rhythmed at speeds (albeit always accelerating) that enabled humans to not only conceive of Enlightenment and modernity and their potentials—but also to go on to *create these* through the same material processes that still underpin the social, cultural, and political forms of the (western) world today.

The Enlightenment is all that we have. However, its canon has been obscured through digital information and has been dissipated by network-driven speed. Chronic distraction increasingly renders stable ideas inaccessible. The time needed to revive them, to regenerate them, to relegate some, and to promote others, does not exist for the billions of Internet-connected drones who comprise (or should comprise) the public sphere. The idea and the practice of the canon (any canon) in a network society with its digital flows of ephemeral information, is impossible. But a canon is necessary as never before. And so what we need in the face of the digital onslaught is a temporal appreciation of *conservation* and a political ethic of *conservatism*.

Conserving the Canon: A Necessary Pause for Thought

Conservatism is the antidote for chronic distraction. But what kind of conservatism are we talking about? I think it is very simple—it's the kind of conservatism (political, cultural, intellectual, technological) that first and foremost seeks to conserve that which works and has a positive and democratic and inclusive function. By "conserve" I mean to hold in time, to pause upon an idea or an issue or problem and think about it, debate it, and then reassess it in the light of other relevant perspectives. It is a cliché that is repeated often in surveys on political opinions that runs something like: "don't ask me, I've got no time for politics." And it is true. Increasing numbers of individuals turn away from politics and any practical political commitment because they have no time to spend on what they have deemed (rationally enough) to be irrelevant to the getting of a job, the paying of the mortgage, and the putting of food on the table. Of course, to stop and actually consider the problems of getting an job, paying for a house, and having enough food for the family is as political is it can be. But the personal issues always seem to be more immediate, and the "solutions" usually seem to be immediate and imperative as well: that to say, to find a job, to get the money, to pay the mortgage, etc.

It takes actual time (the unfolding of duration, the passing of hours and days and weeks and years) for the more fundamental issues to be located and uncovered. And of course this pathway, if chosen, in addition to being fully time-consuming, depends upon the ability to identify the appropriate information: the books and essays, the people, the examples and processes and debates that are able to illuminate the "politics" of our personal situation, the "politics" of our society, and the "politics" of our wider world. But information, or more precisely, its digital and commodified and accelerated and networked "new morphology" (1996, 469) as Castells termed it, is robbing us of our own time and depriving us, as a consequence, of the capacity being able to penetrate the reality of our world. The tyranny of the imperative, of the immediate and the urgent are at the core of our neoliberalized global economy. Not only must we exist on the surface of lived experience, but also we are also condemned, through technological speed and social acceleration, to experience overstimulation and chronic distraction—a double negative that robs us, individually of the knowledge that gives us power and agency and opportunity. The power and the agency such as we might have is only exercisable within the confines of the neoliberal system, a system that has become so deeply engrained, and has so depleted our cognitive faculties, we are no longer able to think of alternatives to it. Such a calamitous situation, as Perry Anderson has noted, is unprecedented in the history of modern western thought—thought that today is seemingly rootless and canonless (Anderson 2000, 17).

Whilst researching for this chapter, I mentioned to a German colleague the value that I had found in the work of Gehlen. "But he is a conservative!" came the rather brusque retort. But that is precisely his value. Here we need to be clear what we mean by "conservative." Mainstream media, in North America especially, use the term to label someone, anyone who is affiliated with the Republican Party, who is against "big government," who is for fewer taxes, who believes in the magic of the free market, who views the "individual" as the primary social unit—and so on. The economic and cultural whirligig of globalization and its constant "creative destruction" of whatever capitalism is able to colonize and squeeze dry, is all of a piece with the background noise of the "conservative" worldview. However, conservatism in this widely understood sense is ironically all about motion and striving and struggling and competition. There is precious little, if anything, about conserving—unless it is the personal vested interest.

Clearly there is a disjuncture between the "conservative" described here, and the conservatism that my German friend imputed into Gehlen's work.

Gehlen was indeed a political conservative, but this conservatism stems from a much longer historical lineage than modern-day conservatives such as, say, George W. Bush or Sarah Palin or the faddish Tea Party in the USA. This historical, or classical conservatism connects with its roots, as does so much of the logic that guides this book, in the European Enlightenment. Perhaps it has been expressed most widely through the writings of Edmund Burke, the so-called "father of conservatism" who lived between 1729 and 1797. The defining political feature of Burke's life was the French Revolution (1789-1799) and his most famous treatise, *Reflections on the Revolution* in France (first published in 1790) emerged from his considerations of these tumultuous events. Much has been written about Burke's arguments against the Revolution, however what shines through clearly in almost all of his *Reflections* is a temporalized perspective that constantly compares *agitation* and *effervescence* with such traits as *prudence* and the need to *suspend judgment*. Consider the following, a typical Burkean paragraph that is speaking of the need to resist speed and hold fast to reason, to reflection, to necessary institutions, before forming an opinion on the nature and the consequences of the contemporaneous French *événements*:

> When I see the spirit of liberty in action, I see a strong principle at work; and this, for a while, is all I can possibly know of it. The wild gas, the fixed air is plainly broke loose: but we ought to suspend our judgments until the first effervescence is a little subsided, till the liquor is cleared, and until we see something deeper than the agitation of the troubled and frothy surface. I must be tolerably sure, before venturing publicly to congratulate men on a blessing, that they have really received one. Flattery corrupts both the receiver and the giver; and adulation is not of more service to the people than to kings. I should therefore suspend my congratulations on the new liberty of France, until I was informed how it had been combined with government; with public force; with the discipline and obedience of armies; with the collection of an effective and well-distributed revenue; with the solidity for property; with peace in order; with civil and social manners. All these (in their way) are good things too; and, without them, liberty is not a benefit while it lasts, and is not likely to continue long. The effect of liberty to individuals is, that they may do what they please: we ought to see what it will please them to do, before we risk congratulations, which

may soon be turned into complaints. Prudence would dictate this in the case of separate insulated private men; but liberty, when men act in bodies, is power. Considerate people, before they declare themselves, will observe the use which is made of power; and particularly of so trying a thing as new power in new persons, of whose principals, tempers, and dispositions, they have little or no experience, and in situations where those who appear the most stirring in the scene may possibly not be the real movers. (Burke 1790/1986, 90–91)

The paragraph is rather long, but I make no apologies (how could I?). It is necessary because it is useful. It drips with a temporal sensibility—with an unstated but undeniable warning on the risks posed by acting too fast and not pondering on the consequences of our actions. It is no coincidence, but not often noted, that Burke titles his book "reflections." The term is almost dialectical, a kind of mirror of reason, where the gaze and the self and the world combine to pause and "reflect" and consider what it is that one sees looking back at you. There is nothing static in Burke's *Reflections*, however. It is highly dynamic in its engagement with effervescence and speed and the "real movers." The imagery it conveys are those of momentum, transformation, and change—but with the underlying principle that change must be managed and organized. As Burke himself put it: "A state without the means of some change is without the means of its conservation" (1790/1986, 90).

Revolution (and the actions of revolutionaries) constitutes a leap into the unknown, a thrusting toward opportunities of unknown dimensions that must somehow be grasped. For some such as Lenin, this was the *only way* that revolutions were possible. Lenin and Burke's contemporary in France, Robespierre, did not deal in canonical works that had stood the test of time and were seen to have practical and positive implications for society. Lenin especially, based his views on abstract ideas, principally, of course, those of Marx. What this necessitated, though, was a conscious sweeping away of the old world and leaping headlong into a future, the nature of which only the revolutionaries themselves were certain. This logic too is deeply temporal in that is denies all that is past, and from the perspective of an evanescent and ever-shifting present they throw the dice of fate toward tomorrow. Burke took his own measure of this accelerated thrusting of events, the act of certainty from the zealot without the pause for reflection or calculation of consequences, when he wrote in a letter dated March 1790, to A. J. F. DuPont:

> I have no great opinion of that sublime abstract, metaphysic reversionary, contingent humanity, which in *cold blood* can subject the *present time* and those whom we *daily see and converse with* to immediate calamities in favour of the *future and uncertain* benefit of persons *who only exist in idea.* (1790/1986, 23) (emphases in original)

Gehlen's conservatism is Burkean in its recognition of the need, the vital need, for structures that act in the same way that Burke sees as evident in, for example, the U.S. Constitution. The American Revolution was a conservative one that for Burke was measured and ordered in that it had—to use Derrida's phrase—the "indispensible guardrails" that were the Constitutional texts consciously held up to be the ideas and principles upon which the modern American society was to be constructed. Gehlen's philosophical anthropology provides us for a means of understanding our species and how, as "unfinished" creatures, we come into the world susceptible to distraction and overstimulation from "a mass of impressions which flood in on him and with which he must cope" (Gehlen, 36) and so therefore need to develop such structures, psychic as much a physical that allow us to lead a life instead of being driven by instinct as are other creatures. This recapping of Gehlen's utility bring us back to a consideration of the canon as the textual basis for the kind of cognitive structure that is indispensible to our species in order to avoid distraction and overstimulation. Here we can synthesize Gehlen's structures with Burke's malleable conservatism, the necessary "means for change" that he argued that it must always have.

It was noted before that to look to immovable ideas (such as contained in a canon) is actually of little use in a culture that is expressed increasingly through social acceleration. This is because the two processes cannot easily connect or synchronize. However, in the actual context of our social acceleration and the chronic distraction that it engenders, the ideas themselves are not so much "immovable" as "invisible." Information overload, the neoliberal promotion of instrumentalized information, the rapidly growing and accelerating webs of data that envelop us like a cloud of digital fog, make the "indispensible guardrails" disappear. Whether we suffer a disconnection from our cognitive center through the dissonance emerging from the seeming irrelevancy of immovable ideas, or from the inability to see those ideas clearly and reflectively because of our networked reality, the effect is the same: we cannot effectively be in contact with the ideas and narratives that have constructed the very world we live in. And so we live afflicted by a kind of cognitive alienation within which, as Adorno and Horkheimer (1998, xii) phrased it, "thought becomes a commodity," and as a commodity finds its echo only in the valorized spaces and times of the neoliberal networked economy.

However, if we blow away the fog of commodification and apply a brake to the hurtling logics of distraction and dissonance—by stopping to read and to reflect—we are able to make the invisible visible. I want to end this penultimate chapter with a short example of the continuing existence and relevance of canonical works; works that express ideas that are so part of what we are as both individuals and as members of a society (national and global) that we do not even consider them (when we consider them at all) as works of canon.

In a recent edition of *Foreign Affairs*, a flagship publication of conservative politics and thought, there appeared an interesting essay that ostensibly has little to do with the arguments I put forward here. It is titled "Conflict of Cooperation?" and was written by Richard K. Betts, a researcher in war and peace studies in the USA, and is a revisiting of the influential political ideas of Samuel Huntingdon, Francis Fukuyama, and John Mearsheimer. It is a good article as far as it goes, and in what it sets itself to do, and follows faithfully in the tradition of the journal's concerns and perspectives. However, it was the essay's opening line that caught my eye. It reads:

> Practical men, who believe themselves to be quite exempt from any intellectual influence, are usually the slave of some defunct economist', John Maynard Keynes once wrote. Politicians and pundits view the world through instincts and assumptions rooted in some philosopher's Big Idea. Some ideas are old and taken for granted throughout society. For most Americans, it is the ideas of the liberal tradition, from John Locke to Woodrow Wilson, that shape their thinking about foreign policy. The sacred concepts of freedom, individualism, and cooperation are so ingrained in U.S. political culture that most people assume them to be the natural order of things, universal values that people everywhere would embrace if given the chance. (Betts 2010)

Keynes may have been a bit too polemical in respect of the dismal science, but his broader point that no one can have a view from nowhere is essentially sound. Often it is simply the case that we do not know how or why we "know" something. Betts goes on to make this valuable point in respect of the "Liberal tradition" and its "sacred concepts." The functioning of invisible power through the invisible structures of tradition is precisely what the process of canonicity achieves. Canonical ideas from people such as John Locke, David Hume, Montesquieu, Tom Paine, Thomas Jefferson—and even Karl Marx (as negative specter in liberal capitalist tradition) seep into the political consciousness (and unconsciousness) of millions in the western democracies. Their democratic and radical "spirit" oversees every election—from the humble multitude that contest council offices across a nation, to the political summits of power in the White House or Downing Street. When drawn upon, this spirit and its ideas can still have far-reaching motivating effects. For example, in the absence of any weapons of mass destruction in Iraq after the invasion of that country in 2003, and in the context of a political inability to *take the time* to make the detailed arguments about why the removal of a Caligula-like regime was justifiable in its own right, George Bush, Tony Blair, and other leaders resorted to canonicity and told us that the West was "democratizing" the Middle East. It was "fixing" Iraq, by moulding it to be more like "us." This was Edward Said's Orientalist perspective written up for a new phase of history, to be sure, but the point remains that the wars in Iraq and Afghanistan could not have been sold in the way that they were (and continue to be) without drawing from the shining canonical tradition that has made the West what it is—but which few know little if anything about (including our leaders).

The very next line from Betts' article, however, steers him away from his sensible musings on the nature of ideas in society, and slides him toward cliché about the capacities of the public sphere. It reads: "In times of change, people wonder more consciously about how the world works" (Betts 2010). If he means the majority of people, well fact they do not, and they never have done. The "people" who do the thinking are the people who write for *Foreign Affairs,* or who pen the Op-Eds in the *New York Times,* or *Die Zeit,* or *Le Monde,* etc. In other words, it is the elites who do the thinking that matters—just as it was in the eighteenth century, so it is today. The difference between the Enlightenment North Atlantic "Republic of Letters" and today's strata of opinion-shapers is that the former debated ideas, whereas the latter mainly promote ideologically slanted assertions. Indeed, in the absence of a canon of ideas to consciously look to, to hold up and test against the present context, we "slave" not under any "defunct economist" as Keynes imagined, but under a virtually unchallenged hegemony of neoliberal assumptions. We are by now familiar with these declarations regarding the "reality" of the world: the capitalist free market is the natural and most efficient state of human affairs; the acquisition of individual material wealth is both "right" and "natural" as well as a justifiable end in itself; and neoliberalism, despite its short-comings, is the least worst form of social organization and therefore to court alternatives would be to run the risk of social catastrophe or political dictatorship. Critically underscoring these assertions is the political assertion that they are all compatible with democracy.

What we get in terms of a public sphere of public values and morality is a public vacuum. Ideas that have not stood the test of time (and the ones just listed certainly have not) cannot be said to be canonical. But nonetheless these are the shallow concepts that are now in the ascendancy. The social (and social democratic) paucity of the current hegemony has been made painfully clear in the wake of the global financial crisis. However, our disengagement from the more solid structuring ideas that could give insight into the economic malaise, and signal possible pathways from it, means that an empty hegemony still holds in the teeth of the crises of its own making. Traditions of social and moral responsibility, ideas that have come to us from Aristotle, and were refined in respect of our relationship with technology in the works of Hans Jonas (1985), have become invisible, or are scattered and fragmentary to the extent that they no longer have any significant conscious effect upon our present-day thinking and actions. Networked capitalism and political neoliberalism—and its chronic symptom of distraction—has made us a Know Nothing society that does know that it does not know, and is becoming morally and ethically bankrupt as a result.

As I write this we pass through the third year of a global economic crisis created by laissez-faire neoliberalism, and brought to fruition by the corporate banking sector. Thus far in the major Anglo Saxon economies, *no one* has claimed moral or ethical or even practical responsibility for what they have done. Millions have lost jobs, homes, and savings and yet our politicians either look the other way as banks cheerfully carry on as before—or they loudly applaud them for doing so. The dignity and humility that goes with social responsibility has likewise evaporated in our networked capitalist society. That there is an acute lack of shame in the personages of our corporate and political leaders is so because they live in a culture of short-termism, where the past is not mined for its canonical lessons on how to live a good and virtuous and dignified life. The moral philosopher Alasdair Macintyre well understood what happens when the connection between government/corporate capitalism and the moral compass of the community is broken. In his *After Virtue* he wrote that:

> When...the relationship of government to the moral community is put in question both by the changed nature of government and the lack or moral consensus in society, it becomes difficult any longer to have any clear, simple, and teachable conception[s]... (2007, 254)

Macintyre is a Christian who believes in many of the precepts of the original canon, the Bible. One does not have to be Christian, however, to appreciate that some of its canonical principles have helped shape our Western moral community. For example, in Jeremiah 6:15 it says "Were they ashamed when they had committed abomination? Nay, they were not at all ashamed, neither could they blush." This ancient value judgment describes well our post-modern lack of capacity for embarrassment. It is a lacuna that stems directly from our inability to know both our world and ourselves, and its logic follows two parallel paths. On one path travel the millions who unabashedly and unreflectively crave the consumerist life and whose ultimate goal is the attainment of celebrity of whatever kind. We see this in our fascination (and identification?) with those who will do anything to get themselves noticed on television in shows like Big Brother and other reality shows, where the faculty for self-reflection and embarrassment are left at the studio doors. The other track is traveled by those at the top of the social pile, the Wall Street or City of London traders and allied professions, who look in the shaving mirror each morning with an untroubled gaze. Making money from money in the abstract circuits of the digital flows of the capitalist economy appears to them as unproblematic—as does, for example, the existence of the current British "Austerity cabinet" wherein eighteen of its twenty-three membership are millionaires, but can nonetheless *vote democratically* to impose drastic funding cuts on the vast mass of its society in order to pay for the economic crisis (Milland and Warren 2010).

Leaders and led no longer take enough responsibility because we function in a context that we do not really recognize any more. We have little time to look to the canons that shaped our society, or to ourselves, or to each other for answers because speed, information overload, and the chronic distraction of everyday life ensures that we tend to look primarily to what is at hand, to that which is most urgent—the increasingly unexpected demands that network society throws our way. But the Know Nothing mind is not the mind of the moron. It is a necessary effect of the over-stimulated and overloaded and distracted mind. Our minds, as Carr argues in *The Shallows*, are becoming rewired for brevity and for speed in order to cope (at least partially) with the demands of the destabilized world. This is the rewiring of the consciousness and modes of thinking that has created modernity and its modes of being in the world, modes that are being dissipated, instrumentalized, or simply forgotten. Carr's arguments and my own are being bolstered daily with evidence from the lab, some of which we have noted already. The most recent confirmation of the inexorable trend toward chronic distraction came across my desk only today, in the form of a *New York Times* article. Titled "Growing Up Digital, Wired for Distraction" it is concerned with exactly what I am arguing in these pages. It begins:

> By all rights, Vishal, a bright 17-year-old, should already have finished the book, Kurt Vonnegut's *Cat's Cradle*, his summer reading assignment. But he has managed 43 pages in two months. (Richtel 2010)

The article continues by relating that, unsurprisingly for this demographic, this youth prefers Facebook and Youtube and other forms of digital media. Indeed, Vishal has a temporal justification for his digital habits. "On Youtube you can get a whole story in six minutes...a book takes so long. I prefer the immediate gratification" (Richtel 2010). The article notes that the so-called "digital generation" face profound new challenges in terms of being able to focus and learn. It goes on to quote a researcher at Harvard Medical School who says that "The worry is we're raising a generation of kids in front of screens whose brains are going to be wired differently" (Richtel 2010). This echoes Carr's concerns in *The Shallows*. The evidence mounts. But the interpretation of a generational "problem" of "dumbing down" is a misreading. The clinical evidence shows that the "rewired" brain is a neurophysiological problem, but it is one that affects all of us. Moreover, the rewiring does not make us "stoopid" or "shallow" as Carr characterizes it—it makes us different kinds of people, different kinds of thinkers from those who developed cognitively and intellectually on the basis of the fixed word on paper.

We have become *post-modern* in the fullest sense of that term. We are moving beyond the cognitively wired human being that came to its fullest potential (in terms of what the written word and the reading of the written word could achieve) somewhere around the 1970s. By that time the time of the clock had exhausted its temporal usefulness for a crisis-ridden economic system that had no alternative other than to accelerate beyond that which rigid clock time could provide for. Computers would digitalize our words into information and information, soon enough, would generate a network time sensibility that allows a typical student less than half a page of Kurt Vonnegut per day. In such a context, ideas of canonicity and the value of the canon for knowing our world and for changing our world for a basis of agency—have little chance. Chronic distraction and the loss of contact with a living and dynamic canon, however, are only a part of it. Let us finish with a recapitulation of the thesis, a examination of the political dimensions of chronic distraction, and then try to identify some points of light that might give hope in what is, I feel, only the beginning of a darkening tunnel.

7

Considerations on the Prospects for Political Change

Do I Still Have Your Undivided Attention?

Maybe not. Going to the "back of the book" to quickly capture its gist is a contagious symptom of our age of distraction, one which most of us exhibit at one time or another, so let me briefly reiterate my main points before moving to some more speculative reasoning on the malaise in order to consider what might be done.

Time is key to my thesis of distraction. Time as a socially produced and experienced phenomenon is a deeply embedded essence of what it is to be human. Over countless human generations, the rhythms of time have functioned as an interaction between individuals and collectives and their natural environments. The beat of the human heart is an individual rhythm, as is the cadence of the breath; rhythms can be coordinated across groups of individuals when they come together to share and create times, such as the commemoration of events, or punctual times like birthdays and weddings, as well as rights of passage into adulthood, etc. Times such as these have been the temporal foundation of human culture making for thousands of years. These biological and social rhythms have also synchronized with the rhythms of nature since the beginnings of our species. Individuals and groups live in and through the rhythms of the seasons, with the rising and setting of the sun, with the changing phases of the moon, and so on. Time, it is clear, is in us, and we experience the rhythms of nature through our unavoidable need to exist within its cosmic temporalities.

If humans are fundamentally temporal, then so too are we essentially technological. Anthropology tells us that as we define our tools, our tools in turn shape us. Through the dialectic between human temporality and human-made technology, we have "entimed" the tools that we invent and use. The tools themselves reflect our individual and social temporal capacities. And so the microchip, say, reflects a

171

certain electronically driven speed of society, just as the invention of a flint axe, reflected a society that was rhythmed fully by biological and environmental temporalities. The former example suggests a highly complex process that perceives a growing dominion over the environment and its temporalities, whereas the latter expressed the basic capacity of ancient peoples to use and interact with what is (literally) to hand.

It is here that we connect these insights into biological–ecological rhythming with what Walter Ong saw as the most important tool ever invented: writing. As a tool, the initial concept and practice of writing reflected our (then very basic) temporal and technological capacities in ancient Babylonia, the place of writing's invention. The physicality of writing, the size and portability of their dimensions, the clay tablets or papyrus inscribed by cut reeds or bamboo, or scrolls giving way to the codex and later the mass printed book, corresponded to (and was shaped by) our human dimensions and temporal capacities deriving from the biological and ecological dialectic. The actual practice of reading and writing was likewise time-loaded with this same biological and ecological rhythming—or more simply expressed: we can only read so fast and write so fast until the cognitive process begins to break down.

The breakthrough technology of writing was what got civilization off the ground. It gave us the capacity to organize our world, to create knowledge and disseminate knowledge, and to make possible the fixing in time and space of new ideas. The stability of words on paper enabled the testing and debating of abstract concepts, to narrate our lives as stories and created the metanarratives or the big stories that became the basis for religious thought and historiography and philosophy and science, and so on. The creation of writing and the acting of the products of writing on the world through reading and more writing wired our brain in a specific way (if we deduce from what cognitive science tells us today). But this occurred also in a way that was random and could not be planned. In other words, the temporal rhythms inscribed in the technology of writing also inscribed the rhythm and pace of the worlds that it itself created. Technology, however, has always developed. Either a technology is replaced by some kind of agreed improvement in its functioning, or else a completely new technology appears to serve a human need. For most of human history, however, the pace of this development was relatively slow: never static, but also never systematic. Crucially, this slower and non-systematic pace did not deplete the human capacity to synchronize with the "speed up in life" if any, that a new technology (say the wheel) brought to our actioning on the world. Indeed, the relatively slow pace of technological development for most of human history was a boon to our cognitive capacities and our ability to continue to construct our world.

Technologies proliferated and human societies became more multifaceted. This growing complexity (and acceleration) created the need for a more rational and manageable civilization. The clock, a technology that had been in existence since seventh-century China, began to find a more widely practical role in a late-Medieval Europe that was entering a new level of technological and economic sophistication. A clock time reckoning began to order ever-widening realms of European society and this acted as a spur to further technological developments on a more systematic basis as societies became more interconnected. Machine and writing converged with the invention of the Gutenberg press. Ideas could now begin to spread more widely. Momentum spurred yet more momentum and the period of the European Renaissance thus created the basis (cultural, scientific, technological, and philosophical) for what became the Enlightenment and the concomitant rise of capitalism and industrialism. Technical, philosophical, and cultural knowledge dissemination gradually became systematic and followed a machine logic in a burgeoning capitalist and industrializing context made possible by the rationalizing and coordinating of time production enabled by the clock.

It can be seen in retrospect that the rise of the Enlightenment and the spread of industrialism represented the high point of what humanity could achieve through cognitive capacities that had been brought about through the acquired effects of the interaction of biological and ecological time and the technology of writing. Clock time, machine-based writing, and a machine-oriented industrialism (all driven by the revolutionary processes of capitalist competition) set us on a new ecological and temporal plane. This not only stimulated our increasingly elaborate societies to new levels of complexity, but also began to draw upon the reserves of cognitive and temporal capacity that our anciently wired brains possessed. Modernity, in spite of all its advances, was in fact a process of ever-diminishing returns in respect of our capacity to control it and direct its trajectory and our ability to synchronize with its increasing acceleration. We managed to keep up with the pace of this logic until the 1970s.

A New Information Enlightenment?

In the age of distraction, destabilized words have become so much digital chaff. The billions of gigabytes of text that flow and flood our networked society are far too much to contend with or even attempt to synchronize with. Even the most important words and texts, those comprising *the political texts which describe our economies and our conflicts and our flagging democratic structures*, get no privileged position for us to hold and reflect upon in our digital media (Davies 2008). Politics and economics blend with entertainment and sports to form a bit torrent of information. In his book *You are not a Gadget*, Jaron Lanier observes that: "It takes only a tiny group of engineers to create technology that can shape the entire future of human experience with incredible speed" (2010, 6). This has already occurred, and "human experience" is now shaped by technology's own logic of competition. Its colonization by the market means that our experience of information is at the same time alienating as it is attractive—but less and less is the experience informative.

Some understanding of politics, or at least an appreciation of its intrinsic importance, is perhaps the most essential key to a life of active and fulfilling and transformative citizenship. A lack of understanding is to leave oneself, or one's class and community, at the mercy of abstract forces such as those that emanate from Wall Street, Silicon Valley, and Pennsylvania Avenue—or their analogs across the world. We can see the extent of the political dissonance caused by overload, speed, and distraction in the case of the website WikiLeaks that emerged in 2006. WikiLeaks uploads to the Internet, secret or sensitive government documents that have been leaked to them in order to allow the world to view and judge their contents in the spirit of "freedom of information." In November 2010, WikiLeaks, in collaboration with five prominent "serious" newspapers from around the world released what one of the newspapers, the *Guardian*, dubbed "The U.S. Embassy Cables." These comprised over 250,000 documents that contained largely unexpurgated communications between Washington and its embassies across the world, many of them in sensitive regions such as the Middle East, Russia, and China. In a supporting piece to the *Guardian's* phased release of what it judged to be the most important of these documents, there appeared on the first day of their release, on the November 29, an article by Heather Brooke, titled "WikiLeaks: The revolution has begun—and it will be digitised" (2010). In it she opined that "The web is changing the way in which people relate to power, and politics will have no choice but to adapt too." Brooke goes on to argue that the age of secretive diplomacy and pre-1914 style intrigues conducted by elites seems set to change through sites such as WikiLeaks. This is moot. But the article ends with a sensible and sober injunction, and contains a time framing with which Edmund Burke might well have agreed:

> This is a revolution, and all revolutions create fear and uncertainty. Will we move to New Information Enlightenment or will the backlash from those who seek to maintain control no matter the cost lead us to a new totalitarianism? What happens in the next five years will define the future of democracy for the next century, so it would be well if our leaders responded to the current challenge with an eye on the future. (Brooke 2010)

In respect of a "New Information Enlightenment," the *immediate* aftermath of the WikiLeaks *exposé* was not promising. After the phased release of the documents, the issues raised (and any political hopes that were raised) fell back into the distractive miasma. Indeed, the "issues" barely got above the swirl of news, sport, and celebrity in the USA where the *New York Times* front-paged with the WikiLeaks trove. The *Times'* lead story on November 29, 2010 online edition was titled "Leaked Cables Depict a World Guessing About North Korea" (Sanger 2010). Well, it seems that the world was not guessing about this particular issue on that particular day. In the USA at least, the Google Trends website—a site which measures Internet trends through key search words—did not even rate the WikiLeaks "revelations" in its top twenty for that day. That penultimate November day was in fact top-billed by the death of the actor Leslie Nielsen, followed by an consumer interest in the "best cyber Monday deals 2010," and in third place was evidence of an apparent thirst for information on "bear gall bladder uses" (Google Trends 2010).

An effect of economic acceleration is that in the context of a global media business they reduce potentially important political information to fleeting moments that must soon move over for the next headline story (Davies 2008). The short shelf life of news has been a feature of the media for many years, but when this is compounded by digital speed and a myriad of other distractions and imperatives in our time-compressed lives, there is a drastically diminished chance that political information will "stick" and have traction with readers.

This was confirmed in early 2011 when the *Guardian* quietly carried a report that cited a U.S. State Department official who stated that though some of the WikiLeaks revelations were "embarrassing" for some, they "had little concrete impact on policy" (Harris 2011).

Compare this, if you will, to a big news story from the 1970s, a political narrative from a very different time, with a very different speed of economy and very different speeds of news media. In 1971 there occurred another leak of secret documents. These were officially called "United States–Vietnam Relations, 1945–1967: A Study Prepared by the Department of Defense." History knows them as "The Pentagon Papers." Photocopied and sent to the *New York Times* by military analyst Daniel Ellsberg, these detailed the disastrous consequences of the Kennedy and Johnson Administration's policies in South East Asia, policies that ran directly counter to what the government had been telling its own people. As R. W. Apple later put it, the Pentagon Papers: "demonstrated, among other things, that the Johnson Administration had systematically lied, not only to the public but also to Congress, about a subject of transcendent national interest and significance" (1996). Apple goes on to show that the publication of the forty-three-volume *Papers* and the victory the *Times* won in the Supreme Court in a dispute over the attempt by the government of Richard Nixon to suppress them, was a major victory for democracy and the freedom of information: "The Nixon Administration responded (to this defeat) by creating the Plumbers unit (so-called because they were to deal with leaks like that of the papers). That step in turn led to the Watergate scandal and ultimately to Nixon's resignation" (1996). Nixon's resignation may have been the most salient effect of the Pentagon Papers, but their actual contents, as they were being debated and reflected upon, stabilized into political knowledge that rocked the U.S. political establishment to its core, lending added impetus to the anti-Vietnam War feelings that were growing in that country and across the world. The print-based processes of democracy and the freedom of information were conducted over *years* and this contrasts starkly with the speed and the (non) effects of the WikiLeaks that characterize political public debate and accountability—and the actual effects of freedom of information in our networked age.

The general inadequacy of WikiLeaks as a modality for the promotion of democracy has been considered in a thoughtful article that appeared in the *New York Review of Books* after the brief fuss had died down. The article, by Christian Caryl, also makes the historical comparison with the Pentagon Papers, and views the impact of the Papers as far more consequential. This article, like so many other analyses of politics and ICTs make the temporal point explicitly, but it is stated as a matter of fact, not as a key element of the whole problem and so is therefore never followed up systematically. Caryl makes the point that "there is simply no way that any editor, however well-meaning, can make an informed judgement about...vast amounts of confidential data" (note that he uses the term "data" and not "information"—much less would he describe it as "knowledge"). Tantalizingly he then moves to the central (but underrated) point:

> I wonder whether preaching restraint [on the seeming free-flow of digital information] can have much effect. The technology has outpaced the ethics, and it seems justified to ask whether the ethics can ever catch up again. (Caryl 2011, 27)

The problem is that he does not ask, and so the issue of WikiLeaks, and the myriad issues that emanate from an outpaced ethics and outpaced politics cannot be viewed with proper account taken for the temporal dimension.

If we say that the Enlightenment and the substance of the politics that it has given us are of a certain human- and environmental-centered temporality, this means that the "New Information Enlightenment" that Heather Brooke posited above, as a possibility for information that is free, is actually an impossibility. The temporal logics of "new information" and the substance of Enlightenment thinking are counterposed to each other. However, the opposition is invisible unless one makes the temporal dynamics salient.

Indeed this suggests that the invisibility of the temporal dynamic of politics is itself another political problem. It is a problem because in much of the popular and academic literature on the subject of new media and its political potential is upbeat, and views the conjuncture as one of immanent positive possibilities for the creation of a "new politics." There is a growing disjuncture, or de-synchronization that is caused by the very technologies that are purported to offer each of us limitless potential and opportunity in our political processes and in our political culture. For some, such as Clay Shirky the organizational and political potential of the Internet speaks for itself; it is there for the taking if we only reach out and grasp its logic and make it work for us. Shirky is an alumnus of the technophile Electronic Frontier

Foundation (EFF), which is a politically neutral but politically active body that seeks to develop civil liberties and civil rights in cyberspace. Groups such as the EFF view the *logic* of computing unproblematically, and view cyberspace as a terrain for struggle that is essentially no different from the material world.

In his 2008 book *Here Comes Everybody*, Shirky argued that Web 2.0 technologies are a breakthrough in that they mirror human interaction capabilities. Not only they do that, but enhance our communicative structures powerfully. He observes that "We now have communications tools that are flexible enough to match our social capabilities" (20). Just what are our "social capabilities" and their political potential, Shirky does not say. What he does supply are examples of how interconnectivity "works" in supposedly beneficial ways. He relates tales of how close digital connectivity in New York allowed a woman to retrieve her lost mobile phone; and he gives us examples from Thailand and Belarus where flash mobs conducted actions against repressive governments. However, whilst the lost phone example was a traditional narrative of lost-fret-found-happy again, the real politics of change from online such as in Thailand and Belarus are far less easy to mark as successful, even marginally so. Indeed, Shirky states as much himself in a line that seems to obviate the whole point of his book: "whenever you improve a group's ability to communicate internally, you change the things that it's capable of. What the group does with that power is a separate question" (2008, 171). There is a conceptual echo with the work of Shields here. Like Shields, Shirky sees himself as an artist, and has studied fine art. He also founded a theater group, according to Wikipedia, and Wikipedia tells us also, rather intriguingly, that the title "here comes everybody" is a line from Joyce's *Finnegan's Wake* (which it is, because I checked on Google Books). Like Shields and like Joyce, Shirky seems to have a penchant for the non-narrative and non-programmatic. As an artist, this is fine, but if you want to analyze politics, you need to analyze the logic of political power—which is still predicated upon modernist and narratable processes of conflict, resolution, and further conflict arising through immanent contradictions. To do this profitably you need to have a sense of the past, a feeling for the present, and an understanding how these times can structure the future. Joyce was notoriously apolitical. For all his EFF credentials, Shirky comes close to this himself. That is to say, to aver that the politics of communication is "another question," something separate to the instrumental processes of technological connectivity indicates that he either does not really care (like Joyce) or simply does not know.

Shirky compounds the problem of the non-salience of a temporalized perspective in his 2010 book *Cognitive Surplus: Creativity and Generosity in a Connected Age*. Given the concerns of this book, the title immediately attracted my eye. But here again technophilia is the dominant trope. The subject of connectivity in *Here Comes Everybody* is built upon and extended through to a novel concept of cognition. According to Shirky, ICTs and the networked society that they have created has bequeathed to us all a *surplus of time*, which may be used to think creatively and more deeply than we already do. All this freed up time allows us to make use of a "cognitive surplus" that we develop through the alleged efficiencies of computing. In this respect, Shirky's book is a counterpoint to Nicholas Carr's *The Shallows*. Where Carr sees a dearth of time through information technologies, Shirky sees its surfeit. How can this be? How can a networked world create so much time that it becomes a surplus and with the gain in time we will be free to recreate ourselves and recreate the world?

To answer the question, we need to first understand what Shirky means by "free time." The free time he is alluding turns out to be the same "cumulative" free time that accrued to workers in the post-WWII era of Fordist production, where new and efficient production techniques, new machines and growing individual wealth gave people access to "leisure time" in spades. However, as Shirky puts it: "all that free time wasn't yet a cognitive surplus, because we lacked the means to make use of it" (2010). We tended to blow it on watching another new technology of the time, television. As isolated individuals (or in families) we watched a monological box from which nothing creative and positive could come. With connectivity and Web 2.0, however, this free time (and Shirky estimates there are a trillion hours of it stacked up each year in the USA) becomes the raw material from which the potential of cognitive surplus may be extracted in countless differing social and cultural ways. This sounds great, but it is simplistic. As an example of how this works today, Shirky points to Wikipedia where people (tech savvy types mainly) devote some of their cognitive surplus to what is an admittedly impressive and worthy project. But Wikipedia editors are a tiny strata of the connected humanity that is the network society, and on its own is no indicator of any general outbreak of cognitive surplus. Who is to say what the thinking processes of individual Wikipedia editors are, and where they get the time to deploy it in such a way?. Are they as "creative" and "generous" in the way Shirky suggests? How would anyone know?

A possible effect of Shirky's enduring technophilia is that he seems not to have applied any cognitive surplus to the positions he takes in the book in order to work them through systematically to consider the premises and their consequences. We see this in his old-fashioned perspective on free time—a *démodé* that is unusual coming from someone so clearly identified as at the cutting-edge of Internet thinking. As noted above, the free time he imagines is of the 1950s "leisure time" type that tended to be wasted before the Internet came along. But if the social context of free time has changed, and more importantly, if the technological context that created free time has also changed, then free time as a concept surely has also changed? That our experience of free time is no longer so clear cut as is once was is shown in the lack of academic consensus regarding whether we have more of it today or not. Juliet Schor in her landmark study *The Overworked American* (1991) (and not mentioned by Shirky) argued that free time was being drastically reduced due to the demands of a globalizing American economy. She cites data showing that in 1987 workers were spending 163 hours per year more at work than they did in 1969. Robinson and Godbey take the opposite view in their book *Time for Life: The Surprising Way Americans Use their Time* and show data that indicate that workers have in fact *gained* five extra hours since 1966 (1999). Something, obviously, is not quite right here.

The conflicting analyses indicate that Schor, Robinson, and Godbey—and Shirky too—are working with an outmoded idea of free time. The post-WWII idea of free time is a high modernist and Fordist relationship with time. This was a clock time world where work time and leisure time were fairly clearly delineated, with regular hours for most people, and with weekends constituting the bounded block of free time for many in the work force. The rise of neoliberal globalization and the concomitant rise of the ICT revolution changed this relationship with time. Shirky acknowledges that technologies produce time, giving us what he sees as abundance of it that baby boomers wasted in front of endless episodes of *Gilligan's Island* and *Star Trek*. Today, however, we have the technological game-changer in the form of ICTs and these are producing what I have termed network time. Work and leisure time blur into the time of the network that we are increasingly connected to, and the network is a space of commodification that was built specifically for that purpose. New relationships with time do not necessarily produce more free time in the network society, but they do indicate a more concentrated and chronoscopic temporal experience (Hassan 2003). Admittedly we do more and more varied things in a measured hour than our parents could ever have imagined. But this "more" does not make any free time. Rather, doing more simply compresses our experience of time. And this is time that is produced in a highly commodified space, so the uses of that time are preponderantly oriented toward commodified ends such as the consumption of commercialized images, texts, and material goods (when not actually working). Even time that could be seen as genuinely "free"—the time where you can "choose" what to do, the time for browsing and blogging and texting, and so on is time appropriated from you (as value) by websites such as Facebook or Youtube, etc., and on-sold to advertisers (Agger 2010). These social networking spaces, the realm of Shirky's cognitive surplus, are therefore not exactly conducive to thinking creatively and reflectively about alternate worlds. Regrettably, in a context where time has been upgraded to reflect the realities of our networked world, there is little cognitive surplus (that is not expropriated as surplus value) that would allow for our creative and generous human traits to act upon the world in the ways in which Shirky envisages.

The book's advice for connecting cognitive surplus to a political program for change is anyway non-existent—or if not missing, then massively sidestepped. For example, Shirky broaches the topic of actual politics in the following way:

> Creating real public or civic value, though, requires more than posting funny pictures. Public and civic value requires commitment and hard work among the core group of participants. It also requires that these groups be self-governing and submit to constraints that help them ignore distracting and entertaining material and stay focused instead on some sophisticated task. (180)

This is a clichéd generality that one could have little dispute with. It merely says that if group mechanisms for avoiding distraction and staying focused are employed, then anything might be possible. However, Shirky follows up this line with the somewhat baleful observation that undermines the generality itself: "This work is not easy and it never goes smoothly. Because we are *hopelessly committed* to both individual satisfaction and group effectiveness, groups committed to public or civic value are rarely permanent" (180) (My emphasis).

In other words we humans cannot stick to the task at hand because we are "hopelessly" torn between the needs and wants of both individual and group. But this dichotomy is the basis of a democracy and the basis of the motivation for a programmatic politics. What is the democratic process (and what use is it) if it does not seek to reconcile the interests of both individual and group? The two are mutually inclusive because our individual identity is derived in part from our identity groups (Gutmann 2003).

Elsewhere, Shirky inadvertently betrays his lack of political sophistication when he notes that "Our cognitive surplus is only potential" (28). So there we have it. Freedom is down to individuals who are democratically oriented, un-distractible, and are in complete control of the technologies they use and the socio-temporal contexts they create. How are we to harness (or even recognize) this "potential" when our surplus-creating cognitive tools (ICTs) are tied to the trajectory of the speed economy of capitalism? Gehlen tells us that "The cognitive process...is a technical process" (1980, 70). It is. The "potential" that Shirky leaves as a very large unanswered question can only remain so unless and until he comes to grips with the nature of time. "Free time" he will then realize is something different from the time of the 1950s spent in front of *I Love Lucy*. The network time of our network society is time of a very differently technological order—and as presently constituted has very little potential in respect of the freedom of the individual or group.

To be able to progress toward what Doug Kellner has dubbed a "techno politics" (1997) or a form of political organization that straddles both network life and its analog counterpart, we must look beyond Shirky's unreflective love of the network expressed in these books because, fundamentally, the network as it is constituted is in fact the problem. Not quite coincidentally, however, we will return to Shirky presently, where his growing technophilic influence took him, in early 2011, to the eminent pages of *Foreign Policy*, wherein he *does* take the subject of politics seriously. But to set the scene for the closing of this book, and in order to understand the parameters of being "committed to public or civic value" we need to look afresh at the notion of the *public sphere* and how in a globalized context, individual and group sovereignty over technologies and the temporalities they produce can be regulated in such a way that politics and technology may once more be in relative synchrony with the cognitive capacities and potentialities of humans.

Communication Above All

The basis of politics is communication. In order to develop political philosophies and move these toward programmatic action, individuals and groups need to create and share information. These can of course take many forms. On one hand, miscommunication or communication that may signal forms of inequality or injustice being visited upon one group or another can be the catalyst for political conflict. On the other hand, communication that carries more socially positive forms of discourse can bring individuals and groups together to share and advance political goals. This much is obvious. Nevertheless it is something that is consistently overlooked or neglected or demoted to an instrumental process, wherein the context and nature of communication take second place to its technological means: the "more efficient the better" syndrome. This has meant that technological developments or improvements in forms of communication are almost always viewed as somehow enhancing democracy. This historically unreflective view of the relationship between communication technologies and democratic processes has for the most part been unproblematic, because, as I have argued, the temporality of communicative processes had not reached the point of breakdown, or asynchronicity, where forms of communication (and volumes of communication) had become too fast for the temporal rhythms of the democratic process. We passed the point of breakdown with the introduction and then rapid hegemony of networked communication in economy, culture, and society.

The realms of economy, culture, and society may be said to make up our public sphere, the "space" (and this descriptor is vitally important as I shall soon show) in which modern liberal democracy acquires its impetus. According to theorists such as Jürgen Habermas and Nancy Fraser, the public sphere contains the civic and democratic possibilities for the shape and nature of any future forms of democracy. In closing this book we need to briefly reacquaint ourselves with the political importance of the public sphere and what it is supposed to do for our democracy. We will then consider whether—and under what circumstances—it can function as sphere for democracy in our networked society.

Habermas is credited with the most in-depth and influential theoretical treatment of what constitutes the public sphere in modern (i.e., eighteenth and nineteenth century) societies. Importantly, Habermas saw the public sphere as being formed and motivated through discourse and *communication above all*. As he puts it in his seminal work on the subject *The Structural Transformation of the Public Sphere*:

> The public of 'human beings' engaged in rational-critical debates was constituted into one of 'citizens' wherever there was communication concerning the affairs of the 'commonwealth'. Under the 'republican constitution' this public sphere in the political realm became the organizational principle of the liberal constitutional state. (1991/1961, 107–8)

Citizens were fashioned from the raw stuff of nature through "rational-critical" forms of communication to constitute the bourgeois public sphere. Habermas is here describing its creation as a fundamental element in the construction of the Enlightenment and the modern world. He uses Kant's definition of what constitutes "enlightenment" as being the sharing of reason (rational–critical debates) across the widest possible circles of literate society. This for Habermas is "publicity as a principle" wherein he observes that (quoting Kant):

> The public use of one's reason must always be free, and this alone can bring about enlightenment among men. The private use of reason, on the other hand, may often be narrowly restricted without particularly hindering the progress of enlightenment. (106)

Habermas adds his own postscript to this, which reads that in this historical intellectual process of the forming of the public sphere: "Each person was called to be a "publicist", a scholar whose writings speak to his public, the world" (106). This is, we can see, a fairly elite conception of the social and intellectual dynamics that constituted the public sphere. To be a participant, one has to be literate indeed a scholar who has something important to say that connects with the affairs of the times. Habermas has been criticized for this, but how could his conception be otherwise? This was a public sphere created from what Habermas called the "world of letters". This world was inhabited by those who generated the ideas that were distilled (those ideas deemed appropriated for commercial bourgeois life) down to the political sphere where they were applied toward the aim of the "regulation of civil society" (Habermas 1991, 52). Communication (or more precisely, philosophical, economic, and political writing) was the basis of the public sphere, and if it was elitist (which it was) then it only reflected the sophistication of the networks of

184

communication of the time. This was, to again use Debray's extremely helpful phrase, the "communication networks that enable thought to have social existence" (2007, 5). And the temporal rhythms of this incipiently modern public sphere reflected the bio- and eco-temporality that words on paper had retained since the time of their invention.

A very large gap sits in this formulation, of course. Although Habermas tracks accurately and invaluably the genesis and construction of a public sphere (the initial political institution of Enlightenment thinking), it nonetheless describes a precise historical time in Europe. This was a Europe where white males (if not all "dead") at least held a monopoly of communicative power. Moreover, they tended to speak for their own class—which was the bourgeoisie; or if they were more radical and with a Jacobin or Reformist tinge, then they would speak primarily *to* the bourgeois' dialectical Other, the proletarian class who were not yet literate enough nor consciousness enough of themselves as a class to speak in their own right and to their own interests. Habermas' worth is that he laid the historical groundwork upon which others could build more universalized structures.

An influential piece in this respect is Nancy Fraser's 1991 essay *Rethinking the Public Sphere: A Contribution to the Critique of Actually Existing Democracy*, which seeks to critique Habermas' work from the perspective of a "critical social theory of the limits of democracy in late-capitalist society" (1991, 56). Fraser begins by acknowledging the value of Habermas' work and argues for the concept of the public sphere as an interpretive framework for the analysis of political democracy. But, for Fraser, the initial conception by Habermas is (perhaps understandably, given its focus) an "historically specific and limited form" of the public sphere (58). Habermas' limitations are rather easy to see, easy once the somewhat more difficult task of pointing them out has been undertaken first—which is what Fraser does in her essay. She makes the observation that whilst developing a theory of the bourgeois public sphere, Habermas "oddly" stops short at developing a "new post-bourgeois model." This is itself "odd" because we still live in a *bourgeois age* and any post-bourgeois theorization would only be speculative. Still, the point is made that the Habermasian public sphere is a thoroughly bourgeois one—wholly white, Christian, middle class, and European in constitution. To be fully democratic, Fraser argues, and to more faithfully reflect at least the beginnings of a "post-bourgeois" age in our own time, the reconstructed framework would need to be vastly more pluralistic and diverse. Communication is still key crucial dynamic here, but it is "constituted by [a political] conflict" that has always existed in the modern public sphere, but has never been given sufficient recognition by Habermas. The elements of conflict, and the elements of Habermas' exclusion, in his theory are what Fraser terms "counterpublics" (61). These today are the publics of women, of people of color, workers, of gays and lesbians, of ethnicities, of culture, of language, and of competing ideologies—be they democratic, or socialist, or even fascistic (67–68). Crucially for Fraser the public sphere is a stratified one, with the counterpublics being *subaltern* ones, and not the "single, comprehensive public sphere" implied in Habermas (68). Fraser's argument, fundamentally, is that only an inclusive and diverse public sphere—within a stratified order that motivates conflict—can give it its dynamism and its ongoing trajectory of change that could, at least in theory, expand society's "capacity to envision democratic possibilities beyond the limits of actually existing democracy" (77).

The theoretical parameters of what constitutes the public sphere (at least in ideal type) are fairly clear today, and as a consequence, the debates, and hence the interest, have gone off the boil with the major theoretical questions more or less settled. Or so it seems. Habermas wrote his path-breaking book in 1962 and Fraser published her critique nearly thirty years later. That was twenty years ago. If communication and information is key to the function of the public sphere, constituting in fact, its very lifeblood, then it is again "odd" that the perspectives of technological change and its effects upon time have not been applied. And things have changed beyond recognition. Interestingly, as an historical inquiry, Habermas' account is more accurate and durable than Fraser gives him credit for. His public sphere at the dawn of the modern age was in temporal synchrony with its communicative technologies. Print was king and literacy the means of ideational and political power. The bourgeois-dominated public sphere was in a real sense the only possible public sphere, given the role development of communication technologies, and the relative development of an adequately literate society. Fraser's "rethinking" of the public sphere as a pluralist space for positively oriented conflict between counterpublics, though formally logical, and properly takes into account a very different world, does not take into account (at all) the vital role of technological—and therefore temporal—change. By 1991, when she wrote, the world was on the threshold of the information age. But from Fraser's account, one would not guess at it. The problem, partly, is one of lack of interdisciplinarity; a dearth of academic sharing of information and disciplinary insights. In respect of the lack of temporal insight shared between scholarly communities, it was a point made with some plangency by Douglass North who observed that historians and political scientists (and not only these) fail spectacularly to take ideas of time into their theorization and interpretations. He writes that:

> For an economic historian, time has always been something that is fundamentally disturbing, because there is no time in neoclassical theory. The neoclassical model is a model of an instant of time, and it does not therefore take into account what time does...I will be blunt: Without a deep understanding of time, you will be lousy political scientists, because time is the dimension in which ideas and institutions and beliefs evolve. (cited in Pierson 2004, 1)

The early 1990s, admittedly, was a time that is even very different from our own. Neoliberal globalization was raging around the world and computerization was playing its pivotal role—but the Internet was incipient and blogging and Twitter and all the rest of it were a glint in the eyes of Silicon Valley's rising stars. But Fraser revisited the subject again in 2009 with her *Scales of Justice: Reimagining Political Space in a Globalizing World.* One imagines that when discussing the politics of a "globalizing world" the role of technology would play some important role. But no. The network society, or the Internet, or digital capitalism is non-existent in this world. Needless to say, the relationship between politics and temporality and between temporality and techniques of communication are absent too. Such lacunae, from such an eminent political theorist, is disheartening. The public sphere remains the central interpretive framework for the analyses of the effectiveness of democratic political practice in our world, in our networked world and in its dwindling off-line manifestations. However, a lack of temporal analysis prevents us from the realization that communication (through new computer-based communication technologies) simply operates too quickly for the functioning of an effective political sphere. The civic world Habermas describes where reading and writing on paper was the primary mode of mass communication has been superseded; and the world in which Fraser tries to balance "plurality of competing frames" of justice (2009, 2), does not account for the new communicative reality in any way at all, a reality that sees the networked public sphere that pulses at high speed, not as a "discursive space" of diverse "counterpublics," but a cacophony of white noise wherein the time for proper debate and reflection and planning and programs for political action are dwindling fast.

Consequently, there is a very large and persistent disconnect between the theory of the public sphere and its reality. Current theories that through disciplinary ignorance fail to confront the dual effects of computing and acceleration upon communicative practices are rendered unable to identify the political consequences of chronic distraction and information overload. Theory is thus not equipped to appreciate that the indelible rhythms of Enlightenment-derived democratic politics cannot be geared up to a high speed. Only authoritarian politics can function rapidly, and this has no place in the public sphere. Moreover, we can expect no *lead from the institutionalized polity in their parliaments and congresses around the world.* On one hand, in the homogenous neoliberal planet, even serious and worthy politicians and their bureaucracies that wish to do well are in thrall to the ideology that ubiquitous computing is self-evidently an economic and social benefit. On the other hand, there is no shortage of self-seeking politician for whom "the corrupt parliamentary game" is anyway the only game in town (Zizek 2010, 94).

Today, the public sphere could hardly be less theorized in a way that takes into serious account not only the technological transformation of its preeminent communicative modality, but also the "space" of the sphere and the *time of the sphere.*, which brings us back to Clay Shirky.

Internet Freedom Is a Long Game

Shirky's books and articles and blogs and Youtube videos have given him an influential voice. Wikipedia has a Shirky entry. And the same Shirky has made several appearances at the prestigious "technology, entertainment, design" (TED) conferences, where the great and the good, from Bill Clinton to Stephen Hawking, relate the latest blue-sky thinking. His work, as we have seen, concerns itself with the connections between the forms of politics we have in our networked society and how they are influenced by networked technologies. Shirky is also interested in the public sphere as an interpretative space for understanding these dynamics. The rising of his star plus the growing discussion on the effects of social media on the political process caused Shirky to be invited (one presumes you have to be invited) to write an essay for the high-status *Foreign Affairs* journal.

Titled, "The Political Power of Social Media: Technology, the Public Sphere, and Political Change" (2011, Vol. 90 No. 1) the essay is an attempt to get to grips with a few increasingly salient questions that are being widely debated in media, academic, and political circles today. Questions such as: does the Internet, with its add-ons such as Facebook, Twitter, basic mobile texting, etc., constitute the basis for a new kind of "bottom up" politics? Do ICTs represent a radical challenge to media corporations with their own agendas, and to political elites who are often viewed as out of touch with grassroots needs? To his credit, Shirky delivers a very useful and sober revision of the overconfident "here comes everybody" thesis he espoused in 2008. He begins with a review of some of the noted instances of widespread social media constituting its own virtual public sphere. There is the Filipino "text-messaging generation" that President Estrada blamed for his 2001 fall from grace and office; then there is the example of the much-suspected rigging of the elections in Iran in 2010, which infuriated millions of ordinary (networked) young people in that country, who then organized themselves online and took to the streets for days of demonstrations that badly shook the confidence of the regime; and then there were the flash mobbing instances in Belarus and Thailand that Shirky had mentioned in his 2008 book. Appearing when it did, in January 2011, the article seemed particularly apt. This was the precise time when the Tunisian government felt the power of a networked constituency gathering *en mass* in the streets of Tunis to drive its president from power and to seek refuge in Saudi Arabia. This was termed a "digitally-driven, leaderless revolution" (Matai 2011). The Tunisian revolution seemed to be the precursor of a wider politicization that was "digitally-driven" across North Africa and the Middle East. Clearly, something different is happening today and answers to such serious questions are needed. Accordingly, an article for the influence-wielding readership of *Foreign Affairs* provides a very useful opportunity to begin a serious discussion.

Reading on, it seems that when commissioned to consider the *politics* of ICTs as the exclusive focus of his assignment, the analysis has become more equivocal (and conservative) than the techno-sunniness of earlier works. Shirky reviews the empirical evidence and realizes early on that there is really little basis upon which to form hard and fast conclusions. And so:

> The safest characterization of recent quantitative attempts to answer the question, do digital tools enhance democracy? Is that these tools probably do not hurt in the short run and might help

in the long run—and that they have the most dramatic effects in states where a public sphere already constrains the actions of the government. (30)

The equivocation is actually analytically very useful. Shirky's "short-term/long-term" dichotomy serves to temporalize the issue, and it opens up the possibility for much-needed time-oriented insights into this very contemporary political problem. Shirky says that for the public sphere to function effectively, it must develop with a view to eschewing the short-termism of neoliberalism and instead invest in it the time necessary to achieve particular political goals. But what is the long-term? A few lines on, Shirky tells us. He writes that "the potential of social media lies mainly in their support of civil society and the public sphere—change measured in years and decades rather than weeks or months" (30). Reiterating the point he stresses that: "A slowly developing public sphere, where public opinion relies on both media and conversation, is the core of the environmental view of Internet freedom" (34).

So there we have it: the commonsense view in cold print—*the public sphere needs its own time*. It cannot function unless "conversation" (reading, writing, debating) is given over to its "natural" temporal rhythms to allow it to work upon the creation and sustaining of its own processes. What this implies is that the Internet, the growing vector for information in the public sphere, must become something other than it currently is, something more oriented to people's needs than to the hegemonic demands of the economy. Shirky notes, again with some acuity, that: "Access to information is far less important, politically, than access to conversation" (35). That the Internet needs to become more human in order to become more democratic is a point I will return to shortly. But what of his tentative temporalizing of the problem of social media and the public sphere? It promises so much and so to develop a temporal critique of politics in a premier journal such as *Foreign Affairs* might well open the door to a much-needed universalizing of the issue in our time-starved and hyper-distracted society. The old Braudelian question of the historical *longue duree* might at last be attached to the processes of politics, and become a salient and urgent agenda item beyond the confines of academic theorization.

Unfortunately, the questions of temporality implicit in Shirky's essay do not get followed up. They are left hanging, to be forgotten or obscured by the vague "environmental view" where the politics of the "long-term" should be prudently pursued in the building of a democratic public sphere. This tells us nothing about the very real barriers to the realization of a long-term political conversation. The public sphere of conversation that Shirky and Habermas and Fraser would wish to see does not exist—or exists only fictively—in our networked neoliberalism. This is a "timescape" that is dominated by the economic imperatives of capital, and "conversations" that are about constructing narratives concerning political goals, simply do not has the time to develop. The network that shapes (disfigures) so much of our lives, is an information network where conversations are truncated and narratives that draw from the past and look to the future for meaning and identity-endowing qualities are increasingly more difficult to form and sustain (Bauman 1998, 18). We are becoming decimated by information.

The tools of network information add to the problem. They are entimed with the speed of the network and are set upon an open-ended continuum of acceleration and multifunctionality. The people of Manila may have literally spelled out the end for President Estrada though using basic text-enabled phones, but that was way back in 2001. Today Smartphone's are *de rigueur*, from Tunis to Tehran and from Seattle to Sydney. The tool itself, moreover, is engineered to distract and not to concentrate the mind politically as the writing or reading of a pamphlet might do—indeed was designed to do. Texting now competes with video and Internet capability for the users' diminishing attention capacity. Multifunctionality leads to the creation of multi-constituencies, each of which are not necessarily technologically compatible, and so the plethora of platforms themselves fractures the potential of the public sphere. These are privately or publicly owned techniques of communication that are compelled to vie with each other for the attention of the revolutionary-cum-commodity. If a headline one day screams that a "Twitter Revolution" has caused this or that authoritarian regime to falter, then the news will be greeted sullenly, no doubt, by the folks at Facebook, or by any other newcomer to the global social networking marketplace, not simply because of the priceless free advertising that Twitter would have enjoyed, but because they are in competition with each other for the market share of the world's would-be regime changers. Efforts will then have to be redoubled, by Facebook or whomever, in order to make challenger platforms more appealing, more functional, more easy to use—and faster.

Social media—or social networking—is in a very real sense a misno-mer. At its root, there is nothing "social" about them. They are private and commercial processes that have millions of coopted users as their raw material-generating nodes. There is not much within these high-speed information flows that is able to sustain mass conversations over the long-term; not much upon which narratives and plans and organizations and choices may be built for the attaining of political goals. The public sphere, in both its classical articulation and its virtual iteration, is simply not capable of producing the basis for a sustain-able democratic politics. The print culture that grew and developed it is too slow for the networked society, and the culture of virtuality is too fast to maintain any political coherence. Through autonomous technological development we have warped our relationship with temporality twice over: we have obscured the nature of bio- and eco-temporality through the domination of clock time since the eighteenth century; and we have now begun to render clock time obsolete through computer-based network time. This cannot be viewed as technologi-cal progress, but as an example of McLuhanesque "autoamputation" whereby we cut ourselves off from our temporal roots. The most alarming factor in this process is that due to our historical inability to properly come to terms with the nature of time—we do not even realize that we are drifting; we have no sense of unease or the feeling that we are stranded.

> *Only through time is time conquered*
> —*T.S. Eliot "Burnt Norton"*

If the public sphere is no good, then what can we do? If the arenas for politics is dominated by a networked economy and we can only ever hope to play constant catch-up to its searing pace, where does this leave the hopes for democracy? Our collective inheritance of de-mocracy comes with its own indelible rhythms, rhythms that stem, in their turn, from our relationship with the technologies of reading and writing. Democracy is slow, and as Shirky says, we need to work with it over "the long-run" (2011, 41). To do otherwise (to make democratic processes faster and more "efficient") means that we also need to redefine what we mean by democracy—and that can only portend a lesser democracy. To redefine democracy in these terms would be to yield to technological determinism and to neoliberal power. And from our squandered inheritance we would be left with a "democracy lite," a formal democracy, but one that has no real substance. There is no shortage of this kind of democracy around the world today, one need only think of Venezuela, or Thailand, or Russia, where people can vote and assemble and form parties—but the reality is that these are democracies for the elites. This is democracy at globalization speed where boardrooms and cabinet rooms hold access to power and the decisive information. And the logic bleeds into our own democracies in the developed countries, because more and more people have less and less time to think clearly about the kind of polity they live in—and still less have the inclination to think in terms of a "temporalized democracy" (Adam 2003). The only slow-moving rhythm still intact in our neoliberal globalization is the election cycle where the participatory charade is carried out regularly and the illusion regularly maintained.

It is a cliché that democracy comes with both rights and obligations. We are, all of us, therefore obligated to save democracy from powerlessness at the popular level. The temporality of the event-horizon of neoliberal globalization offers no solutions. We must be conservative in the spirit of Edmund Burke or, as Sheldon Wolin phrases it, "preservative" and recognize that "political time is out of synch with the temporalities, rhythms, and pace governing economy and culture" (1997). We need to preserve what we have inherited, to look after it and nourish it so it will grow "naturally." The most important inheritance, apart for the canonical works that have shaped our thinking, is the process that gave these ideas concrete expression—the *public sphere*. We have seen that it is currently ineffectual, is in retreat, in denial, or in thrall to the possibilities purportedly stemming from its virtualization. Thinking temporally, however, the term "public sphere" gives us a hint about where to begin honoring our obligations.

Let us begin with the term "sphere." It of course connotes space— *political space*. Nancy Fraser takes up the theme and the concept of political space in her 2010 book *Scales of Justice: Reimagining Political Space in a Globalizing World*. She brings her abiding interest in the public sphere right up to date in the context of "the fraying of nationally based social democracy under pressure from global neoliberalism" (102). On the face of it this would seem a necessary—if not vital—consideration for those who wish to see democracy and justice function optimally in these new and extremely challenging times. The processes of globalization lead one naturally to think of space, the shrinking of space, and the coming together of the myriad "nationally based" political processes to singular sphere. To consider what might be called the "space economy" of global politics is therefore undoubtedly a worthy endeavor, and Fraser's contribution is an important one. However, it is only half the story. A key concern in this book has been to argue that in physics as well as in the social world, concepts of time and space are indivisible. One does not make much sense without the other. David Harvey's theory of "time-space compression," as we have seen, shows that it is our *experience of time that has compressed space* (1989, part III). It is also our *production of time*, through communication networks, that has condensed space almost to the point of instantaneity. Any "reimagining" of politics that considers the contraction of space as a key element must be accompanied by an equal consideration of the acceleration of time (Rosa, 2003; Scheuerman 2004). Unfortunately, it seems that political scientists such as Fraser, as the quote from Douglass North earlier noted, still neglect to take questions of temporality sufficiently seriously. Indeed, it is indicative of the general lack of transdisciplinarity in the academy that Fraser hardly mentions the Internet or the network society or ICTs at all, yet these are processes that must be at the heart of any reimagining of the globalization process. To lament the omission at this point of the book would be futile. One can only direct the reader to insightful works that show the consequences of neglecting the temporal dimension. A key text here is Nigel Thrift and Jon May's edited collection *timespace* (2001). Their introductory essay is a powerful argument for the motivation behind the book, which is that the: "basic formulations of space [in the literature] appears to us curiously one-dimensional and which, at root, seem premised upon a familiar and unhelpful dualism moving around the foundational categories of Space and Time" (1). Any treatment of politics in our networked society must interrogate the politics of both time and space and so Thrift and May's *timespace* is an invaluable beginning to what must be an ongoing process of correction.

It is not always advisable to end a book with the introduction of a new concept. However, in this case it is both unavoidable and necessary. My book has been about distraction, and how it is reaching epidemic and chronic proportions throughout the world due to the dual (and interpenetrative) processes of neoliberal globalization and the revolution in ICTs. Whilst the framing of the problem here has encompassed social and temporal theory, together with sociology, a bit of history and philosophy, and with a more that a dash of economics, all of the narrative is inherently political. It is overtly political in that chronic distraction places most of us outside the circuits of power. The power of information has become a form of political and economic power deriving to whomsoever can best exploit the nexus between the free market as unchallenged hegemon, and instrumentalized ICTs its tool. This power shifts erratically, admittedly, but it does so primarily within the elite networks structured by the owners and controllers of capital (Harvey 2005, 101–8).

Information that becomes knowledge that in turn translates into power constitutes the temporal logic of politics. To be able to grasp, as Georgio Agamben puts it: "the favourable opportunity and choose his own freedom in the moment" (2007, 115) is to possess and experience temporal autonomy. But who has this today? "My time" is not really my time. It is "owned" by the information network that continually makes demands upon it and distracts it into countless different, yet increasingly homogenous commercial and commodified spaces. Autonomy to empty one's mind and think fresh thoughts is a basic element of freedom. Henry David Thoreau wrote that "To affect the quality of the day, that is the highest of arts." The writer of *Civil Disobedience* knew that to affect anything is intrinsically political and yet today we are individually and collectively losing this power due to the nature of the world that we created since the 1970s. This book has attempted to understand it, but what to do about it?

There are no easy answers just as there are no quick solutions. Nor could there be. Shirky's long game for the development of the public sphere is the only way. More dauntingly still, we need to begin at the beginning. I will develop what I am about to propose in a future book, but let me start here with the first step, and with the introduction of a term that is surprisingly new: *temporal sovereignty*. Googling this phrase did not elicit much from the site's hardworking algorithms. The best that it could come up with was various uses of the term to describe the Pope and the Vatican and what they own. The catalogue in my own university library, a good one in the scheme of things, had thirteen matches of which were some more on arcane Popish matters, a chapter in a collection that was concerned with temporal sovereignty in Aztec Mexico (could be useful for later research, and was noted), after which the relevance became progressively tenuous as the list exhausted itself. Given what I have just argued on the neglect in the social sciences, and politics in particular, this came as no surprise. Temporal sovereignty is something we are not so used to thinking about. Spatial sovereignty, however, is etched deep into our political and cultural bones.

So closely related are the terms "space" and "sovereignty" that they are almost identical in what they convey. Wikipedia defines "sovereignty" as "the quality of having supreme, independent authority over a geographic area, such as a territory" (2011). This is easy for us to understand. The government we elect has sovereign power over precisely defined spatial boundaries—and no more. The writ of a government runs only so far, and then power immediately dissolves, or passes to another sovereignty authority with its own laws and rights and so on. The Peace of Westphalia in 1648 began to conceptualize and traditionalize power as requiring to be stable and static (between nations) in order to eliminate what had been decades of continuous warring in Europe. As Kimberly Hutchings noted, the Peace was underscored by the assumption that "the *space* of international politics was thought of as frozen in *time*" (2008, 11) (emphases in original). Wars are fought primarily over the sanctity of sovereign space, and the "frozen" metaphor that Hutchins employs is a useful descriptor for understanding the temporal dimension of the post-1945 Cold War, where borders (and Ideologies) were frozen in time for a generation. Paralleling this meta-concept, and again something that we well used to, is the idea (or in this case primarily the *feeling*) of personal sovereignty—or personal space. Edward T. Hall, in his *The Silent Language*, which, through anthropological studies, showed that "space speaks," pioneered the concept (1959, 158–81). We have culturally determined comfort "zones" in relation to other people, and we know consciously or unconsciously, when these are being trespassed. In other words, and as we saw earlier in the works of Lefebvre (1992), space (being cultural) is socially produced.

Until fairly recently we have had immense conceptual difficulties in relating to time in the same way. We produce timescapes as social constructions but modernity and capitalism—and now post-modernity and late-capitalism—overlay these with a technological time to the extent that our bio- and eco-temporalities have become alien to us. And yet these are what we must recover if we are to survive (cognitively and politically) the onslaught of social acceleration. Relating to time as individually and collectively, sovereign is the first step on the road to a fundamental recognition of ourselves as temporal beings. Our alienation from the human experience of the timescapes we create is a political question that is located in the nexus between neoliberal capitalism and unrestricted technological development, primarily that of networked computing. As so it is to the public sphere, the only possible realm through which we can recover time for society, that we must look for hopes of redress. But first the public sphere needs to function at its own pre-digital, modern, Enlightenment-derived pace. Public intellectuals, social scientists, politicians, and others must take the first step by pointing out that temporally speaking the public sphere cannot function in an accelerated, network-driven context, where information flows and has no time to consolidate into knowledge.

The debates and the analysis can ripple out. That we acutely feel the alienation of our temporal selves is borne out in the growing debates on the "lack" of time in our society. However, it is not enough to center the debates, as most commentators do, on the workplace, or the need to bring some equity to the "life-work" balance. These are important, but they are effects as opposed to causes of our time-starved lives. To conceive of time as we conceive of space would open up a fundamentally new perspective within the public sphere. If time is considered sovereign, as belonging to me in the deepest sense, and belonging to society in an equally profound sense, then the question of *rights* follows logically. Who has the right to take it away? The purchase of "my" time is implicit in the wage relation in capitalist society. However, reflection on the nature of time shows that the appropriation of "my" time by forces over which I have little or no control goes much wider than the workplace. Networked society and neoliberal globalization have brought these forces to a new level, and to a new accelerated tempo. Chronic distraction is but an example of how my time is created in an accelerated informational stream, and appropriated at the very point of its creation. The logic (from the perspective of capital) is clear. But if we understand time more clearly as "mine" and not something abstract, then the argument can be made that this hyper-exploitative colonizing of time is in fact inefficient. Arguments in the public sphere to the effect that a lack of time sovereignty is not only an infringement of rights, but is also poor economics, is a potentially powerful basis upon which to take the struggle for temporalization forward. A temporally aware public sphere would naturally take the debates and the arguments to the state and government bureaucracies, where meaningful action could begin to be undertaken.

It should be pointed out that notwithstanding the power and the influence of computing in our network society, there has never been, anywhere in the world, a wholesale review of the technological beast we have created, one that asks: why do we need this? And what, actually, do we want it to do? To date its development, its sprawl, and its speed, has mostly been shaped by the chaos of market forces. Speaking for individuals and for communities, governments must ask: what is this new product or service for? What social benefits is it designed to bring? The nebulous claims for efficiency and freedom must be measured against the instrumental commercial logic that usually (through acceleration) works against such claims. Thinking slowly and clearly and rationally and temporally about the Internet would throw up many issues that could be acted upon positively. This would mean taking up a serious government claim of interest in what the Internet does and in whose interest it does it. Thinking modestly, with small and achievable steps to begin with: spam mail, pop up ads, phishing, and so on, are something that most people find intrusive and distracting could be cracked down on much more seriously that is now the case in many countries. Internet Service Providers (ISPs) could be shut down if they fail to take concrete steps to stamp such intrusions out.

Thinking more boldly, and thinking over the longer term whilst developing a culture of human control over autonomous technological systems such as the Internet, could make us realize and accept that it would make sense—temporally as much as anything—to functionally split the Internet into at least two "spheres" comprising two "times." A *commercial Internet* would be the sphere for industry, for research and development, for science, medicine, and realms of inquiry where powerful computing and fast-speed connectivity makes sense and has unalloyed positive social and economic outcomes. There will never be any shortage of useful work for networked computing to do. This could be the sphere for entertainment too, for advertising, for spam even, where people could *choose to go to be distracted* by whatever they want, a sphere for movies, for eBay and Youtube, etc., for "social" networking where the emphasis is on friends and sharing interests with them. Content providers (users and businesses) could make available whatever people themselves want in this part of their networked lives. It would be a space that is regulated relatively lightly *but nonetheless consistently* through national and transnational legislation.

A *public Internet* could be engineered so that it could be instantly accessed by the pressing of a key to enter another sphere that is everything the commercial Internet is not, an Internet that is not necessarily slow in that pages take forever to load, etc., but one that is nevertheless at a clearly differing tempo, an Internet for different things. It would be filled not with content that drove you to browse, to flit here and there and never stay still, but with content that will keep you there for longer, "sticky" content that is not oriented toward selling you something, but to offer you another perspective, something to make you think and reflect and stay as long as necessary. It would be an interactive sphere in the fullest sense where the latest and fastest technologies make debates live in real time, but where there is equally no pressure to move to the next thing, nothing to distract you except another compelling idea or debate. This could be "civil society Internet," a public sphere that is also respectful and engendering of public time, created public "timescapes" wherein people can engage in politics and civic affairs in ways we can scarcely dream of today. It would be a realm that is removed from the commercial imperatives of the other sphere, we could switch between the two when we need to—and we could have the power to turn it off altogether when we have had enough. The ubiquitous mobile phone too could be divided into this dual-sphere accessibility: a button for the commercial sphere and another for the public one. The individual would choose, and the phone's social utility could expand exponentially.

This public realm need not be dull; a post-modern replication of state-owned television or radio circa 1980. Dullness comes from a lack of proper funding, a lack of participation and lack of real public interest. It would have to be heavily invested in by both government, interested private sector players, and by users themselves. The public Internet could be a sphere of public interest that conducts innumerable debates at many differing levels and tempos, where the most important of them would percolate up due to a growing public awareness and desire to broaden and deepen the issues. Like an ideal public sphere, anything could be debated through blogs or video forums and the like. Newspapers could get over their current angst and save the paper costs and migrate online wholesale. Part of it could go to the commercial sphere, the rest to the public. People would choose where to go and what to buy. Art, literature, whatever people want to take slowly and at their "natural" unforced rhythms could be situated in the public sphere for open and free public participation. Vitally, the public Internet is where society must site education. From the primary school to the university, education and pedagogy is shriveling under the heat of commercial competition and knowledge is shallowing as an effect of the speed of competition (Barnett 2007). Universities need to decouple from a neoliberal economic logic, be funded fully by government and go online to offer a commitment to knowledge instead of a commitment to profit and credentialism.

Conceivably, this rational realm of the network society would begin—in the fullness of time—to act upon the commercial realm. A humanist and humanizing realm of network life could not fail to have a similar effect upon the feverish ravages of capitalism in its neoliberal mode. The same people would inhabit both realms, after all. With more social control over technological development would evolve a more reasoned (instead of instrumentally rational) capitalism. The *longer-term perspective* would arise logically and naturally as the key sustainable basis upon which economies could flourish. Many people already agree that the environment and its care is the most important challenge facing humanity today, and a temporalized public sphere and a more time-friendly capitalism would make this challenge rather more able to be met. Perhaps the most exciting effect of a temporalized public sphere would be its bringing forth a new politics. A properly functioning public sphere would mean difference of opinion and difference in political outlook. These could be legitimately channeled through the public sphere itself, taking the form of new political groups and parties. Ultimately it is possible that a temporalized and diverse public sphere could form the basis, somewhat counterintuitively, of a *new conservatism* in politics and in the civic structures of society more broadly. This would be conservatism for a temporally awakened age in history, one where meanings deriving from it are from Burke's conservatism in respect of the tempo of politics, and aligned to Wolin's more up-to-date "preservative" philosophy. Such conservatism would preserve the structures of society that give it center and fixity—such as the canon—whilst ensuring through diversity of opinion and perspective that they do not ossify and become reactionary or power-centered. Perhaps most exciting, capitalism in this conservative/preservative milieu, would cease to be the elephant in the room that it has been for the last generation: the fount of much of our troubles, but yet cannot be identified as such. A diverse and temporally attuned conservative society would ensure that capitalism, slowly and gradually, and with none of the "shock doctrine" (Klein 2008) destruction that scars much economic and social processes today, will be oriented more and inexorably toward capitalism's future sustainability. Over the long term it may even be possible that a truly conservative and temporally oriented capitalism will cease to be the Marx-theorized "contradiction" that it currently is, and evolve to be simply a humanistic mode of economic organization.

Just think, the puny claim to the right not to be distracted might be the path to a future state that is hardly even visible today in our digital fog.

Bibliography

Adam, Barbara. "Reflexive Modernization Temporalized." *Theory, Culture and Society* 20, no. 2 (2003): 59–78.

_____. *Time*. Cambridge: Polity, 2004.

_____. *Timescape of Modernity: The Environment and Invisible Hazards*. London: Routledge, 1998.

Adorno, Theodor. *Minima Moralia: Reflections on a Damaged Life*. London: Verso, 2005.

Adorno, Theodor and Max Horkheimer. *The Dialectic of the Enlightenment*. London: Verso, 1986.

AFP. "As World First, Finland Makes Broadband Service Basic Right." *Google Hosted News*, July 1, 2010. http://www.google.com/hostednews/afp/article/ALeqM5iCyviFF-xcoqDvpKRtyymPHxgLsA (accessed November 22, 2010).

Agamben, Giorgio. *Infancy and History: On the Destruction of Experience*. Translated by Liz Heron. London: Verso, 2007.

Agger. "iTime: Labor and Life in a Smartphone Era." *Time & Society* 20, no. 1 (March, 2011): 119–36.

Aglietta, Michel. *A Theory of Capitalist Regulation: The US Experience*. Translated by David Fernbach. London: Verso, 2000/1979.

Amazon.com. *Kindle Reader Website*, 2010. http://www.amazon.com/Kindle-Wireless-Reader-Wifi-Graphite/dp/B002Y27P3M (accessed February 3, 2011).

Anderson, Benedict. *Imagined Communities*. London: Verso, 1991.

Anderson, Janna, and Lee Raine. "Future of the Internet IV." *Pew Internet and American Life Project*, February 19, 2010. http://www.pewinternet.org/Reports/2010/Future-of-the-Internet-IV/Part-3Gadgets.aspx (accessed June 20, 2010).

Anderson, Perry. "Renewals." *New Left Review* 1 (2000): 5–24.

Anderson, Sam. "In Defense of Distraction." *New York Magazine*, May 17, 2009. http://nymag.com/news/features/56793/ (accessed October 11, 2010).

Apple Jr., R. W. "25 Years Later: Lessons from the Pentagon Papers." *The New York Times*, June 23, 1996. (accessed February 19, 2010).

Aristotle. *Physics: Books III and IV*. Translated by Edward Hussey. Gloucestershire: Clarendon Press, 1993.

Arnold, Matthew. *Culture and Anarchy*. London: Cambridge University Press, 1960.

Auletta, Ken. "Publish or Perish." *The New Yorker*, April 26, 2010. http://www. newyorker.com/reporting/2010/04/26/100426fa_fact_auletta (accessed May 20, 2010).

Baran, Paul A., and Paul M. Sweezy. *Monopoly Capital: An Essay on the American Economic and Social Order*. New York: Monthly Review Press, 1966.

Baudrillard, Jean. "The Gulf War did not Take Place." Parts 1–3 originally published in *Libération* and *The Guardian*, January 4–March 29, 1991. Bloomington: Indiana University Press, 1995.

Bauman, Zygmunt. *Globalization: The Human Consequences*. Cambridge: Polity Press, 1998.

BBC 2010. *The Bottom Line*, program broadcast June 29, 2010. http://www.bbc. co.uk/programmes/p00889dh (accessed July 16, 2010).

Beaumont, Peter. "Rwanda's Laptop Revolution." *The Observer*, March 28, 2010. http://www.guardian.co.uk/technology/2010/mar/28/rwanda-laptop-revolution (accessed November 3, 2010).

Beck, Ulrich, and Elizabeth Beck-Gernsheim. *Individualization: Institutionalized Individualism and its Social and Political Consequences*. Thousand Oaks, CA: Sage, 2002.

Beckett, Andy. "The Dark Side of the Internet." *The Guardian*, November 26, 2009, 17.

Bell, Daniel. *The Coming of the Post-Industrial Society*. New York: Basic Books, 1973.

Bello, Walden. *Dilemmas of Domination*. New York: Henry Holt, 2006.

Bergman, Michael K. "The Deep Web: Surfacing Hidden Value." *The Journal of Electronic Publishing* 7, no. 1 (August 2001). http://quod.lib.umich.edu/cgi/t/text/text-idx?c=jep;cc=jep;q1=bergman;rgn=main;view=text;idno=333645 1.0007.104 (accessed October 2, 2010).

Betts, Richard K. "Conflict or Cooperation?" *Foreign Affairs*, November/December, 2010. http://www.foreignaffairs.com/articles/66802/richard-k-betts/conflict-or-cooperation (accessed February 10, 2011).

Blattner, William. *Heidegger's "Being and Time": A Reader's Guide*. London: Continuum Books, 2007.

Bloom, Harold. *The Western Canon: The Books and School of the Ages*. New York: Harcourt Brace, 1994.

Boltanski, Luc, and Eve Chiapello. *The New Spirit of Capitalism*. Translated by Gregory Elliott. London: Verso, 2006.

Bolter, Jay David. *Turing's Man: Western Culture in the Computer Age*. Chapel Hill: The University of North Carolina Press, 1984.

Brent, Jonathan. *Inside the Stalin Archives*. New York: Atlas, 2009.

Brooke, Heather. "WikiLeaks: The Revolution has Begun – and It will be Digitised." *The Guardian*, November 29, 2010. http://www.guardian.co.uk/commentisfree/2010/nov/29/the-revolution-will-be-digitised (accessed December 13, 2010).

Bruner, Jerome S. "The Narrative Construction of Reality." *Critical Inquiry* 18, no. 1, (Autumn 1991): 1–21.

Buchan, James. *Crowded with Genius: The Scottish Enlightenment: Edinburgh's Moment of the Mind*. New York: HarperCollins Publishers, 2003.

Burke, Edmund. *Reflections on the Revolution in France*. Edited and introduced by Conor Cruise O'Brien. London: Penguin. 1790/1986.

Carr, Nicholas. "Is Google Making Us Stupid?: What the Internet is Doing to our Brains." *Atlantic Monthly*, July/August, 2008. http://www.theatlantic.com/magazine/archive/2008/07/is-google-making-us-stupid/6868/ (accessed February 14, 2010).

_____. *The shallows: How the Internet is Changing the Way We Think, Read and Remember*. London: Atlantic Books, 2010.

Caryl, Christian. "Why WikiLeaks Changes Everything." *The New York Review of Books*, January 13, 2011. http://www.nybooks.com/articles/archives/2011/jan/13/why-wikileaks-changes-everything/ (accessed February 20, 2011).

Castells, Manuel. *The Rise of the Network Society. Vol. 1, The Information Age: Economy, Society and Culture*. Oxford: Blackwell, 2000/1996.

Cobbett, William. *A Year's Residence in America*. Charleston, SC: Nabu Press, 2010 (1819).

Coleridge, A. D. *Goethe's Letters to Zelter*. London: George Bell and Sons, 1887.

Cork, Richard. *Vorticism and Abstract Art in the First Machine Age*. London: G. Fraser, 1976.

Cottle, T. J. *Perceiving Time: An Investigation with Men and Women*. New York, NY: Wiley, 1976.

Crowther-Heyck, Hunter. *Herbert A. Simon: The Bounds of Reason in Modern America*. Baltimore, MD: Johns Hopkins University Press, 2005.

Cubitt, S., R. Hassan, and I. Volkmer. "Postnormal Network Futures." *Futures* 42, no. 6 (2010): 617–24.

Daniels, Peter T., and William Bright, eds. *The World's Writing Systems*. New York: Oxford University Press, 1996.

Darnton, Robert. *The Case for Books: Past, Present, and Future*. New York: Perseus, 2009.

_____. "Google and the Future of Books." *New York Review of Books* 56, no. 2 (February 12, 2009): 11–14.

Davies, Norman. *Europe: A History*. London: Pimlico, 1997.

Davies, Nick. *Flat Earth News*. London: Chatto & Windus, 2008.

Davis, Mike. *City of Quartz: Excavating the Future in Los Angeles*. London and New York: Verso, 1990.

Debray, Régis. "Socialism: A Life-Cycle." *New Left Review* 46 (July–August 2007): 5–17.

Derrida, Jacques. *Specters of Marx: The State of the Debt, the Work of Mourning, & the New International*. Translated by Peggy Kamuf. New York: Routledge, 1993.

Doctorow, Cory. "Writing in the Age of Distraction." *Locus Magazine*, January, 2009. http://www.locusmag.com/Features/2009/01/cory-doctorow-writing-in-age-of.html (accessed April 9, 2010).

Dumazedier, Joffre. *Toward a Society of Leisure*. New York: Free Press, 1967.

Durkheim, Emile. *Elementary Forms of the Religious Life*. London: Allen and Unwin, 1964.

Eagleton, Terry. *Reason, Faith, and Revolution: Reflections on the God Debate*. New Haven, CT: Yale University Press, 2009.

Edwards, Paul. N. *The Closed World: Computers and the Politics of Discourse in Cold War America*. Cambridge, MA: MIT Press, 1995.

Elias, Norbert. *Time: An Essay*. Oxford: Blackwell, 1992.

Ellul, Jacques. *The Technological Society*. Translated by John Wilkinson. Introduced by Robert K. Merton. London: Jonathan Cape, 1964.

Enzensberger, Hans Magnus. *Critical Essays*. New York: Continuum, 1982.

Eriksen, T. H. *Tyranny of the Moment: Fast and Slow Time in the Information Age*. London: Pluto, 2000.

Ermath, Elizabeth Deeds. *Realism and Consensus in the English Novel: Time, Space and Narrative*. Edinburgh: Edinburgh University Press, 1998.

Fara, Patricia. *Science: A Four-Thousand Year History*. Oxford: Oxford University Press, 2010.

Federman, Mark. "Touching Culture: Comments on eCulture, Creative Content and DigiArts." *UNESCO Conference on ICT and Creativity*, Vienna, 2005. http://individual.utoronto.ca/markfederman/TouchingCulture.pdf (accessed April 18, 2010).

Feenberg, Andrew. *Questioning Technology*. London: Routledge, 2004.

Ferriss, Tim. *The 4-Hour Workweek, Expanded and Updated*. New York: Crown Archetype, 2010.

Figes, Orlando. *The Whisperers: Private Life in Stalin's Russia*. London: Allen Lane, 2007.

Foucault, Michel. *The Archaeology of Knowledge and the Discourse on Language*. Translated by A. M. Sheridan Smith. New York: Pantheon Books, 1972.

_____. *Discipline and Punish: The Birth of the Prison*. Translated by Alan Sheridan. New York: Vintage Books, 1979.

_____. *Power/Knowledge: Selected Interviews and Other Writings, 1972–1977*. Edited by Colin Gordon. Translated by Colin Gordon et al. Brighton, Sussex: Harvester Press, 1980.

Frankel, Boris. *From the Prophets Deserts Come*. Melbourne: Arena, 1992.

Fraser, Nancy. "Rethinking the Public Sphere: A Contribution to the Critique of Actually Existing Democracy." *Social Text* 25/26 (1990): 56–80.

_____. *Scales of Justice: Reimagining Political Space in a Globalizing World*. New York: Columbia University Press, 2009.

Friedman, Milton. *Capitalism and Freedom*. Chicago, IL: University of Chicago Press, 2002/1962.

Gates, Bill, with Nathan Myhrvold, and Peter Rinearson. *The Road Ahead*. New York: Penguin Books, 1996.

Gehlen, Arnold. *Man in the Age of Technology*. Translated by Patricia Lipscomb. New York: Columbia University Press, 1980.

Gies, Frances, and Joseph Gies. *Cathedral, Forge, and Waterwheel: Technology and Invention in the Middle Ages*. New York: HarperCollins, 1995.

Gleick, J. *Faster: The Acceleration of Just About Everything*. New York: Abacus, 1999.

Glenn, David. "Divided Attention." *The Chronicle of Higher Education*, January 31, 2010. http://chronicle.com/article/Scholars-Turn-Their-Attention/63746/ (accessed February 22, 2010).

Glyn, Andrew. "Productivity and the Crisis of Fordism." *International Review of Applied Economics* 4, no. 1 (1990): 28–44.

Google Trends, 2010. "Leslie Nielsen." http://google-trends.i1corner.com/2010/11/29/leslie-nielsen-spiderman-on-broadway/ (accessed March 5, 2011).

Graham, Lindsey. "This Bill Stinks ... We're Not Being Smart." *Fox News Interview Archive*, February 6, 2009. http://www.foxnews.com/story/0,2933,489007,00.html (accessed November 11, 2009).

Grosz, Elizabeth. *The Nick of Time: Politics, Evolution and the Untimely.* Sydney: Allen and Unwin, 2004.

Gugerli, David. *The Culture of the Search Society: Data Management as a Signifying Practice.* Lecture given at the Society of the Query conference, Amsterdam, November 13, 2009. http://www.networkcultures.org/public/The_Culture_of_the_Search_Society_DavidGugerli.pdf (accessed April 27, 2011).

Gutmann, Amy. *Identity in Democracy.* Princeton, NJ: Princeton University Press, 2003.

Habermas, Jürgen. *The Structural Transformation of the Public Sphere: An Inquiry into a Category of Bourgeois Society.* Translated by Thomas Burger and Frederick Lawrence. Cambridge, MA: MIT Press, 1989/1961.

Hadot, Pierre. *The Veil of Isis: An Essay on the History of the Idea of Nature.* Translated by Michael Chase. Cambridge, MA: Harvard University Press, 2006.

Halavais, Alexander. *Search Engine Society.* Cambridge: Polity, 2008.

Hall, Edward, T. *The Silent Language.* New York: Doubleday, 1959.

Hammonds, Keith H., "How Google Grows... and Grows... and Grows." *Fast Company*, March 31, 2003. http://www.fastcompany.com/magazine/69/google.html (accessed April 11, 2009).

Hardt, Michael, and Antonio Negri. *Multitude: War and Democracy in the Age of Empire.* New York: Penguin Press, 2005.

Hardy, Barbara. "Towards a Poetics of Fiction." *NOVEL: A Forum on Fiction* 2, no. 1 (Autumn 1968): 5–14.

Harmon, Katherine. "Motivated Multitasking: How the Brain Keeps Tabs on Two Tasks at Once." *Scientific American*, April 15, 2010. http://www.scientificamerican.com/article.cfm?id=multitasking-two-tasks (accessed July 21, 2009).

Harris, Paul. "WikiLeaks has Caused Little Lasting Damage, Says US State Department." *The Guardian*, January 19, 2011. http://www.guardian.co.uk/media/2011/jan/19/wikileaks-white-house-state-department (accessed April 17, 2011).

Harvey, David. *A Brief History of Neoliberalism.* New York: Oxford University Press.

_____. *The Condition of Postmodernity.* Oxford: Blackwell, 1989.

_____. *The Limits to Capital.* Newly updated version. London: Verso, 2006/1983.

Hassan, Robert. *The Chronoscopic Society: Globalization, Time and Knowledge in the Network Economy.* New York: Peter Lang Publishing, 2003.

_____. *Empires of Speed.* Leiden: Brill Academic Publishers, 2009.

_____. *The Information Society.* Oxford: Polity, 2008.

_____. "The Speed of Collapse: The Space-Time Dimensions of Capitalism's First Great Crisis of the 21st Century." *Critical Sociology* 37 (May 2011): 233–51.

Heidegger, Martin. *On Time and Being.* Translated by Joan Stambaugh. New York: Harper, 1972.

Hekman, Susan J., ed. *Feminist Interpretations of Michel Foucault.* University Park, PA: Pennsylvania State University Press, 1996.

Hellsten, Iina, Loet Leydesdorff, and Paul Wouters. "Multiple Presents: How Search Engines Rewrite the Past." *New Media & Society* 8, no. 6 (2006): 901–24.

Hendricks, C. D., and J. Hendricks. "Concepts of Time and Temporal Construction among the Aged." In *Time, Roles and Self in Old Age*, edited by J. F. Gubrium, 13–49. New York: Human Sciences Press, 1976.

Hobsbawm, Eric. *The Age of Extremes.* London: Vintage Books, 1994.

Hobsbawm, Eric, and Terence Ranger, eds. *The Invention of Tradition.* Cambridge: Cambridge University Press, 1983.

Hörning, Karl H., Daniela Ahrens, and Anette Gerhard. "Do Technologies Have Time?" *Time and Society* 8, no. 2–3 (September 1999): 293–308.

Hume, David. "Of the Original Contract." In *Social Contract : Essays by Locke, Hume, and Rousseau*, edited by Ernest Barker. London: Oxford University Press, 1980: 207–37.

Hutchings, Kimberly. *Time and World Politics: Thinking the Present.* Manchester: Manchester University Press, 2008.

Illich, Ivan. *Deschooling Society.* Harmondsworth, Middlesex: Penguin, 1973.

Isaacson, Walter. "In Search of the Real Bill Gates." *Time* 149, no. 2 (January 13, 1997). Online edition http://www.time.com/time/gates/cover0.html (accessed March 22, 2010).

IWS (Internet World Stats). 2010. http://www.Internetworldstats.com/stats.htm (accessed January 7, 2011).

James, William. *Pragmatism: A New Name for Some Old Ways of Thinking.* London and New York: Longmans, Green, 1907.

Jaynes, Julian. *The Origin of Consciousness in the Breakdown of the Bicameral Mind.* Boston, MA: Houghton Mifflin, 1976.

Jonas, Hans. *The Imperative of Responsibility: In Search of an Ethics for the Technological Age.* Translated by Hans Jonas with the collaboration of David Herr. Chicago, IL: University of Chicago Press, 1985/1979.

Judt, Tony. "Words." *New York Review of Books*, June 17, 2010, 37.

Judt. *The Memory Chalet.* London: Penguin, 2010.

Kant, Immanuel. "An Answer to the Question: What is Enlightenment?" In *Practical Philosophy (The Cambridge Edition of the Works of Immanuel Kant in Translation).* Translated and edited by Mary J. Gregor. Cambridge: Cambridge University Press, 1996, 1–25.

Kellner, D. "Intellectuals, the New Public Spheres, and Technopolitics." *New Political Science* 41–42 (Fall 1997): 169–88.

Kenyon, Susan. "The Prevalence of Multitasking and the Influence of Internet Use." *Time & Society* 17, no. 2/3 (2008): 213–318.

Kern, Stephen. *The Culture of Time and Space, 1880–1918.* Cambridge, MA: Harvard University Press, 1983.

Kimball, Roger. *Tenured Radicals: How Politics Has Corrupted Our Higher Education.* 3rd ed., revised. New York: Harper & Row, 1990/2008.

Kittler, Friedrich. *Gramophone, Film, Typewriter.* Translated by Geoffrey Winthrop-Young and Michael Wutz. Stanford, CA: Stanford University Press, 1999.

Klein, Naomi. *The Shock Doctrine.* London: Penguin Allen Lane, 2008.

Kleinberg, Jon. "The world at Your Fingertips." *Nature* 440, no. 7082 (March 16, 2006): 279.

Kolko, Joyce. *Restructuring the World Economy*. New York: Pantheon, 1988.

Koselleck, Reinhardt. *The Practice of Conceptual History: Timing History, Spacing Concepts*. Translated by Todd Samuel Presner et al. Stanford, CA: Stanford University Press, 2004.

Kristeva, Julia. *Time and Sense: Proust and the Experience of Literature*. New York: Columbia University Press, 1996.

Laing, R. D. *The Politics of Experience and the Bird of Paradise*. Harmondsworth: Penguin, 1967.

Lanier, Jaron. *You are Not a Gadget: A Manifesto*. New York: Alfred A. Knopf, 2010.

Lash, Scott. *Critique of Information*. London: Sage Publications, 2002.

Latour, Bruno. "Morality and Technology." *Theory, Culture and Society* 19, no. 5–6 (2002): 247–60.

_____. *We Have Never Been Modern*. Translated by Catherine Porter. New York: Harvester Wheatsheaf, 1993.

Laursen, J. C., "The Subversive Kant: The Vocabulary of 'Public' and 'Publicity,'" *Political Theory* 14 (November 1996): 584–603.

Lauter, Paul. *Canons and Contexts*. New York: Oxford University Press, 1991.

Lefebvre, Henri. *The Social Production of Space*. Oxford: Blackwell, 1992/1974.

Le Goff, Jacques. *Time, Work and Culture in the Middle Ages*. Chicago, IL: University of Chicago Press, 1980.

Lorenz, Chad. "The Death of Email." *Slate.com*, 2007. http://www.slate.com/id/2177969/ (accessed May 4, 2011).

Lyman, P., and H. R. Varian. *How Much Information 2003*. Berkeley, CA: University of California at Berkeley, School of Information Management and Systems, 2003. http://www2.sims.berkeley.edu/research/projects/how-much-info-2003/printable_report.pdf (accessed January 14, 2011).

Lyotard, Jean-François. *The Postmodern Condition: A Report on Knowledge*. Manchester: Manchester University Press, 1979.

MacIntyre, Alasdair. *After Virtue: A Study in Moral Theory*. Notre Dame, IN: Notre Dame University Press, 1984.

Mackenzie, Adrian. *Transductions: Bodies and Machines at Speed*. London: Continuum, 2002.

Malcolm, M. L."Automation and Unemployment: A Management Viewpoint." *The Annals of the American Academy of Political and Social Science* 340, no. 1 (1962): 90–99.

Marcuse, Herbert. *The Aesthetic Dimension*. London: Macmillan, 1977.

Marx, Karl. *Capital*. Vol. 1. London: Pelican, 1982.

_____. *Grundrisse*. Harmondsworth: Penguin, 1973.

Marx, Karl, and Friedrich Engels. "The Manifesto of the Communist Party." In *Selected Works*. Moscow: Progress Press, 1975, 1–14.

Matai, D. K. "Tunisia: A Digitally-Driven, Leaderless Revolution." *Business Insider*, January 18, 2011. http://www.businessinsider.com/tunisia-a-digitally-driven-leaderless-revolution-2011-1 (accessed May 22, 2011).

Mathis, Blair. "Laptop Sales Exceed Desktop Sales Globally." *Laptoplogic.com*, December 26, 2008. http://laptoplogic.com/news/laptop-sales-exceed-desktop-sales-globally--20319 (accessed June 22, 2010).

May, Jon, and Nigel Thrift, eds. *Timespace*. London: Routledge, 2001.

McDonough, Robert E., "The Marsden Case for the Canon." In *Ford Maddox Ford and 'The Republic of Letters,'* edited by Vita Fortunati and Elena Lamberti. Bologna, Italy: CLUEB, 2002, 27–44.

McLuhan, Marshall. *Understanding Media: The Extensions of Man.* London: Sphere Books, 1967/1964.

McNamara, Robert. "Krakatoa Volcano Eruption in 1883 Was a Worldwide Weather and Media Event." *about.com,* 2009. http://history1800s.about.com/od/thegildedage/a/krakatoa.htm (accessed June 7, 2010).

Merton, Robert. "Science, Technology and Society in Seventeenth Century England." In *Osiris,* vol. IV, pt. 2, 360–632. Bruges: St. Catherine Press, 1937.

Milland, Gabriel, and Georgia Warren. "Austerity Cabinet has 18 Millionaires." *The Sunday Times,* May 23, 2010. The Times Online http://www.timesonline.co.uk/tol/news/politics/article7133943.ece (accessed July 12, 2010).

Miller, Michael J. "Cisco: Internet Moves 21 Exabytes per Month." *PCMag.com,* December 25, 2010. http://www.pcmag.com/print_article2/0,1217,a=249535,00.asp?hidPrint=true (accessed May 7, 2011).

Negroponte, Nicholas. *Being Digital.* New York: Vintage, 1995.

Norris, Christopher. *Uncritical Theory: Postmodernism, Intellectuals, and the Gulf War.* Amherst: The University of Massachusetts Press, 1992.

Nowotny, Helga. *Time: The Modern and Postmodern Experience.* Cambridge: Polity Press, 1994.

O'Hagan, Sean. "Reality Hunger by David Shields." *The Observer,* February 28, 2010. http://www.guardian.co.uk/books/2010/feb/28/reality-hunger-book-review (accessed March 7, 2010).

OLPC (One Laptop Per Child), 2010. http://laptop.org/en/vision/index.shtml (accessed April 12, 2011).

Ong, Walter J. *Interfaces of the Word.* Ithaca, NY: Cornell UP, 1977.

_____. *Orality and Literacy: The Technologizing of the Word.* New York: Methuen, 1982.

_____. *Ramus: Method and the Decay of Dialogue: From the Art of Discourse to the Art of Reason.* Cambridge, MA: Harvard University Press, 1983/1958.

Ong, Walter J. "Writing is a Technology that Restructures Thought." In *The Written Word: Literacy in Transition,* edited by Gerd Baumann. Oxford: Clarendon Press, 1992, 14–31.

Pappas, Nickolas. *Philosophy Guidebook to Plato and the Republic.* London and New York: Routledge, 1995.

Pierson, Chris. "Globalization and the End of Social Democracy." *Working Documents in the Study of European Governance.* Number 9 (May 2001).

Purser, Ronald, E. "Contested Presents: Critical Perspectives on 'Real-Time' Management." In *Making Time: Time and Management in Modern Organizations,* edited by Richard Whipp, Barbara Adam, and Ida Sabelis, 155–67. Oxford: Oxford University Press, 2002.

Putin, Vladimir. "Working Day," *Prime Minister's Website,* 2009 http://premier.gov.ru/eng/events/news/4814/ (accessed May 19, 2011).

Richtel, Matt. "Growing Up Digital, Wired for Distraction." *The New York Times,* November 21, 2010, 21.

Robertson, Roland. *Globalization: Social Theory and Global Culture.* London: Sage Publications, 1992.

Robinson, John P. and Geoffrey Godbey. *Time for Life: The Surprising Ways Americans Use their Time*. University Park, PA: Pennsylvania State University Press, 1999.

Rochlin, Gene. *Trapped in the Net: The Unanticipated Consequence of Computerization*. Princeton, NJ: Princeton University Press, 1997.

Rosa, Hartmut. "Social Acceleration." *Constellations* 10, no. 1 (2003): 49–52.

Roszak, Theodore. *The Cult of Information*. Berkeley, CA: The University of California Press, 1986.

Sabelis, Ida. "Global Speed: A Time View on Transnationality." *Culture and Organization* 10, no. 4 (2004): 291–301.

Said, Edward. *Culture and Imperialism*. New York: Alfred A. Knopf, 1994.

_____. *Orientalism*. New York: Vintage Books, 1979.

_____. *The World, the Text, and the Critic*. Cambridge, MA: Harvard University Press, 1983.

Sanger, David E. "North Korea Keeps the World Guessing." *New York Times*, November 29, 2010. http://www.nytimes.com/2010/11/30/world/asia/30korea. html (accessed April 17, 2011).

Scannell, Paddy. "Radio Times: The Temporal Arrangements of Broadcasting in the Modern World." In *Television and its Audience; International Research Perspectives*, edited by P. Drummond and R. Paterson. London: BFI, 198, 122–40.

Scheuerman, William, E. *Liberal Democracy and the Social Acceleration of Time*. Baltimore, MD: Johns Hopkins University Press, 2004.

Schiller, Dan. *Digital Capitalism: Networking the Global Market System*. Cambridge, MA: MIT Press, 2000.

Schonfeld, Erick. "Costolo: Twitter Now Has 190 Million Users Tweeting 65 Million Times A Day." *TechCrunch*, June 8, 2010. http://techcrunch. com/2010/06/08/twitter-190-million-users/ (accessed February 9, 2011).

Schor, Juliet. *The Overworked American: The Unexpected Decline of Leisure*. New York: Basic Books, 1993.

Searle, John. "The Storm over the University." *The New York Review of Books*, December 6, 1990. http://www.nybooks.com/articles/archives/1990/dec/06/ the-storm-over-the-university/ (accessed October 17, 2010).

Shaer, Matthew. "Twitter: 20 Billion Tweets and Counting." *The Christian Science Monitor*, August 2, 2010. http://www.csmonitor.com/Innovation/ Horizons/2010/0802/Twitter-20-billion-tweets-and-counting (accessed September 29, 2010).

Shenk, D. *Data Smog*. London: Abacus, 1997.

Shields, David. *Reality Hunger: A Manifesto*. New York: Knopf Doubleday, 2010.

Shirky, Clay. *Here Comes Everybody: The Power of Organizing Without Organizations*. New York: Penguin Press, 2008.

_____. "The Political Power of Social Media: Technology, the Public Sphere, and Political Change." *Foreign Affairs* 90, no.1 (2011): 28–41.

Simon, Herbert. *Computers, Communications and the Public Interest*. Baltimore, MD: Johns Hopkins University Press, 1971.

Simon, John. "Foreword." In *Critical Essays*, edited by Enzensberger, Hans Magnus. New York: Continuum, 1982, 14–35.

Slaughter, Sheila, and Larry L. Leslie. *Academic Capitalism*. Baltimore, MD: Johns Hopkins University Press, 1997.

Smith, Adam. *The Wealth of Nations*. Introduced by Alan B. Krueger. Edited by Edwin Cannan. New York: Bartram Classics, 2003.

Snyder, Timothy. *Bloodlands: Europe between Hitler and Stalin*. London: The Bodley Head, 2010.

_____. *Time*. Cambridge: Polity, 2004.

Southerton, Dale. "Squeezing Time." *Time and Society* 12, no. 1 (2003): 5–25.

Spang-Hanssen, Henrik. "Recommendations of the Association for Progressive Communications at World Summit on the Information Society, Tunis, 2005." *Public International Computer Network Law Issues*. DJØF Forlag. 2006.

Stein, Jeremy. "Reflections on Time, Time-space-compression and Technology in the Nineteenth Century." In *Timespace: Geographies of Temporality*, edited by Jon May and Nigel Thrift. London: Routledge, 2001, 94–119.

Stiegler, Bernard. *Technics and Time*. Translated by Richard Beardsworth and George Collins. Stanford, CA: Stanford University Press, 1998.

Stephens, John, and Robyn McCallum. *Retelling Stories, Framing Culture: Traditional Story and Metanarratives in Children's Literature*. New York: Garland Pub, 1998.

Sullivan, Danny. "comScore: US Has Most Searches; China Slowest Growth; Google Tops Worldwide In 2009." *Search Engine Land*, January 22, 2010. http://searchengineland.com/comscore-us-most-searches-china-slowest-34217 (accessed May 17, 2011).

Sullivan, Oriel. "Busyness, Status Distinction and Consumption Strategies of the Income Rich, Time Poor." *Time & Society* 17, no. 1 (2008): 5–26. (accessed February 3, 2011).

Tabboni, Simonetta. "The Idea of Social Time in Norbert Elias." *Time and Society* 10, no. 1 (March 2001): 5–27.

Taylor, Frederick W. *The Principles of Scientific Management*. New York: Harper and Brothers, 1911.

Thakkar, Johnny. "Why Conservatives Should Read Marx." *The Point* 3, (Fall 2010): 11.

Thompson, E. P. "Time, Work-Discipline and Industrial Capitalism." In *Customs in Common*, edited by E. P. Thompson. London: Penguin Books, 1993/1967, 209–17.

Thompson, Sir George. *The Foreseeable Future*. Cambridge: Cambridge University Press, 1955.

Thrift, Nigel. *Spatial Formations*. London; Thousand Oaks, CA: Sage, 1996.

Toffler, Alvin. *Future Shock*. London: Pan, 1970.

Tonelson, Alan. *Race to the Bottom: Why a Worldwide Worker Surplus and Uncontrolled Free Trade Are Sinking American Living Standards*. New York: Basic Books, 2002.

Tweney, David. "Amazon Sells More E-Books Than Hardcovers." *Wired*, July 19, 2010. http://www.wired.com/epicenter/2010/07/amazon-more-e-books-than-hardcovers/ (accessed May 3, 2011).

UNESCO World Report: *Towards knowledge societies*. Compiled by Jérôme Bindé et al. 2005. PDF available at http://unesdoc.unesco.org/images/0014/001418/141843e.pdf (accessed October 12, 2011).

USA Today. *Officials: Students Can use 'text speak' on Tests*. November 13, 2006. http://www.usatoday.com/news/offbeat/2006-11-13-text-speak_x.htm (accessed June 9, 2011).

Von Hayek, Friedrich. *The Road to Serfdom*. Chicago, IL: University of Chicago Press, 1994/1944.

Weber, Max. *The Protestant Ethic and the Spirit of Capitalism*. Translated by Stephen Kalberg. Oxford: Blackwell, 2003.

Weiser, Mark, and Seely Brown, John. "The Coming Age of Calm Technology." In *Beyond Calculation: The Next Fifty Years of Computing*, edited by Peter J. Denning and Robert M. Metcalfe. New York: Copernicus, 1997.

Whitrow, G. J. *Time in History*. Oxford: Oxford University Press, 1988.

Winchester, Simon. *Krakatoa: The Day the World Exploded: August 27, 1883*. New York: Harper Perennial, 2005.

Winner, Langdon. "Do Artifacts Have Politics?" *Daedalus* 109, no. 1 (Modern Technology: Problem or Opportunity? Winter 1980): 121–36.

Wolin, Sheldon. "What Time is it?" *Theory and Event*, 1.1 http://muse.jhu.edu/journals/theory_and_event/v001/1.1wolin.html (accessed December 12, 2010).

Woolf, Virginia. *Collected Essays*. Vol. 3. London: Hogarth Press, 1966.

Wray, Richard. "Internet Data Heads for 500bn Gigabytes." *The Guardian*, May 18, 2009. http://www.guardian.co.uk/business/2009/may/18/digital-content-expansion

Zimmer, Carl, ed. *The Descent of Man: The Concise Edition*. New York: Plume Paperbacks, 2007.

Zittrain, Jonathan. *The Future of the Internet—And How to Stop It*. London: Allen Lane, 2008.

Zizek, Slavoj. "A Permanent Economic Emergency." *New Left Review* 64 (July/August, 2010): 94. http://newleftreview.org/?view=2853 (accessed June 11, 2011).

Index

abstract exchange value, 53
academic capitalism, 152
acceleration of time, 54–56, 109, 156
Actor Network Theory (ANT), 17
Adam, Barbara, 13, 18, 53, 79, 136–137
Adorno, Theodor, 4, 121, 164
After Virtue (Macintyre), 167
Agamben, Georgio, 195
Age of Extremes (Hobsbawm), 72
agency, technology and, 22–23
alienation, 134–136
Allen, Woody, 121–122
Amazon, 132
American Revolution, 163
Anderson, Benedict, 6
Anderson, Perry, 63, 160
Anderson, Sam, 119–121, 124
Apple, R.W., 176
Archaeology of Knowledge (Foucault), 101
Aristotle, 23–24, 35, 166
Arnold, Matthew, 102, 147
art and science, balance between, 109–110
artificial intelligence, 110–111
atomic weapons, 55
Augustine, Saint, 15
Auletta, Ken, 92–93
autoamputation, 38–39, 45, 80, 192

Baudrillard, Jean, 88–89
Bauman, Zygmunt, xv
Baumgarten, Alexander, 109
Beaumont, Peter, 91
Being Digital (Negroponte), 91, 113
Bell, Daniel, 103, 108, 111, 113, 135
Bergman, Michael K., 129–130
Bergson, Henri, 5, 52

Betts, Richard K., 164–165
Bezos, Jeff, 132
Bible, 154, 167
bicameral mind, 31–32
Blainey, Geoffrey, 56
Blair, Tony, 165
blogging, 42
Bloom, Harold, 151–152
Bolter, J. David, 10–11
book trade, 39–40
books, relationship with, 94–96
bookshops, timescape of, 94–95
Britain, industrialization and, 60–61
Brooke, Heather, 174–175, 177
Brown, Gordon, 64
Bruner, Jerome, 99–100
Burghagen, Otto, 105
Burke, Edmund, 161–163, 175, 193, 200
Bush, George, 165
Bush, Vannevar, 107
Byron, George Gordon, 51

canon
    acceleration and, 156–157
    chronic distraction and, 168–169
    debates on, 147–153
    narrative and, 98–99
    relevance of, 164–167
    role of, 153–155
    transformation of, 101–103, 155–158
Capital (Marx), 20, 52, 57
capital accumulation, theory of, 57–58
capitalism
    academic, 152
    acceleration and, 103
    clock time and, xiii
    geography and, 56
    Marx on, 52–53

capitalism (*continued*)
  public sphere and, 200–201
  spread of, 57–60
  Weber on, 48–49
  work ethic and, ix–x
Capitalism and Freedom (Friedman), 61–62
Carr, Nicholas, 115–117, 168, 179
Caryl, Christian, 176–177
The Case for Books (Darnton), 93
Castells, Manuel, 11, 74, 76, 78–79, 160
Chaplin, Charlie, 70–71
Charron, Sylvain, 125
Christianity, 48–49
chronic distraction
  canon and, 168–169
  disconnection and, xv
  emergence of, 46
The Chronoscopic Society (Hassan), 86
Cities of Quartz (Davis), 25
Civil Disobedience (Thoreau), 195
classical antiquity, thought and, 35–36
Classical Mechanics. *see* Newtonian Mechanics
classrooms, distraction and, 2
clock time
  domination of, 28–29, 173
  encoding of, 26–27
  irrelevance of, 78–79
  Newtonian, 23, 28, 53
  physicality and, 34–35
  rhythm of, xiii
  see also mechanics of time; time
Cobbett, William, 96–97
cognitive dissonance, 163–164
cognitive surplus, 179–182
Cognitive Surplus (Shirky), 179
collaboration, 75
The Coming of the Post-Industrial Society (Bell), 108
commodification of words, 134
communication technologies
  development of, 65–68
  network time and, 79
  in nineteenth century, 56–57
communism, 6
The Communist Manifesto (Marx and Engels), 58
competition, 54–55, 57–58, 64, 70, 78, 103–104

computers
  development of, 74–76, 107
  pragmatism and, 76–77
  speed and, xi, 10–12
The Condition of Postmodernity (Harvey), 64
Confessions (St. Augustine), 15
conservatism
  canon and, 159–160
  description of, 160–161
  societal structure and, 200
Conservatives (British), 62
Constitution, 163
conveyor-belt system, 70
  see also Fordism
The Corrections (Frantzen), 140
Culture and Anarchy (Arnold), 147
culture wars, 147–153

Darkness at Noon (Koestler), 141
Darnton, Robert, 43, 93–94
Davies, Norman, 51
Davis, Mike, 25–26
Debray, Régis, 41–42, 97–98, 158, 185
democracy, redefinition of, 192–193
Derrida, Jacques, 149–150
Descartes, René, 13
destabilization, ICTs and, xiv–xv
devaluation, 58–59
Dialectic of the Enlightenment (Adorno and Horkheimer), 4
Digital Capitalism (Schiller), 75
digital generation, 168
distraction
  chronic, xv, 46, 168–169
  classrooms and, 2
  description of, 118–119
  solutions proposed for, 120–121
division of labor, 50
Doctorow, Corey, 118, 120–121, 124
domination, technology and, 22–23
DuPont, A.J.F., 163
Durkheim, Emile, 15, 17
Dux, Paul, 125

Eagleton, Terry, 47
e-books, 93, 132–133
economic crisis (2008), 122–123, 166
écriture automatique, 105–106
Einstein, Albert, 18

Electronic Frontier Foundation (EFF), 177–178
Elias, Norbert, 15–16, 19
Ellsberg, Daniel, 176
Ellul, Jacques, 55
encoding of technologies, 26–27
Engels, Friedrich, x, 55, 58
Enlightenment
  basis of, xiii
  conservatism and, 161
  Firth and, 73–74
  Habermas on, 184
  impact of, 47
  industrialization and, 145
  material forms and, 158–159
  pragmatism and, 76
  recuperation of, 146–147
  rejection of, 50
  rise of, 173
  writing and, 41
entiming technologies, 23–24
Enzensberger, Hans Magnus, 103–104
Ermath Deeds, Elizabeth, 87
Estrada, Joseph, 189, 191
eternity, 48
experiences, subjective nature of, 4–5
exploitation, x–xi, 135–136
extensionality, 22–24, 26, 39

factory workers, x–xi
Fanon, Frantz, 149
Fara, Patricia, 34
Fascism, 69
Feenberg, Andrew, 23
Feminist Interpretations of Michel Foucault (Hekman), 155–156
Ferguson, Adam, 49
Ferriss, Tim, 90
Finnegan's Wake (Joyce), 141, 178
Firth, Raymond, 73–74, 77
fixity, geographic, 56–57–59
flexibility, 62–64
Ford, Ford Maddox, 102
Ford, Henry, 70–71
Fordism, 60–61, 69–75
The Foreseeable Future (Thompson), 110
Foucault, Michel, 20, 85, 101, 155–156
Frankel, Boris, 149
Franklin, Benjamin, ix, 48, 52
frantic optimism, 121

Frantzen, Jonathan, 140
Fraser, Nancy, 183, 185–187, 191, 193–194
free time, 179–182
French Revolution, 161
Friedman, Milton, 61–62, 102
From Gutenberg to the Internet (Norman), 38
frontopolar cortex, 125
Fukuyama, Francis, 164
functional magnetic resonance imaging (fMRI), 125
Future of the Internet Report (Pew Internet Project), 115–116
Future Shock (Toffler), 108–111
Futurism, 69

García Márquez, Gabriel, 149
Gare, Arran, 13, 36–38
Gates, Bill, 107, 112–113, 119, 124
Gehlen, Arnold, xi–xii, 142–146, 160–161, 163, 182
geographic fixity, 56–57–59
geometric modernism, 69
The German Ideology (Marx), 103
German Unification, 50
Gies, Frances, 37, 40
Gies, Joseph, 37, 40
Glenn, David, 125
Godbey, Geoffrey, 180
Goethe, Johann Wolfgang von, 50–52, 55–56, 69, 73, 103
Google
  book project of, 93
  dynamic information and, 131
  interaction with, 128–129
  limitations of, 129–130
  logic, 127–128
  search algorithm of, 126–127
  stickiness and, 1
  Trends, 175
Graham, Lindsay, 122–123
Grapes of Wrath (Steinbeck), 141
graphoshpere, 42–43
Greenwich Mean Time (GMT), 68
Grosz, Elizabeth, 5–6
Grundrisse (Marx), 53, 57
Gugerli, David, 127
Gullers, Peter, 86–87
Gutenberg Galaxy (McLuhan), 39, 96
Guttenberg, Johannes, 38, 173

Habermas, Jürgen, 66, 183–186–187, 191
Halavais, Alexander, 126
Hall, Edward T., 196
Hammonds, Keith H., 128
Haraway, Donna, 149
Hardt, Michael, 108, 135
Hardy, Barbara, 99
Harvey, David, 22, 57–59, 64, 71–72, 133, 194
Hayek, Friedrich von, 61–62, 102
Heidegger, Martin, 17
Hekman, Susan J., 155–157
Hellsten, Iina, 131
Here Comes Everybody (Shirky), 178–179
Hitler, Adolf, 7
Hobbes, Thomas, 13
Hobsbawm, Eric, 6, 72–73
Horkheimer, 4, 164
Hörning, Karl, 26–27
How to Think About Information (Schiller), 135
Hume, David, 43, 47, 49
Huntingdon, Samuel, 164
Hussein, Saddam, 87
Husserl, Edmund, 5, 25, 52
Hutchings, Kimberly, 196
Huxley, Aldous, 141

Imagined Communities (Anderson), 6
Industrial Revolution, 27, 54–56, 144
industrialization, 40–41, 45, 49–51, 103–104
information
  dynamic, 131
  knowledge vs., 86, 88–89
  logic of, 90–92
  post-industrial society and, 109–110
information and communication technologies (ICTs), xiv–xv, 74, 76, 85, 90, 189
information networks, development of, 74–76–78
instinctual deprivation, 142–143
Interfaces of the Word (Ong), 97
The Invention of Tradition (Hobsbawm), 6
Iraq wars, 87–89

James, William, 87
Jaynes, Julian, 31–32, 41, 44, 100
Jobs, Steve, 107

Jonas, Hans, 166
Joyce, James, 140–141, 178
Judt, Tony, xii–xiii, 133–134, 137

Kant, Immanuel, 41, 121, 184
Katyn, 8
Kellner, Doug, 182
Kennedy, John F., xv
Keynes, John Maynard, 102, 164, 166
Kimball, Roger, 151–152
Kindle, 132–133
Kittler, Friedrich, 104–105
Kleinberg, Jon, 129
knowledge
  capital and, 85–86
  fixity of, 130–131
  information vs., 86, 88–89
  mediated, 87–88
  post-industrial society and, 108
Koechlin, Etienne, 125
Koestler, Arthur, 141
Koselleck, Reinhardt, 49
Krakatoa, 67–68
Kristeva, Julia, 5, 8

Lafargue, Paul, ix–x, xiv–xv
Laing, R.D., 4, 14
Lanier, Jaron, 174
Lash, Scott, 90
Latour, Bruno, xii, 17
Lauter, Paul, 101
Le Goff, Jacques, 37
Lefebvre, Henri, 17–18, 196
Leibniz, Gottfried, 76, 86
Lenin, Vladimir, 71, 162
Lewis, Wyndam, 69
libraries, 95
Licklider, J.C.R., 107
The Limits to Capital (Harvey), 57–59
Liquid Modernity (Bauman), xv
literacy
  see also writing/reading
literacy, criticism and, 84
Lyotard, Jean François, 149–150

machine culture, ix–x, 13, 103–104
Macintyre, Alasdair, 167
Mackenzie, Adrian, 19
Man in the Age of Technology (Gehlen), 142
Marcuse, Herbert, 147
Marinetti, Filippo, 69

Marx, Karl, 20, 52–55, 57–59, 85, 103, 134–135, 143, 162
May, Jon, 194
McCallum, Robyn, 100
McLuhan, Marshall, 22, 32, 38–39, 45, 80, 96, 134
Mearsheimer, John, 164
mechanics of time, 13–14
mechanistic materialism, 36, 38–39, 44, 103
Memorial, 7
mercantilism, 37
Merton, Robert, 15, 17
metanarrative, 100–101, 150, 172
mobile phone example, 24, 26
Modern Times (film), 70–71
money, time and, 52–54
Moore's Law, xi
Moses, Robert, 25
multitasking, 123–125
Multitude (Hardt and Negri), 108, 135

narrative, 98–101, 136–137, 139–140, 172
Nass, Clifford, 125
nation, concept of, 6
Nazi-Soviet Pact of August 1939, 7–8
Negri, Antonio, 108, 135
Negroponte, Nicholas, 91, 113
neoliberalism, 61–63, 76
network effect, 90, 114
network of lines, 69
network time
  basis of, 78
  description of, 65
  emergence of, 45–46, 56
  example of, 79–81
  leisure time and, 180–181
  overview of, 65
  prevalence of, 81–82
networked life
  banality of, 111–112
  extraordinariness of, 112–113
  transformation of, 113–115
New York Times, 67
news cycle, 175–176
Newton, Isaac, 11–13, 36
Newtonian clock time, 23, 28, 53
Newtonian Mechanics, 13
Nielsen, Leslie, 175
Nietzsche, Friedrich, 104–105
Nixon, Richard, 176

Norman, Jeremy, 38
Norris, Christopher, 150
North, Douglass, 187, 194
novels, 139–140

oil shock crises, 61
One Day in the Life of Ivan Denisovitch (Solzhenitsyn), 141
One Laptop per Child (OLPC), 91
Ong, Walter, xii, 30–32, 41, 44–45, 78, 94, 97–98, 100, 103–104, 134, 172
optimism, frantic, 121
Orality and Literacy (Ong), 98
Orientalism (Said), 148, 154–155
The Origin of Consciousness and the Breakdown of the Bicameral Mind (Jaynes), 31
Orwell, George, 141
overaccumulation, 58–61
  see also capital accumulation, theory of
The Overworked American (Schor), 180

Page, Larry, 126
PageRank, 126–127, 130
Peace of Westphalia, 196
Pentagon Papers, 176–177
Pew Internet Project, 115–116
photography example, 86–87
Physics (Aristotle), 23
Plato, 35–36
Plumwood, Val, 149
Poland, partition of, 8
political correctness, 148
The Post-modern Condition (Lyotard), 150
Pound, Ezra, 69
pragmatism, 76–77
Pratt, Mary Louise, 148
Principia (Newton), 13
The Principles of Scientific Management (Taylor), x, 71
print media, decline of, xiv
printing press, 38–40, 42, 173
privatization, 63
prostheticization of thought, 33, 35
The Protestant Ethic and the Spirit of Capitalism (Weber), 48
Protestantism, 48–49
Proust, Marcel, 5, 8
public sphere, 182–188, 190, 193, 195, 197, 200

publishing industry, 92–93
Purser, Ron, xiv, 137
Putin, Vladimir, 7

racism, architecture and, 25
railways, impact of, 50
Rajaraman, Anand, 130
Rand, Ayn, 141
reading. *see* literacy; writing/reading
Reagan, Ronald, 62–63
Reality Hunger: A Manifesto (Shields), 139–141
recurrence, 16
    see also temporality: cycles of
Reflections on the Revolution (Burke), 161–162
regime of accumulation, 60
regulation, 198–199
religion, canon and, 154
Remembrance of Things Past (Proust), 5
The Republic (Plato), 36
republic of letters, xiii, 43–44, 66, 74, 113–114
Rethinking the Public Sphere (Fraser), 185
revolutions, 161–163, 189
    see also Industrial Revolution
The Rise of the Information Society (Castells), 11
rituals, social, 6
The Road to Serfdom (Hayek), 61
Robertson, Roland, 44, 67
Robespierre, Maximilien, 162
Robinson, John P., 180
Romanticism, 50–51
Rosa, Hartmut, xi
Rousseau, Jean-Jacques, 47
Rozak, Theodore, 116
Rushdie, Salman, 155
Russia, 7

Sabelis, Ida, 84–85
Said, Edward, 148, 154–155, 157, 165
Scales of Justice (Fraser), 187, 193
Schiller, Dan, 75, 77, 133, 135
Schor, Juliet, 64, 180
Schulze, Gerhardt, xv
Science: A Four-Thousand Year History (Fara), 34
science and art, balance between, 109–110
search engines, 126

Seely Brown, John, 74–75
sensitivity, capitalism and, 51–52
The Shallows (Carr), 116–117, 168, 179
Shelley, Percy Bysshe, 51
Shields, David, 139–141, 178
Shirky, Clay, 177–182, 188–192, 195
Shiva, Vandana, 155
The Silent Language (Hall), 196
Simon, Herbert, 110–111
Simon, John, 103
skepticism, 47–48
Skype, 79–81
sleep, 5
Smith, Adam, xiii, 43, 49–50, 57, 70
social contract, 43, 47
social networking, xiv, 191–192
The Social Production of Space (Lefebvre), 17
social time, 15–19, 51
socialism, ix–x
Socrates, 35
Solzhenitsyn, Alexander, 141
Southerton, Dale, 2–3
Soviet Union, 6–7
Spivak, Gayatri Chakravorty, 149
stagflation, 61
Stein, Jeremy, 56–57, 68
Steinbeck, John, 141
Stephens, John, 100
sticky content, 1
Stiegler, Bernard, 32–33, 45
The Structural Transformation of the Public Sphere (Habermas), 184
Sturm und Drang movement, 50
Sullivan, Oriel, 123

Tabboni, Simonetta, 15–16, 19
Taylor, Frederick Winslow, x, 71
Techics and Time (Stiegler), 32–33
technological determinism, 65–66
The Technological Society (Ellul), 55
technologies
    development of, xii, 54, 172–173
    Gehlen on, 143–146
    human nature and, 171–172
    role of, 21–22
    social relations and, 19–20
TED conferences, 188
temporal cognitive dissonance, 84–85
temporal emancipation, 47–48
temporal sovereignty, 195–197

temporality
    canonicity and, 156
    cycles of, 8, 16
    diachronicity and, 157
    dynamic nature of, 8
    framing questions on, 4
    gradual change in, 56–57
    philosophical views of, 5–6
    politics and, 177–179
    public sphere and, 190
    rhythm of, 6, 171
    writing and, 9–10
    see also time
Tenured Radicals (Kimball), 151–152
texting, 132, 189, 191
Thakkar, Jonny, 143, 145–146
Thatcher, Margaret, 62
"The Right to be Lazy" (Lafargue),
    ix–x
Thompson, George, 110–111
Thoreau, Henry David, 195
Thrift, Nigel, 194
Thus Spoke Zarathustra (Nietzsche),
    104
time
    ability to reflect on, 14–15
    acceleration of, 54–56, 109, 156
    relationship with, 2–3
    social, 15–19, 51
    squeeze, 3
    value of, ix
    see also clock time; temporality
Time (Adam), 136
Time: An Essay (Elias), 15
Time for Life (Robinson and Godbey),
    180
timescapes, 18, 79, 196
The Timescapes of Modernity (Adam),
    18
Timespace (Thrift and May), 194
time-space compression, 22, 194
Toffler, Alvin, 108–111, 113
tools. see extensionality
Toward Knowledge Societies (UNESCO),
    85–86
Trotsky, Leon, 157
Turing Prize, 110–111
Turing's Man (Bolter), 10
Tweney, David, 132
Twitter, 131–132
typewriters, 104–105
typography, 96–97

Ulysses (Joyce), 140
Understanding Media (McLuhan), 22
UNESCO, 85–86
universal man, 51
U.S. Embassy Cables, 174–175

Versailles Treaty of 1919, 7
videosphere, 42
Voltaire, 40–41
Vorticism, 69

The Wealth of Nations (Smith), 43, 50
Weber, Max, 48, 71
Weiser, Mark, 74–75
The Western Canon (Bloom), 151
Western canon, debates on, 147–153
    see also canon
wheel, 54, 144
WikiLeaks, 174–177
Wikipedia, 179–180
Winchester, Simon, 67–68
Winner, Langdon, 25, 76
Wolin, Sheldon, 193, 200
Woolf, Virginia, 69–70, 103
World Summit of the Information
    Society, 90–91
World War II, 7–8
writing/reading
    digitalization and, 131–133
    emergence of, 29–31
    entiming of, 33–34
    impact of, 32
    inadequacy of, 92
    Internet's effect on, 115–116
    mechanization of, 104–106
    openness of, 97–98
    as prostheticization of thought, 33, 35
    as second nature, 44–45
    as technology, xii–xiii, 9
    temporal cognitive dissonance and,
        84–85
    temporality and, 83, 172
    time required for, 96
    transformation of, 3–4
    see also literacy

A Year's Residence in America
    (Cobbett), 96
You are not a Gadget (Lanier), 174

Zelter, Carl Friedrich, 51–52, 55
Zittrain, Jonathan, 42